THE HISTORY OF

THE BALKANS, ITALY & AFRICA

1914 – 1918

Also in this series:

Eastern Front 1914–1920, by Michael S. Neiberg & David Jordan

Gallipoli and the Middle East 1914–1918, by Edward J Erickson

Naval Warfare 1914–1918, by Tim Benbow

Western Front 1914–1916, by Michael S. Neiberg

Western Front 1917–1918, by Andrew Wiest

THE HISTORY OF WORLD WAR I

THE BALKANS, ITALY & AFRICA
1914 – 1918

DAVID JORDAN

FOREWORDS BY DENNIS SHOWALTER AND GARY SHEFFIELD

amber
BOOKS

This paperback edition first published in 2021

Copyright © 2008 Amber Books Ltd

Published by Amber Books Ltd
United House
London N7 9DP
United Kingdom
www.amberbooks.co.uk
Instagram: amberbooksltd
Facebook: amberbooks
Twitter: @amberbooks
Pinterest: amberbooksltd

ISBN: 978-1-83886-121-6

Printed in United States

Contents

Forewords

World War I was limited in time and space, lasting only four years. Its outcome was determined in a single region—northern France and Flanders. Yet its unprecedented scale and cost created a spectrum of consequences, earning it another name: the Great War. That war was a Great Surprise. It was expected to be decisive and short. Instead it drew the entire world into an attritional death grapple whose outcome was uncertain until the end, and whose graves are scattered from Nova Scotia to Singapore. The Great War marked the end of European hegemony, the rise of the US and the Soviet Union as superpowers, and the emergence of the non-Western world on its terms. This conflict truly was the defining event of the twentieth century.

For all its impact, World War I remains shrouded in myth, mystery, and mourning. It exists as a series of disjointed images: old photographs and fragments of poems; devastated landscapes; anonymous soldiers scrambling over the top; above all, the endless cemeteries of the Western Front. *The History of World War I* returns that tragic conflict to the sphere of history. Based on a half-century of sophisticated research, incorporating state-of-the-art graphics, the six volumes of the series present the war on land, at sea, and in the air in a global context, and in human terms.

Dennis Showalter
Former President
American Society for Military History

When the Berlin Wall came down in 1989, it triggered the beginning of the end of a period of history that began with the assassination of Archduke Franz Ferdinand in Sarajevo 75 years earlier. The death of the heir to the thrones of Austria-Hungary fanned the smouldering embers of international rivalry into life, and within six weeks most of Europe was at war. World War I destroyed the existing international balance; brought down mighty empires; created the conditions that led to the rise of fascism and communism; made a second global conflagration likely, if not inevitable; and even sowed the seeds of the Cold War. When, after the collapse of the Soviet Union in 1991, historians looked back, they readily identified 1914, the outbreak of World War I, as the beginning of the "Short Twentieth Century", the bloodiest period in history.

Such a critical era demands to be properly understood, and I am delighted that such a distinguished Anglo-American team of historians—all of them acknowledged experts in their fields—have written a series of admirably accessible books on the war. As it happens, all of them are colleagues, past or present. They have succeeded magnificently in presenting accounts of the key campaigns that skilfully interweave narrative with some incisive analysis incorporating up-to-date research. This is grown-up history for the twenty-first century.

Gary Sheffield
Professor of War Studies
University of Wolverhampton

OPPOSITE **An Askari soldier in German East Africa.**

The Origins of the War

The act which sparked World War I – the assassination of Archduke Franz Ferdinand – was not the spontaneous expression of anti-Habsburg, nationalist sentiment, but the culmination of a series of events stretching back into the nineteenth century. A mixture of ethnic tensions, nationalism, political opportunism and the quest for power and status within the Balkans helped to plunge all of Europe into conflict.

Nationalism was perhaps the most important source of tension in the Balkan region, and it provided a firm underpinning not only to the outbreak of war, but the way in which different nations conducted their campaigns. During the course of the latter part of the nineteenth century, a growing sense of national identity developed amongst much of the population of Europe, particularly within the Habsburg Empire and its environs. This new-found sense of identity, in which people considered themselves as belonging to a wider construct than simply the city-state or region from which they

Archduke Franz Ferdinand and his wife walk to their car during their fateful visit to Sarajevo. Warned of the risk of an assassination attempt, the Archduke said: 'Our life is constantly in danger. One has to rely upon God'. His fatalistic devotion to royal duty would cost him his life.

9

originated, created a considerable amount of upheaval in the latter half of the 1800s. Nationalist sentiment increased in France and the German and Italian states in particular. In the case of the latter two, it led to the creation of unified nation states. The development of Germany as a nation, and then imperial, state was accompanied by support for militarism, dominated by Prussia, the most martial of the German states. The culminating act of the formation of the new country, the Franco–Prussian War of 1870–71 made German nationalism more confident, while French nationalist sentiment brooded over the humiliating defeat and vowed to regain the territories of Alsace and Lorraine, ceded to Germany in the peace treaty.

The Italian nationalists, seeking to unify a varying collection of Italian states which had been in existence for centuries, finally achieved their goal a decade before the Germans, but they could not see their triumph as complete. There were many people of Italian ethnic origin in territory belonging to the Habsburg Empire, most notably the so-called *Italia Irredenta* of the Dalmatian coast. The feeling that there was more territory to be added to Italy was strong, both amongst the Italians and in the Habsburg Empire, which had been grappling with the discomfort of nationalist sentiment for many years. Under the so-called Dual Monarchy of Austria and Hungary, the emperor was monarch of two separate nations, each of which had its own parliament and political system. This caused difficulties when one parliament felt strongly that its partner nation was in some way advantaged. To complicate the picture, the Austro-Hungarian lands were filled with a variety of ethnic groups, and not just the Italians whom the government in Rome wished to see brought into the new Italian state. Amongst the most prominent groups under Austro-Hungarian rule were the Poles, who had been reluctant members of the empire since the dismemberment of their country

A portrayal of the fighting in the Franco–Prussian War, (1870–71). The defeat of France led to the creation of a unified German Empire. It also helped create the conditions for war, as Germany sought to impose itself within Europe, while the French were determined to regain the annexed territories of Alsace-Lorraine from their erstwhile foes.

The cover of the current affairs magazine *Le Petit Journal* from 8 October 1908. On the left Franz Josef, the Austrian emperor, seizes Bosnia and Herzegovina for the Habsburgs, while in the centre King Ferdinand declares Bulgarian independence. To the right, the Ottoman emperor (portrayed as being ill to represent Turkey's position as the 'sick man of Europe') is unable to keep the further parts of the empire under his control.

in the late eighteenth century, with the old Polish Confederation being subsumed into Prussia, Austria and Russia.

In addition, nationalist sentiment developed with some strength amongst the Serbian, Czech, Bohemian, Romanian, Slovak, Croat, Greek and Slovene minorities, particularly the Serbs and the Czechs. A Serb state had existed since the 1830s (although only as a suzerainty of the declining Ottoman Empire until full independence in 1867), and the Serbian leadership had sufficient autonomy to allow it to provide support to ethnic Serbs in the Habsburg Empire during the 1848 revolutions that swept continental Europe in that year. By the early part of the twentieth century, the Austro-Hungarians regarded Serbia as a major threat, which in turn translated into considerable enmity towards Serbia. At first, the attempts to thwart Serb ambitions were conducted economically, but when it was clear that this would not succeed in weakening Serbia, thoughts turned towards the possibility of war. The empire simply could not remain stable if Serbia became more and more assertive.

In 1908, the Austrians decided to formally annexe Bosnia and Herzegovina, provinces that had been Habsburg protectorates for the past 30 years. The Austrians knew that one obstacle to this lay in the shape of Russia. The Tsar and his government held strong sympathies for their fellow Slavs, and it was important to ensure that any action to annexe Bosnia did not create a situation in which the Russians would intervene to protect the large Slavic population there. The Austrians secured Russian approval by agreeing to the Russians placing naval units in the Dardanelles, a long-held Russian aspiration, giving them access to the Mediterranean. Unfortunately for the Russians, the British and French raised strong objections and this part of the agreement was not to be realized; however,

the Austrians went ahead with the annexation, creating considerable resentment in St Petersburg, and bringing the Russian and Serbian governments closer together. This, in turn, raised mutual hostility between Russia and Austria-Hungary. Since the latter considered that it was too weak to resist Russia alone, a closer relationship developed between Austria and Germany.

THE BALKAN WARS

The picture was further complicated in 1912 when the Balkan League of Greece, Serbia, Montenegro and Bulgaria went to war with the Turks. The Turks, unable to resist, were driven from almost all the land they had held in Europe, but their departure created more problems. The peace settlement that ended the First Balkan War (1912–13) created enmity between the league members. The Bulgarians felt that they had been short changed in the division of the spoils, while the Serbs were denied their aspiration for a port on the

Emperor Franz Josef (1830–1916)

On 2 December 1848, the 18-year-old Franz Josef succeeded his mentally unstable uncle Ferdinand as emperor. He was confronted with the difficult task of keeping the empire together, at a time when revolutionary fervour was spreading throughout Europe; he did so via a series of astute manoeuvres and despite several Austrian policy disasters in the 1850s. Franz Josef's life was marked with tragedy: his brother Maximilian, who had accepted the offer of the Mexican throne, was executed after a revolution; his first son committed suicide; and his wife, Sissi, was assassinated in 1898, a blow from which he never fully recovered. Franz Josef attempted to ensure that Europe remained peaceful, seeing the Dual Alliance with Germany in 1879 as a means of achieving this. Following the assassination of his heir Franz Ferdinand in 1914, events spiralled out of control. An increasingly frail and isolated leader, he was unable to give his empire's war effort the dynamic leadership it so desperately needed. He died in November 1916.

Emperor Franz Josef (seated) at the wedding of his grand-nephew, and successor as emperor, Karl Franz Josef and Princess Zita of Parma.

Adriatic coast thanks to the intervention of the Italians and the Austrians. The Russians failed to support the Serbian demand, and this led to the government in Belgrade choosing not to pursue the matter, fearing that it might provoke a war that it could not win, with the unlikely partnership of the Italians and Austrians defeating them in battle.

The unhappiness over the settlement created the conditions for a second Balkan war in 1913. The Bulgarians attacked Serbia, with the tacit support of the Austro-Hungarians, who hoped that a Bulgarian victory would weaken their by now loathed neighbour. The Serbs, however, were able to gain support from Greece, Romania and Turkey, the latter sensing an opportunity to regain territory that it had lost to the Bulgarians the year before. The end result was a defeat for the Bulgarians and a further redrawing of the maps in the Balkans. Yet again, the cartographers produced maps with which no one was entirely content. The

Serbs, still anxious for a port, attempted to take one from Albania in October 1913, but were again thwarted when the Austrians made it clear that this would lead to war; once again, the Russians failed to support their supposed Slav brothers. The resentment this caused led Tsar Nicholas and his advisers to realize that, at some point, Russia would have to live up to Serb expectations.

THE PROBLEM OF ALLIANCES

As well as the increased nationalist tension within the Balkans, the development of an alliance system within Europe meant that a major war was a distinct possibility, with the main European powers leaping to the aid of their allies. The decision by Germany in 1890 to abandon its treaty with Russia led to Russia and France drawing closer together, and in 1894 they created a formal alliance. This was the source of considerable alarm in Berlin. To make matters worse, despite being related to the British monarchy, Kaiser Wilhelm managed to alienate Britain, in particular through his fixation with the idea of gaining German colonies. The British saw this expansionism as a potential threat to the supply lines to their Indian colony, not least since Wilhelm created a large navy in a bid to project German power overseas. This led to the development of a naval race between the two countries from 1897. The growing mistrust between the two countries meant that Britain moved closer to France, even though there had been a near conflict between the two countries over Egypt in the 1880s. However, British foreign policy was nothing if not pragmatic, and it seemed that reaching an accommodation with the French was a sensible move to prevent the Germans from becoming a major threat to Britain's international position. The end result was the Entente Cordiale between the two nations in 1904, although a healthy degree of mistrust remained between the two partners. Three years later, an understanding between Britain and Russia removed the threat of a Russian invasion of India, but in so doing drew Britain deeper into European affairs. The closer relations with Paris and St Petersburg in effect created an alliance of Britain, Russia and France – the Triple Entente.

These developments, not surprisingly, created great concern in Germany. It was obvious that any future war would leave the Germans facing a war on two fronts, and after 1907 there was a strong possibility of British naval power being added to the large armies of the French and Russians as a challenge for the Germans to overcome. The Germans ultimately came to the conclusion that they would have to launch a rapid attack on France to knock that country out of the war, thus denying the British an opportunity to intervene on behalf of their ally; the Germans hoped that this would allow them a free hand to turn their attention to the Russians.

> 'What is the point of these speeches? I come to visit Sarajevo and I get bombs thrown at me. It is outrageous!'
>
> Archduke Franz Ferdinand, interrupting the Mayor of Sarajevo's welcome address, 28 June 1914

Long before the plan for fighting on two fronts (the Schlieffen Plan) was developed, and in anticipation of a possible two-front war, the Germans had embarked upon an alliance with the Austro-Hungarians and the Italians. Under the terms of the Triple Alliance of 1882, each nation agreed that it would go to the aid of any of the others if attacked by two of the other major powers. The Italians specified that they would not abide by the alliance if Britain were one of the powers involved. They were also deeply uncomfortable with agreeing to an alliance with the Austro-Hungarians; however, the fact that the alliance was a defence against a possible attack by France (perceived as a possibility in 1882) was seen as an acceptable justification. But, as time went on, the Italians became less enamoured with the alliance, and well before war broke out, both the Germans and the Austrians expressed doubts as to whether the Italians would abide by their treaty obligations in the event of a European war.

THE SPARK

On 28 June 1914, in what was at best a spectacularly ill judged move and at worst a deliberately provocative gesture, Archduke Franz Ferdinand visited Sarajevo, the Bosnian capital, with his wife, Duchess Sophie. This would have been an unpopular move at the best of times, but for the visit to take place on Serbia's national day was a cause of great anger amongst the Serbs. Franz Ferdinand did not see it as such: he was in the area inspecting the annual military manoeuvres, and thought that it made good sense to combine the state visit to Sarajevo with this. Although there had been many rumours that his life would be in danger, he was not deterred. A small group of young Serb nationalist conspirators had already decided to make their point by assassinating the Archduke if he ever went to Sarajevo, and were aided by the fact that the Habsburg court helpfully announced the date of the visit.

Their initial attempt on the Archduke's life was almost farcical. Of the six plotters strung out along the route of the Archduke's motorcade, the first was not paying attention and the Archduke had passed before the would-be assassin could draw his revolver. The second conspirator's nationalist ardour was not enough to prevent him from being deterred from doing anything by the close proximity of a policeman, while the third, noting that Franz Ferdinand was accompanied by his wife, chose not to do anything for fear of killing the duchess. The fourth conspirator appears to have decided that he had made an error of judgement in joining the plot, because he went home before the motorcade reached him. The fifth man was made of sterner stuff, and as the motorcade approached, asked a nearby policeman which car the Archduke was in. Thinking that the enquiry was from

The Balkans in 1914 prior to the outbreak of war. The painful, convoluted collapse of the Ottoman Empire's control of its European territories and the tensions within the Habsburg Empire created ideal conditions in which nationalism and pro-independence movements could flourish, making conflict increasingly likely.

Gavrilo Princip (second from the right) is dragged away from the scene of the assassination of Archduke Franz Ferdinand and his wife. Princip became a hero to Serbian and Bosnian nationalists alike as a result of his actions, but he did not live to see Bosnian self-determination: he died of tuberculosis in April 1918 while still imprisoned.

someone anxious to see the Archduke, the policeman helpfully pointed out the correct vehicle, only to be rewarded for his trouble by the young man pulling a grenade from under his coat and hurling it at Franz Ferdinand. The chauffeur saw the object heading towards the car and accelerated to remove his vehicle from the danger zone. The increase in speed meant that instead of landing in the car, the grenade bounced off the folded roof at the back of the vehicle and fell into the road. It went off and destroyed the second vehicle, badly injuring some of the occupants and a number of passers by.

In a move that would horrify protection officers today, Ferdinand ordered his driver to stop and climbed out of his car to commiserate with the casualties while they awaited removal to hospital. Once they were all safely under medical care, Ferdinand

carried on to the lunch reception awaiting him at the town hall. During the lunch, it was decided to abandon the afternoon programme of a visit to the local museum so that the Archduke could return to the safety of either the governor's residence or his own residence. This meant that the motorcade could proceed at full speed from the town hall to whichever venue was chosen. Regrettably, no one thought to inform the Archduke's chauffeur.

Meanwhile, a sixth conspirator, Gavrilo Princip, had positioned himself so that he would be able to shoot at the Archduke's car as it made a right turn to go into the street in which the museum was located. Had the change of plan been communicated to the driver, the motorcade would have gone past Princip at speed and some distance away. However, as the driver of the first car in the convoy made his turn, the mistake was realized and instructions were shouted to the drivers. The Archduke's driver stopped and carefully reversed back around the corner at low speed, and in so doing passed Princip at a distance of less than two metres. Princip pulled out a pistol. He was nearly thwarted by a policeman who tried to grab him, but an unknown sympathizer in the crowd barged the officer to the ground, giving Princip a clear shot. He

Austrian officers receive the blessing of a priest prior to their departure to the front in 1914. While political and religious sentiment within Austria was firmly in favour of the war, the conflict only served to exacerbate the anti-Habsburg feelings in those provinces anxious for independence. This placed increasing strain on the Dual Monarchy as the war went on.

fired two rounds, the first of which passed through the thin metalwork of the car door and into the duchess, lodging in her side. The second shot hit the Archduke in the neck, severing his jugular vein and lodging in his spine. Both of them were dead on arrival at hospital.

REACTION

Unsurprisingly, the Austrians were outraged by the assassination. It seemed to be the perfect opportunity to teach Serbia a lesson, and the desire for this was such that the aged Emperor Franz Josef decided not to invite any representatives from Russia or Britain to Ferdinand's funeral in case they attempted to talk him out of attacking his hated neighbour. Advice over the matter was sought from the Germans, and full support was promised from Berlin. On 23 July, an ultimatum was issued from Vienna to the Serbs.

The Serbs, much to the Austrians' surprise, did not reject the entire document, only point six, which demanded the involvement of Austrian officials in a criminal investigation. They accepted, with some reservations, the other points, and fully agreed to keep Vienna informed of events. However, it was not enough. The Austrians wanted to crush the Serbs. There was, though, a complication. The Russians had decided that they would not let down the Serbs and orders were issued for preparations for a general Russian mobilization. This was meant to show the Austrians that Russia was not going to stand aside, but it had several unintended, fateful consequences. It was impossible for the Germans or the Austrians to allow the Russians to mobilize their enormous army, since this left them at serious risk of being attacked before their own armies were in a position to defend. They therefore began their own general mobilizations. The Germans encouraged the Austrians to try to crush the Serbs before the Russians were able to complete the build-up of forces, in the hope that a swift Austrian victory might allow for negotiations. The Austrians declared war on Serbia on 28 July 1914, and shelled Belgrade the next day.

The Russians were now faced with a dilemma, since they were determined to intervene – but their war plans called for an attack on both Austria-Hungary and Germany, since it was known that an attack on Austria would bring the Germans into the war anyway. The Tsar was also advised that a failure to attack Germany would give the French an excuse to remain neutral. The prospect of the Germans being left unmolested by the French and given time to prepare an attack on Russia meant that the Tsar, somewhat reluctantly, approved full-scale mobilization for operations against both Germany and Austria-Hungary on 30 July.

A series of telegrams between the royal households of Europe, desperately attempting to stop the slide into a major conflict, failed to achieve anything. With Russian mobilization underway, the Germans could not afford to wait with their mobilization, while the French Government, warned by its chiefs of staff that every day's delay meant an extra 32km (20 miles) of French territory lost to an invading German Army, felt that it had to order mobilization as well. Anxious to avoid a two-front war, the Germans issued an ultimatum to

The 23 July 1914 Ultimatum from Austria-Hungary to Serbia

1. Suppress publications inciting hatred of the Austrian monarchy;
2. Dissolve Serbian nationalist societies and prevent their reforming;
3. Eliminate all anti-Austro-Hungarian propaganda from public instruction in Serbia;
4. Remove all officers guilty of propaganda against Austria-Hungary from military service;
5. Accept Austro-Hungarian collaboration in Serbia in the suppression of the subversive movement;
6. Begin a judicial inquiry against the accessories to the plot of 28 June who are on Serbian territory;
7. Immediately arrest Major Vojislav Tankosich and Milan Ciganovich;
8. End the cooperation of Serbian authorities in the illicit traffic in arms and explosives across the frontier, and punish those who had assisted the authors of the Sarajevo outrage;
9. Furnish explanations regarding statements from high Serbian officials who have expressed hostility towards Austria-Hungary;
10. Notify Austria-Hungary without delay of the execution of these measures.

Belgium on 2 August 1914, demanding the right to pass through Belgian territory as part of their invasion of France. The Belgians demurred, and on 4 August German forces drove into Belgium and Luxembourg. Britain, as a guarantor of Belgian independence, felt that there was no alternative but to declare war. By the end of the first week of August 1914, there had been 44 mobilizations and declarations of war amongst the European powers; of the alliance partners, only the Italians – much to the annoyance of the Germans and Austrians – failed to enter the war. The war would soon spread to imperial possessions, but the Balkans were to be the first scene of military activity.

CHAPTER 1

The Balkans 1914

The Austro-Hungarian ultimatum confirmed the suspicions of many Serbs that their powerful neighbour's ambition was to expand eastwards and crush Serbia sooner rather than later. The ageing Austrian Emperor Franz Josef appeared to be reluctant to take such a step prior to 1914, but the assassination in Sarajevo, and the support of the Germans, appeared to galvanize political opinion in Vienna to the point where war seemed inevitable.

The need to protect against a Russian attack on Austria-Hungary meant that troops had to be diverted from the Balkan Army to the Galician front, and this in turn forced amendment of the original Austro-Hungarian plans for the conquest of Serbia. Rather than drive into Serbia from both north and west to directly engage the Serbian Army, the Austro-Hungarians instead looked to encircle Serb forces in the west of the country. Austro-Hungarian forces would seek to undermine the left flank of the Serbian Army by taking Valjevo, while simultaneous operations around Pozega would present a serious

Austro-Hungarian troops advance into Serbia in 1914. Serbia possessed few metalled roads, and the conditions seen underfoot in this photograph are typical of those faced by both sides from an early stage in the first Austrian invasion. The Austrian assault literally became bogged down.

threat to the Serbian forces' rear. The Austrians anticipated a swift victory, and felt that such a success would persuade the Italians, Romanians, Turks and Bulgarians to join the Central Powers, presenting a potentially much more challenging array of opposition to the Allies, particularly Russia.

The Austro-Hungarian forces assigned to the invasion were far smaller than originally planned (308,000 strong), given that a large part of the Austrian Second Army was moved to the Russian front, reducing the number of troops in the Balkan Army to around 200,000. However, the Austro-Hungarians could, upon full mobilization, call upon an army of approximately four million men; moving more men into the Balkan Army to support an attack on Serbia was, therefore, a practicable proposition

Serbs read about the developing crisis with the Habsburgs during the summer of 1914. In the absence of wireless and television, newspapers were the main source of mass communication – and propaganda – in pre-war Europe.

once the mobilization process was complete, and as long as the threat from Russia had been contained. The Austrians anticipated a short and relatively simple campaign of conquest.

Opposing the Austro-Hungarians, the Serbs could muster 450,000 soldiers upon full mobilization. The main elements that would face an Austrian attack were the First, Second, Third and Uzhice armies; between them, they possessed a combined strength of some 180,000 men. The numerical superiority enjoyed by the Austrians was boosted by the fact that they possessed better equipment and a better logistics organization; the Serbs were to be largely reliant upon the arrival of *matériel* support from their allies, but supplies were low. It was estimated that full mobilization would see around 50,000 Serbian troops without any equipment at all. Many units lacked any uniform other than a standard issue greatcoat and cap, leaving the soldiers to wear their own clothes beneath. To compound matters, there were shortages of rifles

The Serbian and Montenegrin Armies, August 1914

Commander-in-Chief: Prince Aleksander
Chief of Staff: Marshal Vojvoda Putnik

First Army (General Petar Bojovich)
Timok Infantry Division I
Timok Infantry Division II (reserve)
Morava Infantry Division II (reserve)
Cavalry Division
Branicevo Detachment

Second Army (General Stepa Stepanovich)
Shumadija Infantry Division I
Danub Infantry Division I
Combined Division I
Morava Infantry Division I

General Stepa Stepanovich, commander of Second Army.

Third Army (General Pavle Jurisich-Sturm)
Drina Infantry Division I
Drina Infantry Division II (reserve)
Obrenovac Detachment
Sabac Detachment
Loznica and Leshnica detachments
Ljubovije Detachment
Debelo Brdo Detachment
Jadar Chetnik Detachment
Rudnik Chetnik Detachment

(source: www.vojska.net)

Uzhice Army (General Milosh Bozanovich)
Shumadija Infantry Division I
Uzhice Brigade
Lim Detachment
Gornjacki Chetnik Detachment
Zlatibor Chetnik Detachment

Montenegrin Army
Pljevalja Division (Brigadier Luka Gojnich)
Herzegovina Detachment (Serdar Janko Vukotich)
Lovchen Detachment (Divizijar Mitja Martinovich)
Starosrbijanski Detachment (Brigadier R. Vesovich)

and ammunition throughout the army. The Serbs were supported by the Montenegrin Army, a slightly misleading term since the kingdom did not have a regular standing force; rather, there were a series of local militias, which provided a combined strength of around 45,000 riflemen.

While the Serbians and Montenegrins may have suffered from equipment shortages, they had a considerable advantage in that they had been engaged in the two recent Balkan wars, giving many of their troops considerable combat experience; this

was something that the Austrian troops lacked. In addition, the Austro-Hungarian forces were made up of a variety of disparate ethnic groupings from within the empire, and lacked the cohesive patriotic fervour of their adversaries.

INVASION

The Austrian invasion began in the early hours of 12 August 1914, as Marshal Oskar Potiorek's Second Army attacked in the northwest. Heavy artillery fire fell along the front, particularly at Belgrade. An attempt

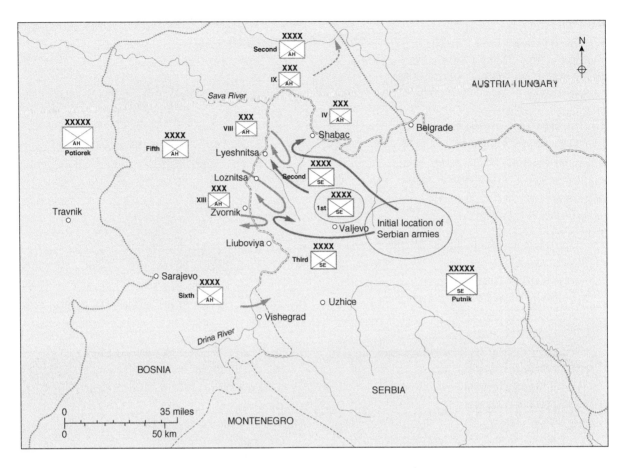

The Austrian invasion of Serbia, August 1914. The Austrian attack was made difficult by the need to force river crossings in the face of determined Serbian resistance, while the Serbs were required to maintain forces to deal with the threat of a possible Bulgarian intervention in the war.

to take the Isle of Ada Ciganlija was forced back by the Serbian defenders, but elsewhere, the Austrians made progress. In the Sava sector of operations, the Austrians captured the town of Sabac, committing a variety of atrocities against the inhabitants in the process of seizing the town. A counterattack was put in by Serbian infantry supported by cavalry squadrons, but they lacked the strength to dislodge the Austrians from their positions. Elsewhere along the Sava, Austrian troops crossed the river against light resistance and captured a number of villages in the area of Mitrovica. The Austrians, however, were unable to exploit their gains in this sector on the first

day, since they needed reinforcement before they could advance further.

On the lower Drina, a heavy preparatory bombardment by the Austrian Fifth Army was followed by an assault against the Isle of Samurovica Ada and the Isle of Ada Kurjacica. The Isle of Samurovica Ada fell swiftly, since it was only lightly held. However, the Isle of Ada Kurjacica, despite being occupied by just two companies of Serbian troops, proved to be a much more difficult proposition. It took most of the day for the Serbian force to be dislodged from its position, and by nightfall the Austrian advance in this area was behind schedule. Only one division of troops had managed to cross the river Drina. Serbian troops carried out harrying attacks at a variety of locations, helping to slow the Austrian advance yet further. After its initial advance, Sixth Army was compelled to move onto the defensive, so as to screen the right flank of the Fifth Army as it sought to overcome tenacious Serbian resistance.

Although the opening attack had been accompanied by heavy artillery bombardment, the effect on the Serbians had not been as disorienting as Austro-Hungarian commanders might have anticipated. Serbian units remained cohesive despite the weight of attack (as illustrated by their fierce resistance across the front), and this meant that the Serb high command was in a position to receive regular and reliable reports from troops as they held positions or made tactical withdrawals in good order. The Serbian leadership was further aided by the survival of most of the telecommunications network within

the country, which made it possible for them to make assessments of the Austrian attack based upon detailed information. As the day wore on, it seemed clear that the Austrian Second Army was carrying out a feint attack, seeking to draw Serbian troops in. Realization that the Austrian Sixth Army had moved to a defensive posture and had all but ended its advance prompted the Serbian commander, Marshal Radomir Putnik, to conclude that the main weight of effort would occur in the northwest of Serbia. It was also evident that while the defending forces were doing well, Shabac and Obrenovac were under threat. The latter location came under persistent, heavy artillery fire throughout the morning of 12 August, and Putnik gave orders that the Serbian First and Second armies should move towards the northwest front, with the Serbian Third Army being employed to block the efforts of the Austrian Fifth Army in its attempts to advance. General Milosh

The announcement of mobilization is received in Belgrade. The prospect of war with Austria-Hungary was regarded with a mixture of satisfaction and trepidation, despite popular opinion being overwhelmingly anti-Habsburg.

Bozanovich's Uzhice Army was ordered to advance to Vishegrad, with the Montenegrin Army providing flank security during the offensive.

While the Serbians were preparing for the attack, Potiorek had instructed the Austrian Sixth Army to dig in, anxious to ensure that the Serbs could not advance towards Sarajevo. Potiorek feared, not without justification, that such a move might provoke a popular uprising amongst Serbs living in Bosnia. Such an insurrection was the last thing that Potiorek needed, with the threat of attacks on his rear echelon and supply lines, hence his considerable care to avoid circumstances that might give rise to such a situation. However, this caution translated itself into exceptionally slow movement by the Austro-Hungarian forces, who failed to maintain the tempo

The effects of Austrian shelling on Belgrade. The Austrians possessed far greater numbers of artillery pieces than their opponents, but problems with ammunition supply and the lack of mobility of the guns meant that they were unable to fully exploit this advantage, allowing the Serbs to put up tenacious resistance.

of the invasion, giving the Serbs the time to make detailed plans for their response to the enemy attack. During 13 August, the Austrian Second Army did not continue efforts to advance, but waited for the arrival of the Austrian Fifth Army. The Austrian VIII Corps had failed to take up its intended position to the north of Lesnica, and this compelled XIII Corps to wait before starting its advance. XIII Corps had been given strict instructions that it was not to start operations until VIII Corps had reached Lesnica, and this meant that it spent an entire day waiting around for news. The delay meant that the Serbs – who might have been hard pressed had the advance gone in on 13 August – were able to bring up reinforcements to meet the projected Austrian advance.

The Serbs were able to move the cavalry squadron from the 1st Drina Division to the southeast of Sabac, and attacked the town of Misar in the afternoon with the Sabac Detachment, in preparation for an attempt to retake Sabac the next day. The 1st Shumadija Division took up positions to the south of the town, and during the 14th both it and the Sabac

Detachment attacked. They failed in their effort to take the town, while the Austrian Fifth Army, having arrived as intended before Lesnica, managed to make some gains, albeit at the cost of considerable losses on both sides. The Lesnica Detachment was driven from its positions by VIII Corps, and XIII Corps, having wasted an entire day, took Loznica. While the delays had not, in the end, prevented the Austrians from achieving their goals, they had given the Serbs time

> 'The Serbians, seasoned, war-hardened men, inspired by the fiercest patriotism, the result of generations of torment and struggle, awaited undaunted whatever fate might bestow'
>
> Winston Churchill, *The Great War*

to reinforce, and the fighting was far heavier, and bloodier, than might have been the case if the Austro-Hungarians had been less cautious in their approach. The day ended with the Austrians apparently holding the advantage after a day of hard-won success. However, Marshal Putnik was far from discouraged. His analysis of the situation during the evening and early hours of 14/15 August was positive. Intelligence information suggested that the general lack of activity from the main body of Austrian Second Army was because its forces were being carefully husbanded to allow the formation to be sent to the Russian front once Serbia had been defeated. As a result, it had only committed certain elements of its strength in the Sabac region, and was content to make limited manoeuvres so as to keep the Serbian First and Third armies opposite it fixed in place, uncertain of whether or not it would open offensive operations against them. It also appeared clear to Putnik that the Austrian Sixth Army was still on the defensive in Bosnia in a bid to ensure that the Serbs did not advance towards Sarajevo and spark the uprising that

Marshal Radomir Putnik (1847–1917)

Putnik was a distinguished soldier, with a record of successful command dating back to the 1870s. By the end of the Second Balkan War (1913), his health was in decline. Following the Austro-Hungarian declaration of war on Serbia in July 1914 he was arrested at the health spa he was visiting in Austria. Putnik was saved by the gentlemanly, but not sensible, decision by Emperor Franz Josef to order his release.

Putnik returned to Serbia immediately, and set about organizing the defences for the inevitable attack. He performed superbly, and the Austrian forces were driven out of Serbia. His success was relatively short lived, as a combination of the typhus epidemic that ravaged his troops and support from the Germans and Bulgarians made the next Austrian attempt at invasion successful. By this point, Putnik was seriously ill, and was clearly unfit to continue in command. He was replaced by his former aide, Marshal Zhivojin Misich, and was taken to France, where he died in May 1917.

Potiorek feared. Putnik's confidence was enhanced by the knowledge that the Serbian Second Army had moved into position alongside the Serbian Third Army, reinforcing the front there. Putnik therefore decided that it was necessary to move onto the offensive in a bid to drive the Austro-Hungarian invasion forces out of the country.

To achieve this goal, it would be necessary for the Serbs to prevent the Austrian Fifth Army from linking up with the elements of the Austrian Second Army around Sabac. This would best be achieved, it seemed, by launching a counterattack in strength against the Austrian Fifth Army. Putnik gave orders that the

A wounded Serb soldier is carried towards a field hospital by his comrades. The medical facilities on offer to Serbian troops were basic but effective. However, the greatest challenge was posed by disease, particularly typhus, which laid low much of the Serbian Army in early 1915.

Serbian Third Army was to block the advance of enemy forces moving into the Jadar Valley, while General Stepa Stepanovich's Second Army was to attack the Austrian left flank. He would move into position, along with the rest of the Serbian forces, during 15 August, with the attack to begin the following day. The Balkan Army continued with its activities during 15 August, unaware of what was to take place the following day. The Austrian Second Army continued to conduct limited operations along its front, while the Austrian Fifth Army made small advances on both flanks to the extent that a continuance might lead to the encirclement of the Serbian Third Army. The Austrian Fifth Army ended the day on the slopes of the Cer, unaware of the fact that the Serbian Second

Army was approaching the opposite side. The Serbian Second Army was equally oblivious of the fact that it would find its opponents so close to hand.

BATTLE ON THE CER

At about 11pm on 15 August, elements of the Serbian 1st Combined Division ran into Austrian outposts on the slopes of the Cer, and fighting broke out. The Austrian positions were lightly held, and their defenders were driven back towards the main body of the Austrian forces. By midnight, fierce fighting was underway. Chaos ensued in the darkness; the commander of the Austrian 21st Infantry Division, General Pschiborsky, found himself at the head of one battalion, so he armed himself with a rifle and led an attack on two Serbian infantry battalions opposite. The Serbs proved too strong, and the Austrians were driven back. By the early morning of 16 August, the Serbs had taken the Divaca range and dislodged the Austrians from their position on the Borino Brdo. The Austrians had suffered heavy casualties during the fighting, and fell back in some disorder. As the day went on, the Serbs prevented the Austrian 21st Infantry Division from linking with Austrian Second Army at Sabac by driving it off the slopes of the Cer. The Serbian 1st Combined Division had spent the past 24 hours marching to the battle area and then fighting without any opportunity to rest; faced by an Austrian assault, the troops on the division's left flank were forced to retreat, beginning a chain of events that left the Austrians on the verge of rolling up the 1st Combined Division's front-line position. The situation appeared to be critical, and General Stepanovich rushed to the front to encourage his troops to hold on. The troops rallied and held the Austrians off until the 1st Morava Division arrived to reinforce them, ending the crisis.

On 17 August, the Serbs attempted to recapture Sabac, but their efforts failed. The 1st Combined Division, having recovered from the travails of the previous day, attacked Trojan and Parlog, before moving on towards Kosanin Grad. The Austrians succeeded in their efforts to drive back the Serbian

Serbian troops cross the Danube River. The proliferation of water obstacles on the Serbian front created considerable challenges for both sides, not least the advancing Austrians, who found it difficult to gain a foothold on the other side of the Danube in the face of determined resistance.

Third Army, forcing it to manoeuvre one of its divisions to protect the approach to Valjevo, which was under threat from the Austrian 42nd Mountain Division. The day concluded with both sides attempting to advance, but with only limited success, their broader ambitions being frustrated by the defensive efforts of their opponents. Early on

Marshal Oskar Potiorek (1853–1933)

Potiorek had the misfortune to be associated with a number of disastrous events that afflicted the Austro-Hungarian Empire at the start of World War I. He was the governor of Bosnia-Herzegovina in 1914, and was travelling in the car carrying Archduke Franz Ferdinand and his wife when they were assassinated. Potiorek had overruled doubts about their visiting those wounded in the initial grenade attack on their lives, and had decided the route the royal car should take to the hospital. He failed to inform the driver of the change of plan, which led to the royal car taking a wrong turn. It then drove past Gavrilo Princip, who seized his unexpected opportunity to shoot the Archduke and his wife. Potiorek was reported to have observed that he was spared from Princip's bullets so that he could die in the effort to avenge the assassination. While he was passionate in his attempts to do so, his leadership skills were inadequate, and after the defeat at Kolubara, he was removed from command. He retired from the army shortly afterwards.

18 August, the Austrians launched another attack, with the intention of driving the 1st Shumadija Division off the Sabac bridgehead, which would allow Austrian Fifth Army to advance. The attack was a spectacular failure, however, since the Serbs destroyed the Austrians at the river Dobrava, forcing the surviving troops to withdraw. The Serbian Second Army's counter-offensive continued along the Cer and Iverak, with the 1st Combined Division attacking at Rashuliacha. The Austrians held Rashuliacha, but came under severe pressure at Kosanin Grad. The first Serbian attack was repulsed, but a wave of further assaults followed during the course of the night. In the early morning of 19 August, the Serbs finally broke the Austrian defences and took the town. The 1st Morava Division drove the Austrian 9th Infantry Division from its positions, and beat off the ensuing counterattack, inflicting heavy losses upon the Austrian troops. Austrian IV Corps renewed the attack on the Shumadija Division, but although the Serbs were forced to withdraw, they did not break before the enemy attack. This meant that IV Corps was unable to alter the direction of its advance towards the Cer, since to do so would have left the Shumadija Division in a position to attack IV Corps from the rear. As a result, IV Corps was compelled to continue the engagement with the Shumadija Division, and was unable to join the battle at the Cer, which was entering its decisive phase.

Rashuliacha fell to the Serbs at noon, and the 1st Combined Division exploited this to advance towards Lesnica. The 1st Morava Division, meanwhile, attacked the Iverak, and after a short, sharp engagement succeeded in driving

the Austrians back. Velika Glava fell just before midday, and by the late afternoon the Rajin Grob Ridge had fallen into Serbian hands. Once this position had fallen, the Austrians began to fall back with increasing rapidity, their will and cohesion apparently broken. The Serbian Third Army enjoyed similar success after a day's hard fighting, driving the Austrian 36th Infantry Division from the field in considerable disorder. The Serbian forces moved to pursue the retreating Austrians all along the front, and by 20 August the Austrians had been thrown back across the river Drina, still harried by the Serbs. Within another 48 hours, all of the Austrian Fifth Army had been driven into Bosnia. With the Austrians defeated at the Cer, the Serbs sought to liberate Sabac. Four days of fighting ensued, and by 24 August the Serbs had driven the Austrians from the town.

The defeat at Cer and the Austrian retreat back across the Drina brought an end to what became known as the First Serbian Campaign. The Austro-Hungarian forces suffered around 37,000 casualties, of which around 7000 were fatalities, while the Serbs endured far lighter losses – around 3000 dead and 15,000 wounded. It represented the first clear-cut victory of the Allies over the Central Powers, but it was not a decisive end to the conflict between Serbia and Austria-Hungary: the Austro-Hungarians would try once more to conquer Serbia, but only after the Serbs had embarked upon offensive operations of their own.

A Serbian reservist. The Serbs were critically short of supplies, and as can be seen from this soldier's footwear, troops were often forced to go into battle wearing a mixture of official army uniform and their own clothing.

OFFENSIVE PLANNING

The failure of the Austrian attempt to defeat Serbia presented the government in Vienna with a dilemma. It had the option of resuming the offensive and attempting to defeat the Serbs, or of moving onto the defensive on the Austro-Serbian border and sending its troops to the Russian front. The Germans had urged the second course of action upon the Austro-Hungarians from the start of the war, perceiving the Russians as the greatest initial threat. However, the humiliation inflicted upon his forces meant that Potiorek was determined to resume the attack on Serbia through an offensive across the Drina. The Austrian high command gave Potiorek permission to launch another invasion, provided he did not 'risk anything that might lead to a further fiasco'.

The Serbs were also considering their next move. The success of operations against the initial Austrian invasion led to a degree of over-confidence on their part, since they thought it would be profitable to carry the war over the border and into Austro-Hungarian territory. Further justification for this view appeared

The corpses of Serbian soldiers from the Timok Division, alleged victims of a massacre by Austrian troops after they had surrendered. Accusations of atrocities were a common feature of the first Austrian invasion of Serbia, and only served to increase the enmity between the two sides.

to be provided by the fact that the Austro-Hungarian forces confronting the Russians on the Galician front suffered a number of defeats, which suggested that the Austro-Hungarians were militarily weak. This was a dangerous view for the Serbs to adopt, as they still had serious problems with lack of equipment and the army had been exhausted by its efforts to expel the invasion. Although the withdrawal of the invading forces gave the Serbs the chance to recover, the Serbian high command's decision that its forces would be fit to embark upon an offensive after just a week seems daringly optimistic, even without the benefit of hindsight. It may have been the case that the Serbs were blinded from a sober assessment of the problems facing their army by the fact that the Austrian withdrawal opened the enticing prospect of being able to attack into the province of Syrmia, as a prelude to an invasion

29

of Bosnia, with the ultimate goal of separating Bosnia from the Austro-Hungarian empire.

THE SERBIAN OFFENSIVE

The first move was made by the Serbs, who invaded Syrmia on 6 September 1914. Although they achieved surprise, they did not gain any major benefit from this. The Serbian First Army led the invasion, and rapidly established a bridgehead across the Sava at Kupinski Kut. From this lodgement, the First Army began to advance further into Syrmia. While First Army was enjoying success, the same could not be said elsewhere. The Timok Division had run into difficulties near Yasenova Grada, having been sent there to protect the left flank of the invasion force. The Timok Division crossed the Sava between the towns of Mitrovitz and Yarak, both of which contained small Austrian garrisons. The crossing of the Sava was met

Serbian officers examine a map in a posed photograph. The geography of Serbia meant that there was little need for close study of maps by the defenders, since it was fairly clear where the enemy attack would fall.

with considerable opposition from Austrian forces on the opposing bank, and although overcome, this delayed the Timok Division's advance. This prompted the Serbian forces to seek to make up time by pressing on, and to do this, they moved on from the bridgehead without fortifying it. Rather than seeking to take either Yarak or Mitrovitz, the Serbs pushed a regiment (the 13th) between the two towns, seeking to avoid contact and thus further delay. The decision to do this was unwise. The 13th Regiment advanced beyond the two towns, leaving both flanks dangerously exposed, and with only a tenuous link to the units behind it, which were having some difficulty in crossing the river. The Austrian forces in the two towns promptly came out and attacked the flanks of the advancing 13th Regiment, which came close to being encircled and cut off. The lack of a fortified bridgehead meant that the Timok Division was unable to remain on the Austrian side of the river, and it was forced to withdraw to the opposite bank. This, of course, meant that the plan to protect the flank of the Serbian First Army had failed, compelling First Army to advance with a far greater degree of caution than might otherwise have been the case had its flank been secure. The Serbs took a number of towns as they advanced, but even five days after the successful assault across the Sava, the Serbian First Army was well short of its initial objective of the Frushkagora Mountains. Without control of the mountain range, an invasion into Bosnia was simply not viable. Events elsewhere were to compromise Serbian intentions.

THE AUSTRIAN RESPONSE

The Austrians launched their offensive late in the evening of 7 September 1914, attacking in strength along the Drina. They faced Serbian forces arrayed along the opposite river bank in a continuous line, which meant that there was little option for the Austrians other than to engage in an attritional battle, with much heavy fighting. In the northern sector, the Austrian assault was unable to make any ground, and five days of bloody fighting produced no result for either side other than heavy casualties. In the southern sector, the Austrians were able to make some headway, not least because Marshal Putnik had judged that the Austrians would not attack into an area noted for its difficult mountainous terrain, and had withdrawn units from the area

to reinforce the attack into Syrmia. Putnik had failed to appreciate the proficiency of the Austrian mountain corps, which forced the Serbs into a retreat, allowing the Austrians into the mountains. A series of fierce and costly battles to gain control of various summits now ensued, with control of these locations changing hands frequently in assaults and counterattacks. The Austrian high command halted the offensive when the Serbian Uzhice Army advanced into southern Bosnia. As September 1914 drew to a close, the Austrians were no nearer to obtaining their initial goal of a swift, decisive victory over the Serbs and had little to show for their efforts other than a few insignificant territorial gains and a large casualty list. There was little doubt that the failure of the second Austrian attempt to subdue the Serbs was a cause of some embarrassment in Vienna. Determination to overcome this would lead to further attempts to destroy the Serbs. The Austrians dug in and fought a series of minor engagements during October, with the most notable success being the expulsion from Bosnia of the Serbian forces that had invaded a few weeks before.

POTIOREK'S OFFENSIVE

Although the threat to Bosnia had been overcome, the Austro-Hungarian high command became increasingly irritated with Potiorek's inability to defeat the Serbs. The Austrian chief of staff, General Conrad von Hotzendorf, had anticipated that it would take at most two weeks for Serbia to be overcome, and the continuing failure to secure a positive result was a source of some embarrassment. The high command was unimpressed when Potiorek

A private soldier in the Austro-Hungarian Army, holding his Mannlicher Modell 1895. The latter was of sound, reliable design, and although it could never be described as the best rifle of the war, it was robust and effective enough to see over 50 years service as the standard service weapon of many of the Central European armies through to 1945.

complained that he had been deprived of success thanks to the removal of the Second Army from his command, and a lack of munitions. Both the Second Army and the munitions had been sent to the more important Galician front to fight the Russians. The complaint would have been of minor concern had it not been regarded sympathetically by the emperor, who decreed that Potiorek should be allowed to act independently of the high command in Serbia.

With this new freedom of action, Potiorek decided that it was necessary to launch another offensive against the Serbs. It is not unreasonable to suggest that Potiorek was allowing his determination for success to override his judgement; bad weather had set in,

with flooding in low-lying areas, and the first snow of the year in the mountains, rendering the primitive road system in Serbia almost impassable in places. The Austrians had the advantage that the indecisive fighting during October had worn down the Serbian Army, which was holding an over-extended line along the front. The troops were exhausted from

Serbian troops on the march in the early part of the war. The Serbs were compelled to move around a great deal in the face of the Austrian advance, retiring to better positions in their ultimately successful bid to blunt the Austrian attack. Nevertheless, it was a close-run affair.

days spent in the front line, under almost continuous bombardment from the Austro-Hungarian guns. In the face of this, the Serbs withdrew their troops from the Machva Plain to the foothills of the Cer mountain range, with the intention of moving out of range of the enemy artillery.

In response, the Austrians pushed forward onto the Machva Plain in the first week of November 1914, and on the 6th Potiorek issued orders that his troops should begin their third invasion of Serbia, with Valjevo as the initial objective. As the town was a major rail junction, the intent was to use the railway lines to supply the Austrian advance on the Serbian arsenal at Kragujevac. Potiorek knew that the heavily forested mountain terrain between his forces and Kragujevac was not conducive to defensive operations, and considered that his chances of success against an outnumbered, exhausted opposition were high. He was to be disappointed.

THE SERBIAN DEFENCE

The first heavy fighting between the Serbs and the invaders came on 7 November, when the Austrian Fifth and Sixth armies attacked across the Drina after a heavy preparatory artillery bombardment. The Serbs put up fierce resistance, but the weight of enemy numbers told against them and they were forced to withdraw. The Serbian Third Army withdrew to defend the Jadar road, in an attempt to block the Austrian advance towards Valjevo, while to the south the Serbian First Army was forced to retreat. In contrast, the Uzhice Army managed to stop the Austrians crossing the Drina. The next day, the Austrians attacked the Serbian Second Army in the foothills of the Cer. The Serbs were desperately short of ammunition, while the attacking Austrians enjoyed support from a considerable amount of artillery. The Austrians were able to get within a mile of the Serbian front line, and dug in. The Second Army was given orders to hold for as long as possible, but if the position became untenable, they were to retire to the right bank of the Dobrava River, and then swing around to cover the approach to Valjevo. The situation was equally serious for the Serbian Third Army, which found itself unable to hold on in the face of the Austrian advance, with Austrian forces driving between the Serbian Third and First armies, forcing another retreat.

Marshal Putnik did not panic; he knew that, as the Austrians advanced, they would extend their supply lines, while Serbian forces would be nearer to their major railheads. He therefore ordered a general retreat away from the positions on the Jadar, moving the Serbian First, Second and Third armies into defensive

positions that covered the approaches to Valjevo, while the Uzhice Army was pulled back to defend the town from which it took its name. However, the Austrians exceeded Putnik's expectations, and managed to bring their heavy artillery along the rutted, muddy roads. They established firing positions and began to inflict heavy casualties on the Serbians. This was the final straw for many of the Serbian troops, demoralized by a lack of cold-weather clothing, a shortage of ammunition and their experiences of the retreat, which had taken place in some confusion as refugees from border areas intermingled with the withdrawing soldiers. It became clear to Putnik that his forces had now become ineffective, and needed to regroup; however, to achieve this it was necessary to make another withdrawal, which involved abandoning Valjevo to the enemy and taking up positions on the river Kolubara.

The Austrians reached Valjevo on 15 November, provoking wild public celebrations in the Habsburg capital. This success lulled the Austrian high command

Montenegrin artillery in position just behind the front line. The Serbs and Montenegrins were painfully short of artillery pieces, and even less well supplied with ammunition. The numerical dominance of the Austro-Hungarian artillery inflicted a heavy toll upon the defenders, but was not enough to bring about victory.

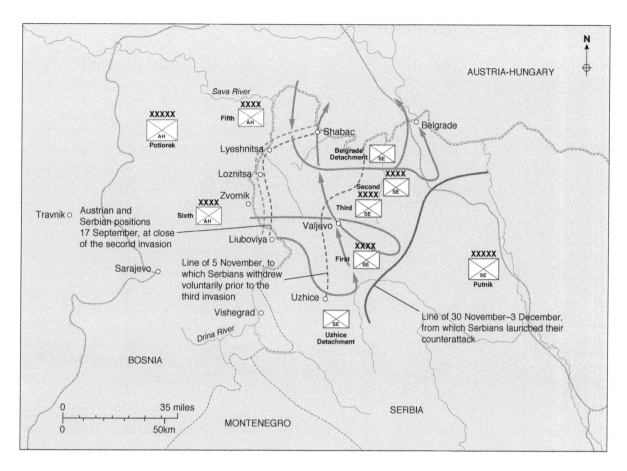

into believing that victory was in its grasp, and that the Serbian Army was finished as a coherent fighting force. This was a serious underestimation of the enemy; while it was true that the Serbians were on the back foot, they were not yet broken. They had lost much equipment on the way back to the Kolubara, but their position was far from hopeless. On the retreat, the Serbs were careful to ensure that they destroyed bridges and telephone lines behind them, denying their use to the Austrians and thus complicating their advance.

TO THE KOLUBARA

While the Serbian Army was now on the verge of exhaustion, its defensive positions on the Kolubara had been prepared for several months and were well founded. Putnik's carefully timed withdrawals had ensured that his losses were lighter than if he had stood and fought pitched battles. The terrain favoured

The second and third invasions of Serbia came as the Austro-Hungarians grew increasingly frustrated with their inability to crush an opponent who they had assumed would be forced to capitulate within a matter of weeks. The defiance of the Serbs surprised their opponents and earned the admiration of their British and French allies.

defensive operations, since although the Kolubara itself did not represent a particularly difficult obstacle to cross, the approaches did not offer any cover to an advancing force, and at various points the land was overlooked by mountainous terrain. The Serbs had taken particular care to fortify the Jeljak and Maljen mountain ranges, which gave a commanding position over all the routes that led to Kragujevac, while they had also established earthworks that blocked the approach to Nish, to where the government had been evacuated when Belgrade came under threat. This meant that the Austrians faced the prospect of

35

Serbian artillery on the move. The appalling conditions underfoot can be clearly seen, and the lack of robust communications infrastructure was a major problem for both sides, particularly as they attempted to move their artillery into position. The poor transport network proved a serious obstacle to Austrian ambitions for a swift victory.

conducting operations in arduous terrain, in which lines of communication were almost non-existent.

The Austrians reached the Kolubara on 16 November, and put in an attack the next day. The Serbian Second Army bore the brunt of the assault, which took place in appalling weather. Over the course of the next five days, the two sides fought a series of battles to the accompaniment of heavy rain and snowfall, with a large number of their men succumbing to frostbite and cold-related injuries. The Austrian assault began with an attempt to seize Lazavarec, which would have given them access to the railway line to Mladenovac and the ability to outflank the Serbian forces holding the centre of the front. Further south, the Serbian First Army came under attack, but the Austrians misjudged the operation, and made the mistake of attacking the Serbs' stronger flank; had they attacked at the junction of the First and Uzhice armies, they might have managed to split the Serbian positions, leaving them with a reasonably clear route to the Morava River. However, by attacking the First Army's right flank, the Austrians ran into stiff opposition and were unable to gain any ground. The Serbs, appreciating that any subsequent attack on the left by the Austrians would be less easy to rebuff, conducted a rapid reinforcement and strengthened their weaker flank. During the night of 18 November, the Austrians moved into position to carry out a further assault, which began the following morning. The Austrians sought to break through the Serbian Second Army's defences around Lazarevac, and to drive the Serbian First Army back towards Gornji

Milanovac, while simultaneously conducting a further attack upon the Serbian positions at Chovka and Vrache Brdo, which threatened the Austrian flank. By the end of 19 November, the Austrians had gained a foothold on Vrache Brdo, and had taken higher ground further to the south. The Serbian First Army was compelled to fall back in the face of the Austrian onslaught, giving the Austrians the ability to push on down the main routes to Kragujevac. Potiorek recognized that there was a danger that Putnik might be attempting to lure him into a trap which would see them attacking the flanks of the Austrian advance, but correctly assessed that the Serbian forces were in no position to carry out such an attack.

On 21 November, the Austrians made a renewed attack on the Serbian First Army, and forced their opponents back after some particularly fierce engagements. The Austrians next headed for Mount Maljen, with the aim of driving the Serbian First Army from its positions there. A further three days of heavy

fighting saw the Serbs withdraw, but Potiorek chose not to pursue the retreating forces, giving them the opportunity to retire in good order. Furthermore, the hard fighting over the course of the preceding three days meant that the Austrians had lost some of their cohesion as a result of casualties suffered, and as fatigue set in amongst the attacking troops who were advancing over terrain that was increasingly difficult to traverse.

While the Serbian First Army was being forced to retire, the Serbian Second and Third armies were offering vigorous resistance to the Austrian advance against their positions. Potiorek reinforced his formations around Lazarevac, with the aim of seizing

Casualties at a Serbian field hospital. The photograph gives little insight into some of the terrible conditions in which the both sides attempted to treat their wounded. The severity of the fighting led to a considerable number of casualties on both sides, exacerbated for the Serbs by the spread of disease throughout their malnourished and exhausted troops.

the town and then driving on to Kragujevac, while the right flank would push down the Western Morava Valley. Potiorek was convinced that he held the upper hand and was increasingly optimistic about the prospect of manoeuvring his forces so that they would roll up the surviving enemy troops from the Serbian Second and Third armies. Potiorek further envisaged that the Serbian First and Uzhice armies would be enveloped by breaking through their lines between Lazarevac and Belgrade and then surrounding them.

This meant that the fighting around the Lazarevac Salient intensified once again. Despite a lack of ammunition, the Serbian troops managed to fend off every Austro-Hungarian attack. The Serbian artillery began to run out of shells, and Marshal Stepanovich asked for permission to send them to the rear, since he felt that their inability to contribute to the defence was a source of frustration to his troops and bad for morale. Putnik refused permission, advising Stepanovich that the Russians had sent supplies of ammunition that included shells for the guns. Stepanovich was sceptical – unsurprisingly given the lack of supplies since the outbreak of the war – but kept the artillery pieces as instructed.

THE FALL OF BELGRADE

The Austrians made further gains, forcing the Serbs back from Vrache Brdo and Chovka with an intense artillery bombardment, but their attempt to cross the Kolubara at its junction with the Sava on 26 November was rebuffed. The initial attack by the Austrians managed to get across the river, thanks

An officer from the Austrian Hussars in a classic duelling stance, aims a Steyr-Hahn M12 self-loading pistol. His uniform is classically nineteenth century in design, and soon proved unsuited for the rigours of modern warfare. The M12, on the other hand, was an excellent pistol that saw service in both world wars, albeit on a more limited scale between 1939 and 1945.

to the heavy artillery support the first wave of the attack received. However, while the Serbs were forced back, they counterattacked and inflicted over 50 per cent casualties on the Austrians, who were forced to halt. They followed this with a counterattack on Chovka on 27 November, and succeeded in driving the Austrians out. While the Serbs were putting up fierce resistance, Putnik was still not content with the situation he faced. Concerned that his line was still too long, he pondered another retirement, even though this meant that Belgrade would have to be evacuated. The decision was made for the Serbs when an attack by the Austrian Sixth Army during the night of 27/28 November made considerable progress, highlighting the parlous situation in which the over-extended Serbian front line found itself. Belgrade was evacuated during 29 and 30 November. The Austro-Hungarians entered the enemy capital on 1 December, prompting yet more wild celebrations in Vienna. The Austro-Hungarians believed that the fall of Belgrade meant that the Serbian campaign was entering the final stages, but the situation was about to change dramatically.

AUSTRIAN REVERSES

Potiorek gave orders that his Sixth Army was to halt, and to wait for Fifth Army to secure its supply lines to the east of the Valjevo railway: it became increasing clear both to Potiorek and Putnik that the Austro-Hungarian forces had over-extended their supply lines. There was a four-day pause in all Austrian operations – and coinciding with this, the Serbs finally began to receive long-promised supplies from the Allies, which restored Putnik's confidence in his ability to make a counterattack. On 2 December Putnik gave orders that all his forces were to attack, informing his officers that the offensive was intended to have the specific purpose of restoring morale. King Peter was

determined to play his part, despite his advancing years, and on 3 December headed to the front with a rifle in a bid to inspire his troops.

The Serbian offensive came as a considerable shock to the Austrians, who now found themselves defending along an over-extended front. To make matters worse, Potiorek had begun to strengthen his left flank, so that the front line was even more lightly held. Despite this, the Austrians were in a position to avoid a serious reverse if they could only prevent the Serbian First Army from reaching the watershed of the Kolubara and Western Morava rivers. The respite presented by the Austrian pause had been exploited by the First Army's commander, General Mishich, who had ensured that his men took the opportunity to rest. Reinvigorated and resupplied, they were confident; they also discovered that the forces opposing them had failed to make adequate preparations to fend off an offensive – their transportation difficulties had

Tired Serbian troops withdraw with their artillery during the desperate days of the Austrian offensive in November 1914. Despite widespread exhaustion and a thinning of the ranks thanks to heavy casualties and illness, the Serbs not only blunted the enemy attack, but launched a successful counter-offensive.

led to the Austrian artillery being left well behind the front line, meaning that the defending Austrians were unable to call upon their heavy guns to break up the Serbian advance. By nightfall, the Serbian First Army had advanced several miles, while success had been enjoyed by the Serbian Second and Third armies, as well as the Uzhice Army. The latter met fierce resistance, but made progress, while the Second and Third armies retook a number of key positions on high ground. First Army enjoyed the greatest success, however, taking a large number of prisoners and inflicting heavy casualties in several sharp engagements during the course of the day. The success of the first

day of the offensive, although relatively modest, did much to enhance the morale of the Serbian troops, just as Putnik had intended. The Austrians had been forced onto the back foot, and did not have sufficient time to recover before the offensive resumed on 3 December. The Serbian assault gathered increasing momentum during the course of the day, and the enemy forces were firmly on the retreat by the end of the day.

On 6 December, it became clear that the Austrian positions were broken – their forces in the centre and on their right had been comprehensively defeated and were in full retreat, abandoning weapons and equipment as they went. The retreat was in danger of turning into a rout, and the Austrian commanders did well to maintain any semblance of order amongst their troops. The Austrians arrived at Uzhice and Valjevo on 8 December, and the Serbs anticipated that the retreating forces would dig in and attempt to block their advance; however, the over-confidence of the Austrians earlier in the campaign meant that they had failed to construct the additional defensive works required to block the Serbian attack. The Austrians had

Montenegrin troops move forward, watched by an admiring crowd. Despite the apparently hopeless odds against them, the Serbian and Montenegrin populations refused to accept defeat, and fought determinedly against the Austro-Hungarians. The civilian population suffered terribly as the war progressed, short of food and often displaced from their homes by the fighting.

ensured that the defences of Valjevo were fortified, and artillery fire plans had been laid down. However, the lack of prior preparation meant that the hilly terrain surrounding the town was devoid of meaningful defensive positions, and the Serbs simply exploited this by moving round the hills and enveloping the defending Austrians at relatively little cost.

The lower reaches of the Drina were retaken by the Serbs on 10 December, by which time the majority of the surviving Austrian forces had been thrown back across the river. The Austrians appeared to be in a better position around Belgrade, not least since they had the benefit of reasonably reliable supplies. An attack by General Frank's forces in Belgrade against the Serbian right gained some ground on 7 December, and the renewal of operations the next day enjoyed some success. This was only temporary, since the arrival of Serbian reinforcements blunted the Austrian assault and began to force them back . By the latter part of 9 December, the Austrian attack had lost momentum, and Frank realized that there was little point in attempting to push the issue further; he ordered his men to fall back on Belgrade. Although Frank considered continuing resistance, it became obvious to him that this was impractical, and on 13

RIGHT King Peter of Serbia came to the throne in 1903 after a coup, and became immensely popular with the Serbian people. Although he retired from public life after the Balkan Wars, with his son becoming regent, Peter played an active part in World War I and paid many visits to the front line.

BELOW A gun crew attends a Serbian heavy artillery piece. Such guns were extremely difficult to move, and were better suited for static defensive warfare, rather than the sort of mobile war which the Serbs found themselves forced to fight in the face of the Austro-Hungarian invasion.

Marshal Zhivojin Mishich (1855–1921)

After the assassination of King Aleksandar Obrenovich in 1903, Mishich was forced to retire from the Serbian Army over his loyalty to the dynasty. However, the chief of staff of the army, Radomir Putnik, insisted on recalling him to become Putnik's aide.

Mishich was promoted to general following his performance at the Battle of Kumanovo during the First Balkan War. At the Battle of Bregalnica in the Second Balkan War, when Putnik was advised by his staff officers to withdraw in the face of a Bulgarian attack, Mishich persuaded Putnik that he should advance. Putnik took his advice and won a great victory. At the Battle of Kolubara, Mishich led the First Army to victory, and was promoted to marshal. Mishich retreated with the rest of the Serbian Army in the face of the 1916 invasion, and suffered exposure on the way to Albania. In September 1916 he resumed command of the First Army and was appointed as chief of staff at the end of the war. He died on a visit to Paris in 1921.

December he informed Potiorek that he considered it impossible for him to remain in Belgrade for much longer. As a result, the Austrian forces in Belgrade were given permission to withdraw; they left the city on 14 and 15 December, retiring in good order back into Austria-Hungary, supported by the guns mounted upon river monitors patrolling the Danube. The Serbs re-entered their capital on 15 December and were in complete control of the city by the end of the day.

ASSESSING THE FIRST ROUND

The failure of their attacks on Serbia came as an unpleasant surprise to the Austro-Hungarian Empire, which had anticipated an easy victory. The Austrians had come close to success at the end of November

Serbian artillery at Belgrade, preparing to fire on enemy forces at Semlin. The Serbs made good use of their artillery during the retaking of their capital, exploiting the fact that the over-confident Austrians had failed to emplace enough of their own guns to defend the city adequately.

Casualties of war. Dead Serbian troops and their transport lie on the road where they fell victim to enemy fire. Serbian casualties in 1914 were enormous, with over 170,000 troops and large numbers of civilians killed or wounded; losses of animals, vital for food and transport, were similarly high.

1914, but the tenacious defence by the Serbs, coupled with judicious command decisions by Putnik, had bought the defenders time. The arrival of supplies came at just the right moment for the Serbs, who were then able to exploit the Austrians' supply problems and over-confidence to inflict a serious reverse upon the invaders. The Austro-Hungarians suffered over 227,000 casualties during the fighting; this represented a casualty rate of over 50 per cent for the Austro-Hungarians – a catastrophic outcome to the opening round of the conflict for the Habsburg Empire. Potiorek was removed from command, although his reputation was such that this was couched in terms of his being forced to step down as a result of ill-health rather than a dismissal for the maladroit manner in which he had attempted to conquer the Serbs.

The Serbs were relieved and jubilant at their success against the Austrians, and Putnik's reputation reached new heights thanks to his organization of the defence and success against what had, at times, appeared to be overwhelming odds. However, removing the Austrians from Serbian territory had come at a heavy price. The army was now on the brink of utter exhaustion, and there had been over 170,000 casualties

amongst the Serbian troops. While the Austrians had been comprehensively defeated in the opening rounds of the conflict, the question now arose of whether the Serbs would be able to recover sufficiently to fend off any further attempts at conquest. It was clear that the Austrians would not abandon their ambition to destroy Serbia, and the Serbs now had to make preparations for the renewal of hostilities that would undoubtedly occur in the not-too-distant future. Austrian involvement in the war against Russia meant that the Serbs were granted a breathing space for much of 1915, since the Austro-Hungarians were unable to contemplate carrying out offensive operations on two fronts. However, this respite occurred in conjunction with changes in the overall strategic situation of the wider European conflict, and when the fighting resumed, the Serbs were to find themselves at an even graver disadvantage than had been the case in the summer of 1914.

CHAPTER 2

The Balkans 1915–17

The demands of fighting the Russians meant that the Austrians were unable to carry out a renewed attack on Serbia for much of the early part of 1915. When the fighting resumed, the Austro-Hungarians were joined by their allies. German allegiance to Austria had been clear from the outset, but the decision of the Bulgarians to commit themselves to the Central Powers made a notable difference to the war in the Balkans.

The Bulgarians had remained neutral at the outbreak of war for a variety of reasons. Although the monarch, King Ferdinand, was pro-German in his views, many members of his government did not share his enthusiasm. This played a part in the country remaining on the sidelines in 1914. More important, though, was the question of Bulgarian self-interest. Whether pro-German or not, the Bulgarian establishment was united in its view that it would only participate in the war if it was clear that joining would bring the nation advantages in its pursuit of more territory. The Bulgarians, thanks to

Serbian troops march to their camp at Mikra in April 1916. After the exhausted Serbian Army had succumbed to the German-led invasion of 1915, the French and British set about re-equipping and refitting their allies, while new Serbian recruits were turned into an effective fighting force.

their geographic location, were not short of suitors. Both the Central and Entente powers sought to woo Ferdinand by promising that his country would receive land if he brought Bulgaria into the war on their side. By the end of November, the Allies changed their offers: these were now conditional on Bulgarian neutrality. The Bulgarians decided not to accept any of the offers made by either side; if the Allies were prepared to offer substantial territorial gains for doing nothing, then it appeared that following that course of action was in the Bulgarians' best interests, unless the Central Powers returned with better inducements.

Erich von Falkenhayn (1861–1922)

Falkenhayn succeeded Moltke after the failed attack on France and the defeat at the First Battle of the Marne. His attempts to outflank the French and British forces ended with the First Battle of Ypres in November 1914, before moving onto the defensive in the west and sending troops to fight the Russians on the Eastern Front. The successes in the east were credited to Hindenburg and Ludendorff, but Falkenhayn's insistence upon the German intervention that led to a swift, decisive victory over Serbia enhanced his standing with the Kaiser, and enabled him to gain permission for a renewed offensive in the west – the disastrous and bloody February 1916 assault on the French fortresses at Verdun. Falkenhayn was then removed and sent to command Ninth Army, where the capture of Bucharest in December 1916 restored his reputation. Sent to Palestine in 1917, he failed to stop the British forces in that theatre, and was subsequently posted to command the German Tenth Army in Lithuania. He retired from the German Army at the end of the war.

The initial success of the Austrian attacks on Serbia impressed the Bulgarians, although the Serb counterattack at the end of November 1914 dented this view a little. Bulgarian sympathy towards the Central Powers increased when it became clear that the Allies were attempting to negotiate with the Greek Government: Ferdinand and his ministers feared that such an accommodation would inevitably disadvantage Bulgaria. As the Germans and Austro-Hungarians enjoyed increasing success in 1915 in their fight against the Russians, the Bulgarian attitude hardened, particularly when it became clear that the Romanians were on the verge of joining the Allies, a sure sign that their territorial ambitions had been recognized as a condition of their entering the war. In addition, there appeared little evidence that the Allies would be able to defeat the Germans in France and Belgium, and even if the war ended in a stalemate, the Central Powers would hold the upper hand in the peace negotiations. The final consideration came when the British and French failed to persuade Serbia to surrender Macedonia to the Bulgarians. In their negotiations, the Germans had promised Ferdinand not only Macedonia, but also a considerable amount of additional territory if only Bulgaria would join the Central Powers. Ferdinand was at last swayed, and determined to enter the war on their side.

However, there was one final consideration that concerned the Bulgarian monarch – the failure of the Austro-Hungarian forces to conquer Serbia at the end of 1914, despite their initial successes during the invasion. Ferdinand therefore attached a notable condition to his joining the Central Powers, and it was that Serbia should be attacked once more – with the forces conducting the invasion coming under German command. If this requirement were met, the Bulgarians would attack Serbia from the east within a week, leaving their beleaguered opponent fighting a war on two fronts against overwhelming odds. An agreement to this effect was signed on 6 September 1915. Under its auspices, the Bulgarians were promised ownership of Macedonia at the end of the conflict, along with territory taken from north and eastern Serbia.

The Austro-Hungarians were both pleased and mildly indignant with these developments. They had achieved their desire to bring Bulgaria into the war, but there were some concerns about the conditions the Bulgarians had imposed. First, the clear lack of confidence in their high command offended their *amour propre*, but this was something that could be tolerated if it brought the Bulgarians into the war. However, they were more concerned at the thought of turning their attention away from Russia towards the Balkans once more. Serbia, they argued, should

RIGHT **King Ferdinand of Bulgaria was careful to play off his neighbours against one another to secure the best interests of his country. This led to his fateful decision to join with the Central Powers. While initially successful in the invasion of Serbia, the end result would be disastrous for his country.**

BELOW **A column of artillery passes by the dead body of a gunner, somewhere on the Serbian front. Although the Serbs had been weakened by a typhus epidemic, they fought hard during Mackensen's invasion, sustaining many casualties.**

not be regarded as a military priority. There were two reasons for this: first, defeating Russia would remove the Serbs' nearest and closest protector, as well as the need for another invasion; and, second, the Italians had entered the war (see Chapter 4), and the Austro-Hungarians saw the Italian front as being of greater importance than Serbia. The Turks, who had recently joined the Central Powers, also expressed reservations about prioritizing another assault on the Serbs.

The Germans, however, saw matters differently. General Erich von Falkenhayn, the German chief of staff, felt that Germany's allies had missed the point. In his view, an attack on Serbia seemed to offer several opportunities. First, if Serbia were removed from the war, it effectively ended Russian interest in the Balkans, and might prompt them to negotiate a settlement to the war, releasing German forces for operations against the French and British. Second, the weather conditions in Russia were worsening with the onset of autumn, and this reduced the chance of conducting major offensive operations, let alone the prospect of gaining success before spring 1916. The conditions in the Balkans, while deteriorating, were better than in Russia, so a window of opportunity existed in which an attack on Serbia would not have a deleterious effect on the conduct of the war on the Eastern Front. Finally, Falkenhayn addressed Turkish doubts by pointing out that if Serbia was overrun, it would open a direct land route between Germany and Turkey. Although the road communications infrastructure in Serbia was in need of substantial enhancement to make this route easily traversable, the rail and river communications were such that a much-increased level of German supplies to Turkey

An occupied Serbian village. Many Serbian civilians joined the army in its retreat to safety in Salonika, with the authorities ensuring that as many youths as possible did so, in order to preserve manpower for the rebuilt army.

August von Mackensen (right) with the Kaiser (left). Possibly the most effective German general of World War I, Mackensen's assignment to command the invasion of Serbia was conducted with considerable skill and efficiency.

could take place. If this were done, Falkenhayn noted, it might provide the Turks with the means to defeat the ongoing Allied operations at Gallipoli, and by securing Turkey against the Allies, offer the Central Powers a means of attacking British imperial possessions in the Middle East and possibly beyond. It would also ensure that attempts to supply Russia through the warm-water ports in the Black Sea – the rationale for forcing the Dardanelles Straits via the Gallipoli campaign – would be thwarted. This might also persuade Russia to consider whether or not a continuation of the war was within its interests and seek a peace treaty that would leave Britain and France at a serious disadvantage. As a result, the Bulgarian demand commended itself to Berlin on a number of levels, and it was agreed that operations to defeat Serbia should begin quickly.

THE ASSAULT ON SERBIA

Although there were few initial indications of a forthcoming attack during early September 1915, the Serbs knew that they would be at a considerable disadvantage if their enemies attacked again. The efforts of the Serbian Army during the last days of 1914 had exacted a considerable toll upon the troops, despite their ultimate success in driving the Austrians from their territory. Many Serb troops had succumbed to illness, and their supply situation had not improved notably over the intervening months. To make matters worse, the already weakened Serb soldiers were afflicted by a typhoid epidemic that swept through their ranks, weakening their ability to resist a forthcoming attack yet further. It was clear to Putnik and other Serb leaders that they would have to

hope that the enemy did not launch an attack while the army was at this low ebb; but, circumstances were not to favour them.

The Serb Army was already at a considerable disadvantage, not least since it possessed only 11 divisions by the end of 1915, and had ranged against it 18 divisions equipped with large amounts of artillery. Serbian guns were still relatively few in number and ammunition supply remained problematic. To make matters worse, the Serbs knew that they could not hope for rapid assistance from their allies, since it was extremely difficult for British, French or Russian troops to get through to reinforce them. The French decided that they must try to help, and planned to send a number of divisions to assist. However, the only way that these troops would be able to reach Serbia would be through the Greek port of Salonika. This was problematic, since while Greece was sympathetic to the Allied cause, it was neutral. Sending troops to Salonika would have consequences: if the Greeks agreed, they would be unable to maintain their status as neutrals, something they were reluctant to do. The Greeks had agreed to send 150,000 men if Serbia was attacked by a Balkan power, and had reached an

49

August von Mackensen (1849–1945)

Mackensen saw active service during the Franco-Prussian war in 1870, and joined the general staff of the German Army in 1891. He became a brigade commander in 1901, and a divisional commander from 1903. He was in command of the XVII Army Corps when war broke out in 1914, and his unit fought at the battles of Tannenberg and the Masurian Lakes as part of German Ninth Army. Mackensen replaced General Paul von Hindenburg at the head of Ninth Army and in April 1915 was given command of Eleventh Army and Army Group Kiev. When Mackensen led the breakthrough at Gorlice-Tarnow in May 1915, which led to the expulsion of Russian forces from all of Russian Poland and most of Galicia, he became one of the most famed – and feted – German commanders. His successful campaign against Serbia in November 1915 and the defeat of Romania in August 1916 enhanced his reputation. At the end of the war he was briefly interned by the French, before being allowed to return home.

understanding with the British and French that would allow the two allies to make use of Salonika in the event of a conflict in the region. However, there was a substantial obstacle to this being realized, since while the Greek Government was in favour of supporting the Allies, the king was not. He insisted on neutrality being maintained for as long as possible, and this militated against any attempt to allow the early deployment of troops who might have been able to help the Serbs resist another invasion of their territory. Ironically, the king's restatement of his determination to prevent the government from permitting the Allies to land at Salonika prompted a decision by the British and French to send troops anyway. Given that the landings represented a gross violation of Greek neutrality, it was perhaps surprising that the British and French did not commit as many troops as their expressed desire to aid Serbia might have suggested. The French found that they did not have enough troops to send to Salonika, which compelled the British to assist. The conflict between the so-called

> 'Only a few miserable remnants escaped into the Albanian mountains, losing the whole of their artillery and everything else that they could not carry. There was no longer a Serbian Army.'
>
> Erich von Falkenhayn

'Easterners' in the British Government, who saw the possibility of winning the war in a location other than France, and the 'Westerners' who felt that the Western Front would be the place where the war was decided, led to considerable friction over the deployment. The Westerners, already irritated by what they saw as the diversion of the Gallipoli campaign, were frustrated to discover that the government now wished to commit more troops to a 'sideshow'. The end result was that, when the demands of the two camps were taken into account, it was impossible to redeploy enough men from France or Gallipoli to send a meaningful force to Salonika.

This almost farcical situation may have been of little importance to the British and French, concentrating upon the fighting in other places, but for the Serbs the small size of the Anglo-French force was a matter of major concern. By mid-1915, it was quite clear to the Serbs that they would have to depend upon the French and British for assistance, and they based their strategy upon the assumption that adequate help would be forthcoming. They were to be sadly disappointed.

The Central Powers' preparations for the attack were briefly dislocated when the Austrians suffered a reverse against the Russians, forcing them to reduce the number of divisions committed to the offensive from six to two. This was not as great a problem as it might have been, since the Germans had sent 11 of their divisions to carry out the invasion, with the intention of simply steamrollering the Serbs out of the way. The German commander, Field Marshal August von Mackensen, had been successful against the Russians through the use of massive artillery bombardments to shape the course of the battle, a technique he intended to employ against the Serbs. He also had a far greater appreciation of the necessity of establishing a robust logistical network than the Austrians had demonstrated in their earlier efforts to subdue the Serbs, and he therefore took considerable care to make sure that his supply lines were secure; without a secure logistics chain, it would be difficult to maintain the supply of shells needed to keep the artillery fed with ammunition.

The need for good supply lines meant that Mackensen constructed a simple, set-piece campaign, which would see his forces advance along the Belgrade to Salonika railway. The German forces were to attack across the Sava and the Danube, driving the Serbs back along the Morava Valley, giving Bulgarian forces the opportunity to attack the Serbian rear. The

British, French and Serbian troops manhandle a field gun as the Entente builds its strength in Salonika. The deployment to Salonika, supposedly a bid to aid the Serbs against the German-led invasion, came too late to affect the outcome, but they would eventually inflict a crippling defeat on the Central Powers in the region.

51

Austrian Third Army was given the task of occupying Belgrade and then advancing on Kragujevac, while the German forces, in conjunction with a variety of specially selected elements of the Austro-Hungarian Army, would advance into the Morava Valley.

This presented the Serbs with formidable difficulties, since their disease-ridden, under-equipped and weakened army was being asked to defend against attacks from both north and east. Marshal Putnik realized that his best hope lay in the British and French sending troops to help with the defence of the country, but recognizing that such help would be insufficient – if it arrived at all – he proposed launching a pre-emptive attack on the Bulgarians before they had managed to mobilize their forces. This daring plan was rejected as impractical by the British and French, and the Serbian Government chose not to implement it. The Serbs instead were forced to deploy their forces in a more conventional defensive posture

German and Austrian soldiers conduct military tourism around the streets of the fallen Serbian capital in late 1915. The supply convoy of pack animals behind them demonstrates that, unlike the Austrian commanders in 1914, Mackensen recognized the need for a robust supply chain.

King Constantine of Greece, with his youngest daughter upon his knee. Constantine had been educated in Germany, and was married to Kaiser Wilhelm's sister, Sophie. It was, therefore, unsurprising that his sympathies lay with the German cause, much to the displeasure of many of his subjects, and particularly his government.

along the frontier. The Serbian First and Third armies were in the front line while the remaining troops were held in reserve. Putnik was faced with the dilemma of how to deploy his forces; unfortunately for the Serbs, he chose to concentrate them to the west of Belgrade on the Machva plateau, since this appeared to be the most likely area for a German attack, leaving only 20 battalions of troops in the capital. All along the front, the Serbs were considerably outnumbered, particularly when it came to artillery pieces. As a number of historians have observed, the Serbs had an advantage over their opposition only in the sheer

tenacity of their soldiers, who were determined to resist attempts to occupy their small country. In the face of a German-led invasion, under-equipped and without Allied support, this was a daunting prospect.

THE ATTACK BEGINS

On 7 October 1915, German troops began to cross the Danube and Sava rivers, covered by heavy artillery fire, although the German gunners found that the arsenals at Kragujevac were a tough nut to crack and did not achieve the sort of effect that had been desired. As the best crossing points were at Belgrade and Ram, Mackensen sought to seize these at the outset of the operation. The weather on 7 October was appalling, making the task of the attacking troops trying to cross the river opposite Belgrade extremely difficult. Serbian defensive fire added to their difficulties, and several German units suffered heavy casualties, notably General Trollman's XIX Corps. The Austrian VIII Corps suffered fewer losses, and although several of the steamers being used to transport the troops were sunk, the bulk of the corps was able to cross the river and establish a bridgehead. Despite its difficulties, XIX Corps managed to force a crossing, although the bridgehead established relied upon a number of rather poorly constructed bridges.

Once across, the Germans and Austro-Hungarians moved on to Belgrade itself, and vicious street fighting ensued for the rest of the day. Fighting continued in the capital throughout 8 October, and Mackensen's troops were in complete control of the city by the end of the following day.

The crossings at Ram were less difficult, aided by the better weather in that area which enabled observers to call in a massive artillery bombardment against the Serbian positions – the driving rain at Belgrade had forced German gunners to fire almost blind. The two German corps attempting to cross further down the river at Semendria ran into difficulties, losing all but eight of their 50 boats. This was a setback, but German troops further to the east of the town exploited the thick fog of 8 and 9 October and managed to get across and outflank the defenders, taking high ground overlooking Serbian positions.

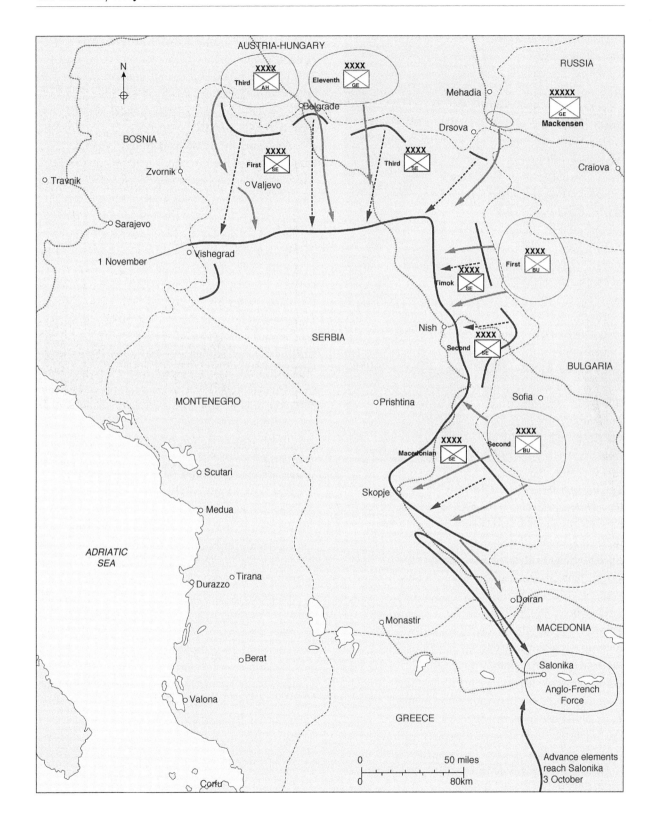

AUSTRIA-HUNGARY

RUSSIA

XXXX
Third
AH

XXXX
Eleventh
GE

Mehadia

XXXXX
GE
Mackensen

Drsova

BOSNIA

Belgrade

Craiova

Travnik

Zvornik

XXXX
First
SE

Valjevo

XXXX
Third
SE

Sarajevo

1 November — Vishegrad

XXXX
First
BU

Timok

XXXX
SE

Nish

XXXX
Second
SE

BULGARIA

SERBIA

Prishtina

Sofia

MONTENEGRO

XXXX
Macedonian
SE

XXXX
Second
BU

Scutari

Skopje

Medua

ADRIATIC
SEA

Tirana
Durazzo

Doiran

Monastir

MACEDONIA

Berat

Salonika
Anglo-French
Force

Valona

GREECE

0   50 miles
0   80km

Corfu

Advance elements
reach Salonika
3 October

Despite these advances, the success of the invasion was still not certain. In the southern sector, Austrian troops had attempted to cross the Drina, but a lack of bridging equipment led to near disaster when the sheer weight of equipment being ferried across led to every single bridge that had been established collapsing. Furthermore, as Mackensen had understood from the outset, getting the first wave of troops across the rivers was not going to be decisive. It was essential to establish robust bridgeheads and to use them to bring *matériel* and equipment across before the advance could continue. While the Serbs were at a considerable disadvantage, Mackensen was painfully aware that unless he could get his heavy artillery and supplies across the river, and ensure that the supply lines were maintained, he would be unable to guarantee success.

This meant that the attackers had to pause to consolidate their supply lines, giving the Serbs a limited opportunity to regroup. The Austrian Third Army made its way across the river, but without its heavy guns, since none of the river bridges were able to sustain the weight of the howitzer batteries. This meant that some of the Austrian units, notably VII Corps, were totally lacking artillery support and would have to try to rely upon weight of numbers to overcome the enemy defences. As VII Corps advanced, it found it extremely difficult to penetrate the Serbian defences using infantry alone, and took over 7000 casualties around Belgrade – more than twice the losses of the German forces there. The Austro-Hungarian/German advance therefore took longer than anticipated to surround Belgrade, and even then did not completely seal off the city.

Elsewhere, the Germans were able to use their artillery to make the Serbian position at Semendria untenable, and the town fell on 11 October; Pozharevac succumbed soon afterwards. Even in these areas, though, supply problems slowed the advance and

The final invasion of Serbia in late 1915 was a much more accomplished affair than the embarrassing failures experienced by the Austro-Hungarians at the start of the war. The intervention of highly proficient German troops and the involvement of Bulgaria meant that the Serbian position swiftly became untenable.

Crown Prince Alexander of Serbia (1888–1934) became noted for his military prowess during the Balkan Wars, and after his appointment as regent in June 1914, was supreme commander of Serbian forces. He went on to become the first king of Yugoslavia in 1921.

allowed the Serbs to withdraw in reasonable order. By 16 October, the Germans had managed to advance only 13km (eight miles), and a gap of 16km (10 miles) existed between them and the Austrian forces. As the Serbians retired, the Germans and Austrians finally linked up on 18 October. An improvement in the weather meant that some of the supply difficulties were alleviated as road and river conditions made movement of equipment easier, particularly of the heavy guns. Being able to bring up artillery meant that the pace of advance increased, as the Austro-Hungarians and Germans used their heavy guns to blast their way through the Serb defences. The Germans were particularly successful in employing artillery to dislodge the Serbs, and there were a number of instances where the weight of bombardment was such that the Serbs were left with no option other than to retreat immediately, leaving vital transport infrastructure intact for the enemy to exploit. With 10 days of October remaining, Mackensen's forces were sitting on a line running from the rivers Kolubara and Pek on a west–east axis. Although the Germans had five more divisions than the Serbs, they were at full stretch and lacked sufficient reserves to exploit further. It was now imperative that the Bulgarians add their weight to the invasion, allowing the Germans to advance on Kragujevac and round up the Serbian forces there.

The Bulgarians finally declared war upon Serbia on 14 October 1915, after much hesitation, mobilizing a force of 450,000 men. Although the Bulgarians were short of artillery and other items of equipment, the soldiers were considered to be of high quality. The Bulgarian First Army, commanded by General

Cheerful Bulgarian troops march through a Serbian town during the 1915 invasion. The Bulgarian soldiers were of high quality, despite deficiencies in their supplies and equipment, and fought with considerable skill and valour.

Boyadiev, was placed under Mackensen's control so that it could aid the attack on Nish. This was problematic, since the Bulgarians had to negotiate their way past two major defensive positions in the form of fortifications at Pirot and Zajechar. The lack of heavy artillery to reduce these forts meant that the Bulgarian troops had to make their way into Serbia by outflanking the positions via mountain passes. The Bulgarian offensive began with the crossing of the Timok River, and enjoyed initial success. However, this swiftly bogged down as the Bulgarians ran into difficulty with their supply lines. To make matters worse, the Serbs succeeded in holding the advance through the mountain passes, leaving the northern flank of the Bulgarian advance in danger of grinding to a halt. To the south, the Bulgarians enjoyed greater success, despite the stern resistance offered by the enemy. The Bulgarian Second Army pushed into Macedonia, and by driving on to Kumanovo succeeded in breaking contact between Serbia and Greece. Despite this success, the Germans were concerned that the failure of the northern part of the offensive would

prevent the capture of Kragujevac. Mackensen therefore requested reinforcements, and was given a Bavarian mountain division. The strengthened forces gained control of more of the rail network, and this alleviated many of the supply difficulties that had delayed the advance. As the weather improved, the German advance gathered pace, with the tired and weakened Serbian Army being unable to hold back the attack for any length of time. There was one saving grace: the lack of coordination between the Germans and Bulgarians, thanks to the earlier difficulties in the north, meant that the Serbs were able to avoid being trapped in a pincer movement. This was nothing more than a temporary respite in the face of the enemy advance. As October drew to a close, Putnik was painfully aware that an increasing number of his units were surrendering after being worn down by constant bombardment from enemy guns.

On 31 October, Putnik ordered a general retreat onto Kragujevac, attempting to keep his exhausted army together as it sought an escape route to friendly territory. Many of his troops were farmers, who slipped away from the retiring army to resume their rural lives. Putnik's declining forces continued their withdrawal towards Albania during the first week of November, a process aided by the fact that the Germans, Bulgarians and Austrians began to lose interest in prosecuting the campaign further. The Germans felt that the war against Serbia was won, with most of the nation under the control of the Central Powers. Regarding Russia as the main threat, Mackensen was eager to move his forces back to the Russian front. The Bulgarians were more than

An Austrian soldier surveys the ground below from his vantage point atop high ground somewhere in Montenegro. The wintry conditions in the Balkans in late 1915 hindered the Central Powers' invasion, but only delayed the inevitable.

happy with their territorial gains in Macedonia and northwest Serbia, while the Austrians were equally content with the notion that the Bulgarians would not move to establish a Greater Bulgaria. The Austro-Hungarian General Conrad felt that failing to conquer Albania and Greece was a major error, however, since this might allow the British and French to gain a foothold from which they could ultimately attack. He expressed his views forcefully, and was outraged to discover that the Germans were withdrawing troops for employment on the Russian front. Even though this wrangling slowed the momentum of the advance and gave the Serbs the opportunity to escape, victory for the Central Powers was assured. The final major confrontation came at the Field of Blackbirds on the plain of Kosovo between 19 and 24 November 1915. The Serbs were afflicted by a new outbreak of typhus, while food and ammunition was in extremely short supply. The result was inevitable. On 25 November, Putnik issued his final orders for the retreat, and his troops began to trek over the snow-covered mountains into Albania. Putnik's health collapsed, and he had to be carried by his ever loyal troops; on 7 December, he resigned as commander-in-chief, aware that he was no longer capable of exercising command. He had, however, managed to ensure the survival of his army.

Some 140,000 Serbian soldiers completed the journey to the coast, and after suffering further privations thanks to lack of supply, they were evacuated by Allied ships. The defeat had cost Serbia greatly: nearly 175,000 men had been taken prisoner or were missing, while another 94,000 were known to have died in the fighting. Casualties amongst Serbian civilians were not accurately recorded, but were known to be extremely heavy. As 1915 drew to an end, Serbia had been occupied, but the survival of the army offered at least some hope for the future.

SOJOURN IN SALONIKA

The final destination for the Serbian Army was to be Salonika, something that the Greek Government was not entirely happy with. While there was only one offensive on the Salonika front in 1916, a great deal of political activity reshaped the way in which Greece was governed. At the outset, the country was

> 'The relentless severity of the Bulgarian pursuit exposed the retreating Serbian forces and population to the worst horrors of war and winter. Scores of thousands of defenceless people perished.'
>
> Winston S. Churchill, *The Great War*

split between those who thought that Greece should support the Allies, those who felt that the Germans merited the country's support (despite the fact that this would mean allying with the much-loathed Ottoman Empire and the mistrusted Habsburg Empire as part of the Central Powers) and a third camp who preferred neutrality. King Constantine was sympathetic towards the Germans: he had received his military training in Germany, and was married to a German princess, Kaiser Wilhelm's sister Sophia no less. However, as noted earlier, his Prime Minister, Eleutherios Venizelos and the members of the Cabinet were strong advocates of joining the Allies. It ended with total confusion, with Venizelos inviting the Allies to land at Salonika before being dismissed, and, despite the invitation being withdrawn, the Allies choosing to land anyway. Constantine now faced the uncomfortable prospect of being ignored by the Allies, whatever wishes he expressed. However, part of the rationale behind the Allied landing beyond attempting to offer some form of aid to Serbia had been to boost Venizelos's position in Greece, and having been compelled to leave office, the presence of Allied forces in Salonika made little military sense, and as Conrad had noted, it was little more than a large internment camp for the 150,000 British and French troops under the command of the French general Maurice Sarrail.

However, the Allies were not dissuaded from attempting to persuade, cajole and coerce the Greeks into joining the war on their side. The British and French had been granted the position of 'Protecting Powers' under the treaty that had led to the creation

The Serbian Army's withdrawal proved to be a terrible trial of endurance for the troops and the accompanying civilian refugees, who were faced with harsh winter conditions and a lack of food supplies. Some 140,000 troops reached the Albanian coast and were evacuated.

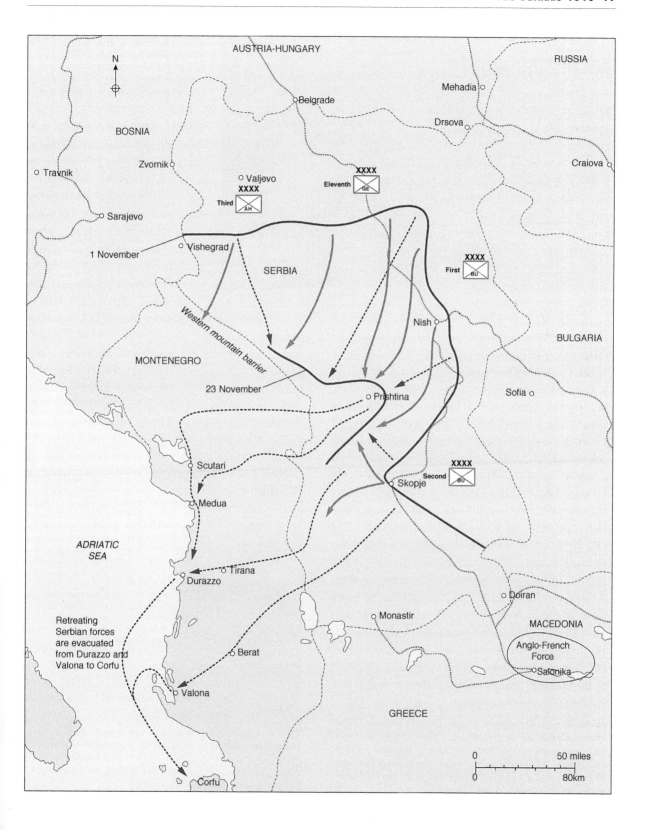

N

AUSTRIA-HUNGARY

RUSSIA

Belgrade

Mehadia

Drsova

BOSNIA

Craiova

Travnik

Zvornik

Valjevo

XXXX
Eleventh GE

XXXX
Third AH

XXXX
First BU

Sarajevo

1 November

Vishegrad

SERBIA

Nish

BULGARIA

Western mountain barrier

MONTENEGRO

23 November

Prishtina

Sofia

Scutari

XXXX
Second BU

Skopje

Medua

ADRIATIC
SEA

Tirana

Durazzo

Doiran

Retreating
Serbian forces
are evacuated
from Durazzo and
Valona to Corfu

Monastir

MACEDONIA

Anglo-French
Force

Salonika

Berat

Valona

GREECE

Corfu

0   50 miles

0   80km

Bulgarian troops at Monastir. The city was at risk to from an Allied attack, despite the strong natural defensive positions surrounding it. It became a key objective for the Serbs in 1916.

One Greek corps handed itself over to the Germans *en masse* and was sent away to be interned in Germany for the rest of the war. Eastern Macedonia was then overrun by the Bulgarians and taken under their control, much to the distress of the local civilian population who came to loathe the Bulgarians as harsh occupiers.

This was the final insult to Greece as far as Venizelos was concerned. Brooding over what to do after his dismissal, he decided that he had to take revolutionary action to bring Greece into the war. On 29 August 1916, his supporters in Salonika, headed by some army officers and the gendarmerie, staged a coup against the local administration and declared their support for the Allies as part of a national defence movement of which they claimed to

of the Greek state in the nineteenth century, and using a liberal interpretation of their responsibilities under this they argued that the king's refusal to listen to the Prime Minister, and his subsequent dismissal of Venizelos, were a threat to the Greek constitution. In such circumstances, they argued, they had a duty to intervene to restore the constitutional status quo. This was not the strongest of arguments put forward during World War I, but it carried sufficient legal weight for the French and British to feel comfortable in employing it, despite the objections of King Constantine. The Greek Government became less and less willing to cooperate with the Allies, and refused to allow the Serbian forces that had been recuperating on Corfu (upon which the Allies had landed the Serbs without the consent of King Constantine) to join the Allies on the Salonika front. Then, to compound their sins in the eyes of the British and French, an incursion into Eastern Macedonia by the Germans and Bulgarians in May 1916 was met with firm orders to the Greek garrisons in the area that they should not offer any resistance.

Prime Minister Venizelos of Greece. Firmly opposed to Greek intervention in the war on the side of Germany, Venizelos and his government were dismissed by King Constantine in 1916, and he went to Salonika as head of an alternative government. Allied support for Venizelos would lead to the abdication of the King and Greek entry into the war.

Serbian troops withdraw across the remains of a bridge during the fighting in the summer of 1916. A surprise Bulgarian offensive thwarted Allied plans for a major attack of their own, which had to be delayed until September.

be the vanguard. Although the Allies said little, it was quite clear that Sarrail had given tacit support to the coup attempt, not least since it now offered Venizelos an opportunity to become a major influence in Greek politics once more. Venizelos decided that he would go to Crete and Salonika, and did so with the French intelligence service protecting him from any interference from the Greek Government as he set off on his journey. He reached Crete on 29 September 1916 and declared the formation of a provisional government. After spending a few days in Crete, he headed for Salonika, and reiterated his declaration of a Provisional Government on 9 October. It claimed jurisdiction over Crete, the Aegean Islands and all those parts of Macedonia that were not occupied by the Bulgarians, and called upon the Greek population

to join the Allies so as to allow the Bulgarians to be driven from Greek territory. Venizelos presented his call to arms as an opportunity for Greece to regain its honour, which Constantine had been unwilling to defend when he had permitted the Bulgarians to march into the country without resistance.

Venizelos's Provisional Government did not gain immediate official recognition from the Allies, but their sympathies were quite obvious. The creation of a Venizelist government in certain parts of Greece effectively divided the country into two: the part under the control of the king and his government in Athens was at peace, but that under Venizelos was, to all intents and purposes, at war with the Central Powers. The Allies kept up the pressure on the Athens government; a day after the Venizelos declaration, they issued an ultimatum demanding that the Greek Navy surrender to them. Constantine was left with little option than to capitulate to the demand, and the fleet surrendered the next day. This was not the end of the Allied efforts, however, and on 19 November a further ultimatum was presented, insisting that Constantine dismiss all the diplomatic representatives of the Central Powers in Athens, and that all Greek war *matériel* should be handed over to the Allied powers. The Athens government was not at all pleased with the Allied ultimatum, and rejected it on 30 November, a step that prompted the arrival of Allied landing parties in Piraeus. The local garrison resisted, and the landing parties were withdrawn the next day. The Allies instead chose to instigate a blockade of Greece by sea, before imposing yet another demand on Constantine on 14 December, insisting that all Greek Army units in Thessaly be withdrawn; the Athens government complied. The final insult to Constantine came on

19 December 1916, when the Allies recognized the Provisional Government in Salonika, and ceased to view Constantine and his ministers as the legitimate constitutional authority in Greece.

The political manoeuvrings partly overshadowed the offensive planned by Sarrai, which was due to take place at the end of August 1916. Sarrail had planned to launch an assault to test the strength of the Bulgarian units south of Doiran, but shortly before the attack was to begin the Bulgarians pre-empted the offensive by launching an attack of their own on 9 August. The Allied forces responded with a counterattack, and although the French made little headway, the British succeeded in capturing high ground in front of their positions, putting them in a better position for the forthcoming offensive.

Fighting died down towards the end of August, and Sarrail was able to resume plans for the offensive. He revised his original thinking, deciding that the natural line of advance along the Vardar River was impractical,

The Allied offensive on the Salonika front in 1916 was delayed as the result of a Bulgarian attack, which was eventually beaten back in time for the planned assault to begin in September. The offensive did not achieve the success that had been hoped, but saw the recapture of Monastir.

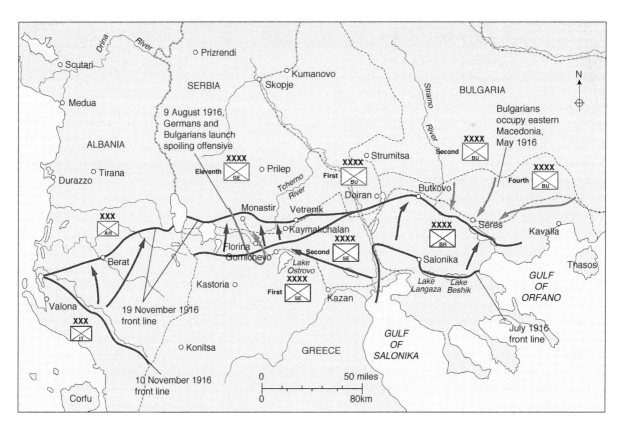

Serbian troops fire a lightweight mountain gun against enemy positions on the Salonika front. Such weapons proved of great value in the campaign, since they were man-portable and could be used to provide much needed fire support in terrain not easily accessible to standard artillery pieces.

since the fighting earlier in the month suggested that the area was too heavily defended to achieve success. Therefore, he decided to redirect that attack against the town of Monastir. Capturing it would give the Allies a means of advancing into Serbia while being able to turn the enemy defences along the Vardar Valley. Sarrail also appreciated that there was a political benefit to attacking Monastir. It was a Serbian town, and taking it would represent the first stage of the liberation of the country, inspiring the Serbian troops under his command to even greater efforts.

The offensive began on 12 September 1916 with the capture of Kajmakchalan Mountain by the Serbs. However, this success was offset by the heavy casualties suffered by the French and Russian troops as they ran into stiff resistance from the well dug in Bulgarians. Fierce fighting continued for two months, but on 19 November Monastir was captured. This occurred at almost the last possible moment at which success could be achieved, since winter had begun to set in.

All this took place against the background of the political machinations between Constantine and Venizelos, which had compelled the British commander, Major-General George Milne, to divert some of his attention to the possibility that he would have to attack elements of the Greek Army, fearing that pro-royalist units might launch an attack into the Allied rear. Sarrail even went so far as to advocate a pre-emptive attack, but Milne talked him out of this course of action, and his troops were left to guard against the possible repercussions of a Greek royalist

General Maurice Sarrail, the French commander at Salonika, owed his prominent position as much to his political connections as to his military ability. His high-handed behaviour exasperated his allies to the point where it became necessary to replace him to ensure that coalition relations on the Macedonian front did not break down completely.

revolt. To everyone's relief, this did not arise. The September offensive could, therefore, be regarded as something of a success. Around 1000 square kilometres (400 square miles) of territory had been taken, and the political situation in Greece, although still confused and unstable, appeared to be moving in the Allies' direction. Perhaps most importantly, though, the capture of Monastir gave new heart to the Serbian troops. It may only have been a single town on the border of their occupied country that fell, but in the eyes of many, it marked the beginning of the liberation of their homeland, suggesting that removing the occupying powers was a possibility that could be realized in due course.

THE ROME CONFERENCE

In the first few days of January 1917, the inter-Allied conference in Rome concluded with the British Prime Minister, David Lloyd George, expressing the opinion of his government that the British troops in Salonika must be employed for more than simple garrison duties, and that efforts should be made to take action against the Bulgarians occupying Eastern Macedonia. Lloyd George implied that if the Allies did not agree upon more vigorous action in the theatre, the British would give serious consideration to redeploying their troops to Egypt.

Perhaps the most significant aspect of the conference, though, was the fact that Sarrail took its conclusions – that there should be an increase in French forces deployed to Salonika, and that development of improved rail communication links in Greece should be undertaken to permit preparation of a possible offensive against Bulgaria – as being a sign of political confidence in his leadership. This was something of a misjudgement, since Sarrail was far from popular, thanks to his high-handed approach that alienated his subordinates and infuriated the British and Italian commanders who had to work with him. Buoyed by what he saw as approval for his style of command, and conscious that the British wanted to see action, Sarrail decided that it was necessary to embark upon another offensive in the spring. In early February 1917, he set his staff to work on a plan that would involve his forces in carrying out an offensive along a 225km (140-mile) front, with the aim of achieving a decisive victory.

Evidence from the autumn 1916 offensive suggested that while the Bulgarians fought well when things appeared to be roughly even between the attacking and defending forces, if their opponents managed to gain the upper hand many units lost confidence and crumbled. Both Sarrail and Milne hoped that a wide-ranging attack would bring about a rapid retreat. Sarrail planned that the French forces would seize the area between Lake Prespa and Lake Ohrid, while a Franco-Italian force supported by a Russian brigade would attack from Monastir towards Prilep, advancing along the Crna River. The Serbian units would attack east of the Crna in the Moglena Mountains region, with the aim of turning the Bulgarian defences on the Vardar. Two British divisions would cross the Struma River and capture Seres, while a third British division was tasked with making a diversionary attack in front of the Belascia Mountains to tie down Bulgarian forces there. Once the first phase of the attack was completed, the French, Serbian and Italian divisions would launch a new attack towards Sofia, while the British would threaten the Bulgarian capital by forcing the Rupel

Italian troops arrive in Salonika. The Italians sent troops to Salonika as a sign of their commitment to the Allied cause, despite the pressing need for soldiers on their home front. The commitment to the Macedonian front gave the Italians the prospect of placing forces on the Dalmatian coast, an area which Italian nationalists had long coveted.

Pass. Milne did not fully approve of the plan, arguing that attacking in the Struma sector was unlikely to succeed because his troops would be operating over marshland around Seres, making it difficult to consolidate any gains. He instead suggested that the British effort should take the form of an attack on the main Bulgarian defensive line above Lake Doiran. Taking this position would give the Allies a commanding position above the communication routes into southern Serbia and Bulgaria.

With hindsight, Milne's proposed alternative seems questionable. He was suggesting that his forces be used to assault difficult mountainous terrain that had been heavily fortified and which was covered by artillery positions that had been carefully sited to allow interlocking fire against an attacking force. In addition, the natural vantage points provided from this series of rocky outcrops meant that the Bulgarians would

have advance warning of any British movements in the area. However, Milne was undoubtedly looking at the wider picture, understanding that while the attack represented a major challenge, the possible gains from the success of the attack would be substantial: if the British managed to break through, they would have made a major step towards shortening the duration of the campaign in Salonika, whereas success in the Struma area would have left the Bulgarians in command of their vantage points. Milne reasoned that the Allies, and most probably the British units, would have to attack the mountainous terrain if they wished to break into Bulgaria, and he felt that the proposed 1917 spring offensive was as good a time as any to attempt this. Sarrail accepted Milne's proposed modification to the plan, and the offensive was scheduled to take place in the middle of March.

THE BEST-LAID PLANS

Unfortunately for the Allies, their preparations were rendered much more difficult by the weather. A severe blizzard disrupted the shaping operations around Lake Prespa, and heavy snowfall meant that launching an offensive was going to be extremely difficult. The Bulgarians also gathered that an Allied offensive

was increasingly likely, from collating reports of the various movements that had been observed from their vantage points in the mountains.

As a result, the Bulgarians responded by making serious efforts to disrupt preparations. For the first time in the campaign in southeast Europe, gas was employed: the Bulgarians bombarded the ravines south of the Doiran with chemical weapons, with the aim of making them impassable. Air raids were carried out by the German air service units supporting the Bulgarians, with attacks being made on known supply dumps and troop concentrations. To make matters worse, the Bulgarians and the Germans defending the Doiran were convinced that any Allied attack was going to take place in that location, and so reinforced it. Just hours before the offensive was due to start, intelligence information gathered from captured Bulgarian soldiers was passed to Milne, telling him that the whole Doiran area which his forces were about to attack had been heavily reinforced. Milne was faced with a dilemma: while it was clear that the element of surprise had been lost, rescheduling the

Russian troops arriving in Salonika. The Russians joined the fighting on the Macedonian front in the summer of 1916, in limited numbers, at the same time as the Italians.

offensive by the British would risk wrecking the attack on the other sectors, and nor could the preliminary bombardment that had been brought down on the Bulgarian and German positions since 21 April be simply turned off and started again at a later date, resupplying the guns with at least three days' worth of ammunition. Milne therefore came to the conclusion that he would have to launch the attack, as scheduled, in the evening of 24 April 1917.

The British advance therefore began on schedule, and ran into immediate problems. The 26th Division was subjected to heavy artillery fire, while a battalion of the Wiltshire Regiment which made it to the enemy lines found that the defenders had rushed machine guns in to cover any gaps in the wire caused by the Allied bombardment. In attempting to force a way through, the battalion suffered 60 per cent casualties,

French troops peer from their positions during fighting along the Doiran. The rocky terrain provided a great deal of natural cover for the defending Bulgarian troops, and made the Allied task extremely difficult. Although the Bulgarians were able to fend off numerous attacks, their defeat in the Vardar Valley made their position on the Doiran untenable.

including all but one of the officers. Although the 10th Devonshires and 12th Hampshires both gained some ground, they found that it was impossible to consolidate their positions in the face of constant machine-gun and artillery fire. The 26th Division was therefore ordered to fall back. Elsewhere on the British part of the front, the 22nd Division enjoyed marginally more success, and gained ground. However, because the 26th Division had been unable to hold the small amount of ground they had taken, the 22nd Division was unable to remain in position, since it would have

Sir George Milne (1866–1948)

George Milne's service career began with the Royal Artillery in 1885. He fought at the Battle of Omdurman in 1898, and in the South African War (1899–1902). In 1913, he became the artillery commander for 4th Division with the temporary rank of brigadier-general. Early in 1915, he was made Brigadier-General General Staff of III Corps, a post he held for only a few weeks before being promoted to major-general and becoming chief of staff for Second Army. He held this post for four months and was then given command of 27th Division, part of XVI Corps. This division was part of the force sent to Salonika, and within six weeks of arriving, Milne had left 27th Division to become the corps commander. He then assumed command of all the British forces in Salonika, attempting to maintain some sort of coalition harmony with General Sarrail, and then working on far better terms with Sarrail's successor

George Milne (second from left), pictured with Sarrail (third from left), examining a captured enemy machine gun with a group of senior officers.

Franchet d'Espérey. After the defeat of the Bulgarians, Milne took his forces into Constantinople, and remained there until 1920, when he returned home.

been vulnerable to heavy enfilade fire from the right flank. As the night went on, it became quite clear that the Bulgarians, using searchlights to pick out the advancing British formations, were not going to be dislodged, and all the attacking units were ordered to pull back to their start line. By the early morning of 25 April, it was clear that the attack had failed.

Ironically, Milne's dilemma regarding whether to upset the timing of the whole operation by delaying the British assault was rendered nugatory by the weather. Heavy snow meant that it was absolutely impossible to consider launching the attack in the Moglena Mountains, and Sarrail decided that it would have to be called off. Given the lack of success enjoyed by the British, he decided that he would postpone the offensive. Milne was given the option of consulting with the government in London to gain guidance on whether the British should attempt a second assault, although it seemed unlikely that it would enjoy any more success than the first gallant efforts to seize the Bulgarian hilltop positions had achieved.

As a result of the setbacks, Sarrail had decided that it was no longer possible to consider an advance on Sofia during the course of the offensive: it would have to wait until a later date. However, the offensive could still be of value in clearing the enemy out of the region of Monastir, regaining more Serbian territory in the process. Sarrail felt that this was a reasonable goal to aim for, particularly since continuing the offensive into the summer would expose troops to excessive daytime temperatures (which could reach over 40° Celsius) and an increased risk from malaria as they operated away from regular supplies of anti-malarial drugs and medical facilities. He told Milne of his intention to abandon campaigning before the onset of summer, which might have been a factor in dissuading Milne from launching a second attack on the Doiran. However, Milne was convinced that if he could dislodge the Bulgarians from the Doiran, they would collapse in short order. Milne was also aware that the British Government had given instructions that the 60th Division and two cavalry brigades under his command were to be redeployed to Palestine in June, a sure sign that the government had no grand ideas of success in Salonika – yet even the lack of political pressure for success did not change Milne's views about the need for a second attack, and he determined that he would make an assault before the troop reductions made such a venture impossible.

THE SECOND BRITISH ATTACK ON THE DOIRAN

Milne decided that the next British attack would have to occur at night, since it would be impossible for the infantry to dig in unmolested in daylight given that their positions would be in full view of Bulgarian troops on the Gran Couronné. Milne gave orders for a shorter preparatory bombardment, and Sarrail was informed that the British would advance at 10pm on 8 May 1917. Sarrail therefore planned to begin his offensive in the Moglena Mountains and Crna loop areas at dawn on 9 May.

The British attack began reasonably well, with a section of the Bulgarian front line being seized with relatively light casualties, but when dawn broke on 9 May, it was clear that the attack had not managed to take the main Bulgarian defensive line. The British troops were exposed to fire from higher up the hill, and it proved impossible to make any progress in the face of this. Milne was forced to order another withdrawal, and by the end of 9 May all the British units had fallen back on their start line, having taken heavy casualties for no obvious gain.

Sarrail's part in offensive operations also went badly. The attack began with considerable promise when the Russian 2nd Brigade managed to take a mountain spur 1.6km (one mile) into enemy

British troops use a periscope to observe enemy positions from behind cover. The British found the Salonika campaign a source of considerable frustration, particularly in the hard fighting around the Doiran, where they suffered heavy losses for no appreciable gains.

territory, while the French and Italian units on their flanks managed to gain ground also. However, the flank units could not move up sufficiently to support the Russians, who were cut off and destroyed, taking over 50 per cent casualties in the process. Also, the Germans moved up reserves to support the Bulgarian defenders, and it soon became clear that the offensive was in serious trouble. A lack of coordination made matters worse, when a breakdown in communications led to an Italian attack at 8am on 10 May going in when their supporting units had been ordered not to advance; unsurprisingly, the Italians suffered heavy casualties. Continuing misfortune befell the Italians on 11 and 12 May as they sustained more heavy casualties while attempting to advance; this led to

The May 1917 Allied offensives on the Salonika Front were far less successful than had been hoped. This ultimately led to the dismissal of General Sarrail when his political patrons found the new French Prime Minister, Georges Clemenceau, unprepared to leave Sarrail in command any longer.

growing anger towards Sarrail amongst his Italian allies, who began to feel that he had lost control of the battle. They were forced to suspend further attacks by more bad weather, and by the time it had cleared on 17 May it was obvious that the Bulgarian lines had been substantially reinforced by German troops; further offensive operations were therefore called off. The only troops to enjoy any success were the Serbs, who managed to establish positions on Dobropolje Mountain. The Serbs hoped to be given orders to advance, but these never came: with the failure of the offensive in other sectors, it was impossible to allow the Serbs to advance unsupported, so they were forced to remain in their recently won positions.

ASSESSMENT

There was little doubt that the 1917 spring offensives in Salonika had failed, and this meant that the war in the Balkans was now almost certain to drag on well into 1918, unless there was some dramatic development

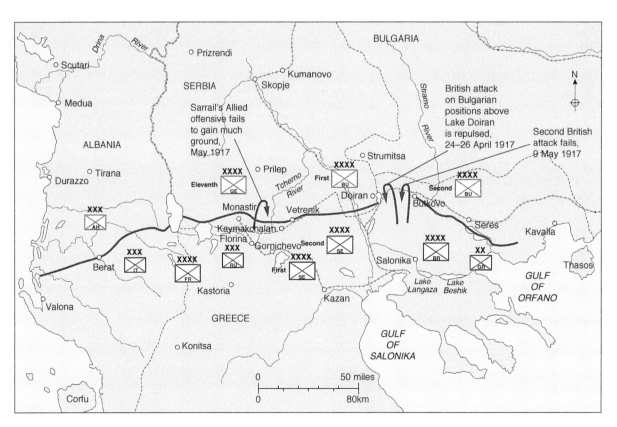

French officers inspect a section of Greek troops. Greece lost around 5000 men during the short period that the country was committed to the war. The relatively late Greek entry into the war led to the other Allies all but ignoring Greek aspirations at the peace conference.

that brought peace. The various Allied commanders contemplated the reasons for failure. Milne blamed a lack of intelligence about Bulgarian artillery strength, since the enemy guns had been the prime cause of the British being unable to advance. The Italians blamed Sarrail, who had annoyed them once too often with his aloof approach. Sarrail himself decided that the blame lay upon one of his subordinates and upon the Serbs, who had reorganized their First Army just before the offensive began at the behest of their exiled government, a situation which meant that it was unable to support the Serbian Second Army in its successful attack onto the lower slopes of the Dobropolje. Some 14,000 Allied casualties had been sustained for very little return, and it became clear that there would have to be some changes before the Bulgarians could be defeated. The major change required seemed to be the replacement of Sarrail. However, as a man who enjoyed the personal support of many politicians, and whose appointment to the Salonika command had

been at their behest, he appeared destined to retain an important command position. Sarrail therefore felt secure and began further plans for offensive action. His confidence, though, was misplaced. When the French Government changed in November 1917, the new Prime Minister, Georges Clemenceau, a man unafraid of political controversy, made an assessment of the effort in Salonika and decided that Sarrail had to go. To Sarrail's considerable surprise, Clemenceau dismissed him in December 1917, and the voices of his political patrons were conspicuous by their absence. Renewed efforts to make progress in Salonika would be someone else's task, and the Allies would have to wait until 1918 before any further attempts to gain victory in the Balkans.

CHAPTER 3

War in the Colonies

At the outbreak of war, the British authorities in Africa were totally unprepared, with relatively few forces available. Although it seemed unlikely that the Germans would mount major operations on the continent, precautions had to be taken against any attempt to seize British territory. Neither the British nor the Germans had any great wish to see Africa brought into the conflict, save for supplying raw materials to help equip their armies.

Neither the British nor the governor of German East Africa had reckoned with the commander of the latter's defence force (the Schutztruppe), Lieutenant-Colonel Paul von Lettow-Vorbeck. He argued that he should take the offensive, since doing so would compel the British to retain troops in Africa that might otherwise be sent to Europe to fight against German forces there. The governor was far from convinced, but this did not stop Lettow-Vorbeck from embarking upon operations. The first attack was made on Taveta, a small outpost at the foot of Mount Kilimanjaro, which was seized on 15

The unusual sight of two German soldiers riding zebras in East Africa. Although zebras substituted for horses in a number of pre-war sporting events, they were not of great use, since the vast majority of the beasts did not take kindly to being pressed into service as mounts or pack animals.

August 1914. This was followed with a move towards the Uganda railway, but the Germans ran into troops from the King's African Rifles (KAR), who stopped the German advance. The governor of British East Africa immediately signalled the Colonial Office in London to ask for reinforcements, and the request was passed on to the India Office in the hope that elements of the British Indian Army might be spared for operations there. The India Office had already received requests for troops to be sent to the main theatres of operation, and thus handed the request on to the Committee for Imperial Defence so it could decide upon how to handle this. It was decided that the Indian Army should provide two expeditionary forces, imaginatively designated Indian Expeditionary Force B and Indian Expeditionary Force C. These would be used to seize the main German port in Africa and to

'No criticism or suspicion of German methods of colonization exists such as that which was levelled (with justification) against the French and Belgians prior to the war … On the contrary, there are many tributes to German colonial activity.'

Heinrich Schnee, *German Colonization Past and Future*

reinforce the KAR. Expeditionary Force B was under the command of Brigadier-General J.M. Stewart, while Major-General Arthur Aitken was given command of Expeditionary Force C.

Expeditionary Force C was not of the highest quality, since the two Indian battalions that made up the bulk of the force had not seen any active service on campaigning for some 20 years, and had not worked alongside one another before. Furthermore, they had been equipped with outdated rifles, and prior to being sent overseas it was decided that they should

Africa just prior to the outbreak of war in 1914. The continent had been largely ignored by European powers until the last two decades of the nineteenth century, when the 'scramble for Africa' saw them expanding their colonial possessions and securing their lines of communications.

be re-equipped with the standard rifle of the British Army, the Short Magazine Lee-Enfield. This weapon, possibly the best bolt-action service rifle ever made, was completely unfamiliar to the Indian troops, and it was clear that it would take a considerable degree of training to make them proficient in its use. It was not altogether clear whether or not they would gain the necessary skills by the time they reached East Africa.

NAVAL CONFRONTATION

While reinforcements were on their way to Africa, the British had to deal with the challenge presented by the German naval presence in African waters, notably the cruiser *Königsberg*, since this represented a potential threat to the supply route. *Königsberg* illustrated this fact by sinking the British merchant ship *City of Winchester* on 6 August before heading into the open sea; on 20 September the ship reappeared off Zanzibar and sank the cruiser HMS *Pegasus*. This led to a reinforcement of British naval strength in the area, with three more cruisers being dispatched to hunt down the German ship. In fact, the arrival of the British squadron led to the *Königsberg* heading up the Rufiji River, where it was to remain, more of a threat to British forces inland (thanks to its guns) than to the Royal Navy units operating in the open sea.

When Expeditionary Force B arrived at Mombasa after a cramped and unpleasant journey, it disembarked. Aitken discussed the issue of where he should take his force with the governor, and it was agreed that it should take the port of Tanga in German East Africa. Aitken was advised that the Germans could easily reinforce the port, but he had a decidedly racist view of the local troops that the Germans would be forced to employ there, suggesting that the Indian troops were far more effective than African troops ever could be. This flew in the face of recently acquired knowledge about the KAR, and there seemed to be little reason to pre-suppose that the Germans'

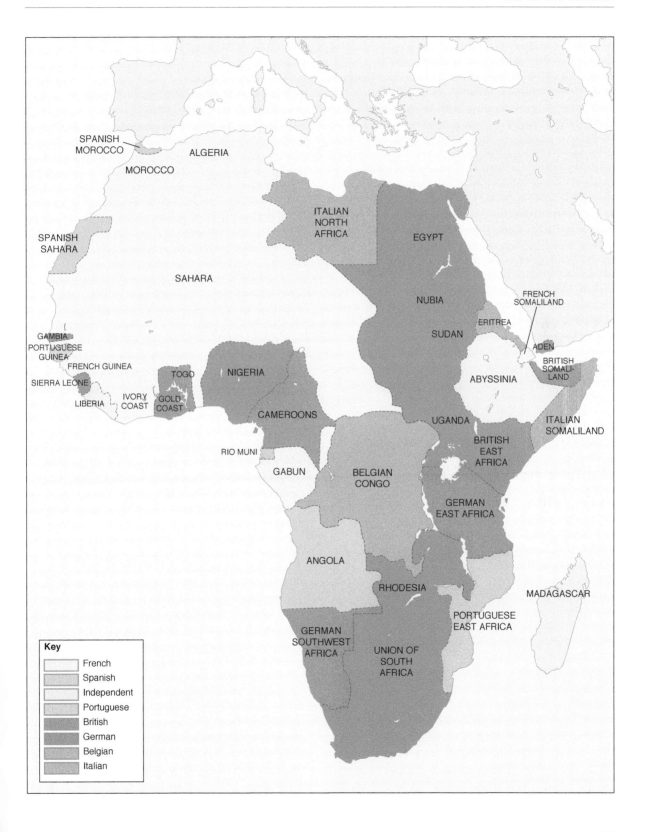

SPANISH MOROCCO

ALGERIA

MOROCCO

ITALIAN NORTH AFRICA

EGYPT

SPANISH SAHARA

SAHARA

NUBIA

FRENCH SOMALILAND

ERITREA

SUDAN

ADEN

GAMBIA
PORTUGUESE GUINEA

BRITISH SOMALI-LAND

FRENCH GUINEA

SIERRA LEONE

TOGO

NIGERIA

ABYSSINIA

LIBERIA

IVORY COAST

GOLD COAST

CAMEROONS

UGANDA

ITALIAN SOMALILAND

RIO MUNI

BRITISH EAST AFRICA

GABUN

BELGIAN CONGO

GERMAN EAST AFRICA

ANGOLA

MADAGASCAR

RHODESIA

PORTUGUESE EAST AFRICA

GERMAN SOUTHWEST AFRICA

UNION OF SOUTH AFRICA

Key

	French
	Spanish
	Independent
	Portuguese
	British
	German
	Belgian
	Italian

Paul von Lettow-Vorbeck (1870–1964)

Lettow-Vorbeck served as part of the German contingent in the suppression of the Boxer Rebellion in 1900, and was then posted to German Southwest Africa (now Namibia), where he saw action during the Hottentot and Herero rebellions of 1904–08. Wounded in one eye, he was sent to recuperate in South Africa where he met and became friends with Jan Smuts – later, his adversary. In 1913, he assumed command of the garrison in German East Africa, a force of around 14,000 men. His creative and skilful use of his forces throughout the war, coupled with the fact that he was undefeated in battle, made him a national hero in Germany, and gained him the admiration and respect of his opponents. He was the last German officer to be promoted to general officer rank by Kaiser Wilhelm II before his abdication, and his reputation was such that the Allies allowed his Schutztruppe to hold a parade through Berlin upon their return home in 1919 – the only German officer to be accorded this accolade by the occupying powers.

local troops were going to be inferior to the KAR. Nevertheless, Aitken's mind was made up, and he set about planning for the operation.

He was immediately confronted with a problem when the Royal Navy informed him that they had concluded a truce with the Germans at Tanga and Dar es Salaam, and that it would be necessary for him to inform the German force at Tanga if he intended to break the ceasefire. While the reasoning behind this was sound from the navy's point of view, it meant that Aitken was in effect being forced to inform the Germans that he was going to attack. Remarkably, he chose to do so, giving them time to prepare their defences, just as had been predicted by the officers already in East Africa.

The attack on Tanga occurred on 2 November, and proved to be a disaster. Aitken's assumption that British-trained Indian troops would be superior to African soldiers was rudely disproved, and Expeditionary Force B retreated in disorder, arriving back in Mombasa on 8 November. It had been a less than auspicious start to the war in the colonies for the British, and it was clear that much had to be done to gain victory in a campaign that nobody had fully anticipated.

EVENTS IN 1915

In the aftermath of the failures in East Africa in 1914, the British decided that they needed to reorganize their forces in the area. Two new commands were created: the Mombasa Area under Brigadier-General

Brigadier-General Michael Tighe returned to service at the outbreak of war, having retired some years previously. He had considerable operational experience, and was regarded as a courageous soldier. Tighe later took command of the Voi Area, but was removed by Jan Smuts in 1916.

Michael Tighe and the Nairobi Area under Brigadier-General Stewart. The Indian Expeditionary Forces that had been deployed were amalgamated into a single Expeditionary Force, and their regiments then distributed amongst the two new commands. A final command change occurred when Major-General Aitken was recalled to London and replaced by Major-General Richard Wapshare. Wapshare was told by the Secretary of State for War, Lord Kitchener, that he should adopt a defensive attitude, since it was most unlikely that any reinforcements would be sent to East Africa, due to manpower requirements in other theatres of war.

Lettow-Vorbeck, however, hoped to create a situation where the British would be forced to divert forces away from the main theatres of war as a result of his plans. As 1915 began, Lettow-Vorbeck suspected that the British units at Jasin would attempt to move along the coastline toward Tanga. It appeared that the best method of addressing this potential threat was to launch a pre-emptive attack. After carrying out a detailed reconnaissance of the area, Lettow-Vorbeck drew up a plan for an attack on the advanced British positions at Jasin, which would draw the British reserves onto the Germans. Lettow-Vorbeck made use of the well run railway line to ferry troops up towards Jasin, so that by 17 January 1915, an attacking force made up of nine companies of troops and two artillery pieces was in position to the south of Jasin. Lettow-Vorbeck issued orders on 18 January: four companies were to attack on the flanks of Jasin (two companies per flank), while the Arab Corps would move to the

Paul von Lettow-Vorbeck (second from the right), possibly the most successful practitioner of guerrilla-style warfare in the modern era, relaxes in an almost stereotypical African colonial setting.

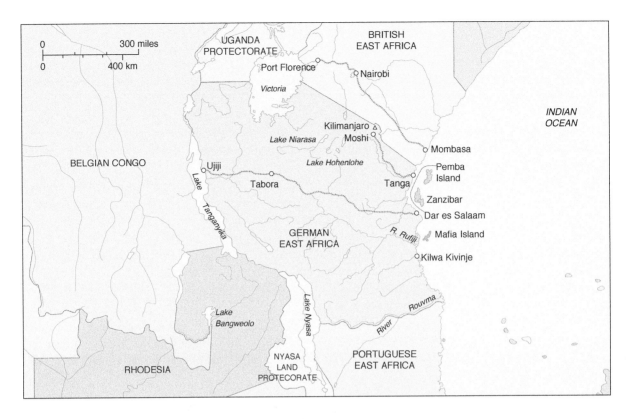

East Africa in 1914. Despite the considerable size of the German possessions in the east of the continent, there were few German troops in the area, and it appeared inevitable that German East Africa would soon fall into British hands.

northwest of the town. Finally, another company would advance on Jasin from the front, followed by Lettow-Vorbeck's headquarters and the main body of the German force, comprising two Askari companies, a third company of German troops and the two artillery pieces. The attack began at 6.45am, and it was not long before the Germans had surrounded the camp and the town's sisal factory. Three companies of the King's African Rifles attempted to relieve the camp, but were unsuccessful, while the members of the 2nd Kashmir Rifles, positioned in the factory, were forced to retire when they ran out of ammunition. In the camp, the battalion commander of the 2nd Kashmirs was killed, and his second-in-command took over. He swiftly realized that there was little he could do to defend the camp, particularly in the face of the German field guns. As a result, the camp surrendered

on 19 January. Lettow-Vorbeck's decision to go onto the offensive was vindicated.

The defeat had a deleterious effect upon British morale, and Lord Kitchener signalled Wapshare to reinforce the advice that he should move onto the defensive in view of the fact that he was unlikely to receive reinforcement at any point in the near future. Lettow-Vorbeck, on the other hand, reviewed his performance with mixed feelings. Although he had gained a notable success at Jasin, it had come at a price. He had lost a number of his regular officers, and over 200,000 rounds of precious ammunition had been fired during the attack; he estimated that he would be able to fight another three Jasin-type actions before his troops began to run out of ammunition and officers to lead them. He therefore decided to move to a campaign of guerrilla warfare; among his targets would be the Uganda Railway.

Wapshare was equally aware of the importance of the railway, and he set about attempting to make it defensible. This was something of a challenge, since it required the 'penny packeting' of troops into small, isolated defensive garrisons along the length of its line. Wapshare also had to protect the frontier, so more small groups of men were sent out to establish some form of defensive position in the hope that there would be enough of them to deal with any German attack. He had no reserves, and the need to maintain a defence based upon fixed lines meant that he was compelled to cede freedom of manoeuvre to Lettow-Vorbeck, handing him the initiative. To make matters worse, there were a number of border outposts where it had been impossible to provide officers or experienced NCOs, and the relatively poorly trained soldiers failed to fulfil some of the basic functions that they would have done as a matter of routine with proper leadership, such as putting out sentries. The Askaris, who had been given far superior levels of training by Lettow-Vorbeck, did not make such mistakes, and were to exploit the errors of their opponents on numerous occasions.

In April 1915, the British changed commander yet again: Wapshare was sent to the Persian Gulf and replaced by Brigadier-General Tighe. Tighe's senior intelligence officer, Captain Richard Meinertzhagen, made a pessimistic assessment of the situation facing the new commander, noting that, as well as the lack of any reserves, the majority of the men in the command were poorly trained and often poorly led, while the orders from Kitchener suppressed any offensive spirit amongst the troops. To make matters worse, the British forces

A corporal of Lettow-Vorbeck's Schutztruppe, German East Africa, 1914. The German troops were lightly armed and short of supplies. They made up for these deficiencies through their skill at arms, and proved good trainers of indigenous troops, who helped prolong the campaign until 1918.

were suffering from increasing levels of disease, to the point that, by June 1915, some battalions had only a quarter of their men fit for action due to sickness; the Rampur Infantry and 13 Rajput regiments both had over 95 per cent of their men unfit for service with malaria. The only troops who were unaffected were, perhaps unsurprisingly, the local troops in the King's African Rifles. However, the War Office – quite wrongly – felt that the native African troops were inferior to the British and Indian troops and refused to allow Tighe to set about recruiting them in greater numbers.

GUERRILLA WARFARE

Lettow-Vorbeck broke his forces down into small units of around eight to 10 men, and sent them to patrol through the bush, where they would conduct lightning attacks on enemy targets, particularly the Uganda Railway. The troops sent on these missions were well trained, highly disciplined and self-sufficient. They carried all their supplies with them, and thus presented Lettow-Vorbeck with few concerns regarding his logistics chain – something that could not be said for the British forces, who had to grapple with the problem of keeping the numerous small outposts along the railway and the border regions supplied. Lettow-Vorbeck's small patrols quickly began to cause serious difficulties to the British, who were quite unable to prevent the German forces from blowing up sections of railway line, destroying communications infrastructure and carrying out a variety of raids in which they captured arms and ammunition (neatly overcoming one of Lettow-Vorbeck's major concerns) and stole horses, helping to enhance their own mobility. Unable to go onto the offensive against the Germans – and not even knowing where the enemy was – the British were compelled to use their manpower to attempt to guard the railway and vulnerable outposts. Being tied down on such duties was not conducive to high morale.

One stretch of railway near to Mombasa, running between Simba and Sambura, came under attack so frequently that it became very difficult for the railway to run effectively. In the space of two months in 1915, over 30 trains were blown off the tracks, and 10 bridges were destroyed. The British had experience of attacks on railway lines from the Boer War at the start of the century and adopted a tactic from that conflict in a bid to mitigate the German efforts at disrupting the transport. They took to placing a light truck in front of the locomotive so that it would run over any explosive charge, leaving the locomotive intact and able to continue. While this was briefly successful, the technique quickly became known to the Germans, who simply gave their explosive charges a delayed setting so that the light truck would trigger the timer and pass safely over the explosives, which would detonate just as the locomotive passed above them seconds later. British efforts to build a new railway were hampered by constant attacks.

The success of the raiding was such that it was not long before Lettow-Vorbeck was able to form two mounted companies of raiders from the horses captured. These parties were able to range far and wide through the bush, carrying out a series of attacks on a wide array of targets. Although the campaign was going well, Lettow-Vorbeck did not sit on his laurels, and made plans to ensure that his forces would be self-sufficient for a considerable time without having to rely upon any supplies from outside Africa. The German territories were given the task of turning their normal peacetime output to the production of war *matériel*, and they did so with notable success. German East African companies produced clothing, rubber, tyres, boots and even synthetic fuel. Also, the German East African Biological Institute in Usambara was put to work on the production of quinine tablets to lessen the risk of the troops catching malaria.

While the original reorganization of forces into raiding parties had been a success, Lettow-Vorbeck thought that he could achieve greater efficiency, and undertook the cross-posting of Europeans and Askaris, so that instead of there being racially distinct units, all of his companies had a mix of nationalities within them. He also increased his troop strength through local recruiting, so that by the end of 1915 he had 3000 Germans and 11,300 Askaris under arms, all of whom were fighting in the guerrilla campaign against the British.

THE BRITISH RESPONSE

To compound the problems and failures within the British forces in East Africa, British commanders

A German Askari soldier. Popular European perceptions that Africans would not make good soldiers were swiftly disabused by both the fiercely loyal Askaris and their counterparts in the British forces, the King's African Rifles.

A stylized depiction of the action in which Lieutenant Wilbur Dartnell won a posthumous Victoria Cross in September 1915. Dartnell was wounded in a German raid near Maktu, Kenya, but refused to be evacuated in the hope that he might somehow prevent the more seriously wounded (who had to be left behind) from being killed by the enemy.

command. Unwilling to abandon their own local intelligence efforts in favour of Meinertzhagen's centrally collated and distributed information, British commanders tended to be using much less precise assessments of the enemy's strengths and intentions, and were unable to respond as effectively as they could, and perhaps should, have done.

The inability to deal with the guerrilla tactics in use by the Germans was a source of great frustration, and led to the decision to send a variety of troop formations from May 1915 into the area to try to overcome the threat, just as Lettow-Vorbeck had hoped would occur. However, in contrast to German practice, prejudices against raising local troops remained. Only in 1916 were these doubts about the suitability of locals overcome, and the KAR expanded dramatically. The British also took some time to establish a carrier corps, which allowed everything that could be manhandled to be conveyed around the theatre of operations; eventually, the carrier corps would reach a peak strength of 200,000 men.

Tighe was concerned that the War Office in London was not taking his concerns with sufficient seriousness, and sent numerous signals endeavouring to gain some action. Eventually, in August 1915, he signalled to suggest that the position in the area was becoming critical. Too many of his men were non-effective as a result of disease, while it appeared that the Germans were successfully replenishing their stocks

tended to downplay the intelligence information accumulated by Meinertzhagen. He had established an intelligence collection system that was remarkably effective, not least in terms of assessing the strength of the enemy. As early as March 1915, he had issued an assessment of German strength that included the exact figure of machine guns available to the Germans, and figures for the number of troops under Lettow-Vorbeck's command that were remarkably close to the true ones, although he had somewhat overestimated the strength of the Askaris fighting under German

Jan Smuts (1870–1950)

Smuts had distinguished himself as a Boer military leader during the Second Boer War (1899–1902), and following the creation of the Union of South Africa in 1909, a process in which he played a leading role, held three key ministerial positions. When World War I broke out, Smuts's first task as head of the newly created South African Defence Force was to suppress a rebellion by Boers seeking to overturn the union of South Africa. This done, Smuts focused on the occupation of Southwest Africa, before being made commander of British imperial forces in East Africa. Sent to London to head the South African delegation to the Imperial War Conference, he impressed David Lloyd George, and was invited to become a member of the British War Cabinet. Smuts was given the task of reporting on the state of the British air services, which led to the creation of the Royal Air Force. At the end of the war, he represented South Africa at the Versailles Peace Conference, and then returned to his homeland, becoming its prime minister in 1919.

of ammunition from production in their colonies, and from supplies looted from British ammunition dumps during the course of the raids. Even news that Southwest Africa had fallen to the Allies was not as encouraging as might have first appeared, since it meant that the South African troops who had been used to take over the colony were being employed away from other theatres of war where they would have been most useful.

The War Office finally accepted that more needed to be done, and Brigadier-General Jacob van Deventer was sent to East Africa to work on plans for the deployment of South African troops. Van Deventer

quickly came to appreciate that there was a clear need for troops, and it was not long before South African units began to arrive. In December 1915, the War Office appointed General Sir Horace Smith-Dorrien to take command of East African forces, while the Committee of Imperial Defence sitting in London made a recommendation to the British Government that a substantial increase in the number of troops was required to overcome Lettow-Vorbeck's guerrilla campaign. While this represented a major shift in the British attitude to the campaign, it played into Lettow-Vorbeck's hands, since it represented the achievement of his desired goal – namely forcing the British to employ large numbers of troops who would have been most welcome on the Western Front, or (at the time) in the Dardanelles campaign.

Smith-Dorrien approved the development of plans originally sketched out by Tighe for engaging the Germans around Mount Kilimanjaro, while another force was to land at Dar es Salaam to engage the Germans from that location. In addition, and finally taking notice of the major issues regarding supply of their forces, the British set about constructing another railway line and a water pipeline to help improve the quality of logistics, particularly in the Kilimanjaro area. Furthermore, in the south, forces on the Rhodesian/German East African border areas were brought under the command of Brigadier-General Edward Northey, who arrived in Capetown to take up his appointment on 30 December 1915. Northey turned out to be a commander for whom Lettow-Vorbeck gained considerable respect. His task was to build up a large force in the area, drawn from the South African and Rhodesian armies, with the aim of attacking into German East Africa in due course. British plans suffered a minor setback at this point, when Smith-Dorrien contracted pneumonia on the voyage to South Africa. It became clear that he would take some time to recuperate, so he resigned his command. It now became necessary to find an alternative commander of similar quality, and the British approached General Jan Smuts, who had been offered command of the East African theatre, but who had turned it down on the grounds that there were political problems in the Union of South Africa which required his attention. These problems had been overcome, and Smuts now felt able to take up the position.

EVENTS IN 1916

Smuts arrived just as Tighe began his offensive operations around Kilimanjaro in February 1916. The offensive started badly, with the Germans inflicting a sharp reverse on the British forces at Salaita Hill, and Smuts immediately sought to ensure that his forces did not suffer heavy casualties. He was determined

RIGHT **Sir Horace Smith-Dorrien was appointed to lead all British East African forces in late 1915. A highly proficient soldier with a ferocious temper, Smith-Dorrien made a number of preliminary plans, but became seriously ill on the voyage to Africa and felt obliged to resign his command.**

BELOW **The results of a raid by Lettow-Vorbeck's men. German forces were particularly adept at attacking the British communications infrastructure. The British hoped to exploit their burgeoning rail network in the area to outflank the enemy forces, but they were never able to do so.**

Men of the King's African Rifles cross the Ruwu River in March 1916 while participating in British offensive operations. The offensive did not go to plan, and led to the new commander, General Jan Smuts removing several senior officers in whom he had little confidence.

to avoid a frontal assault on the enemy, and hoped to outmanoeuvre the Germans, forcing them to fall back from their positions until their hold on the area became untenable. He therefore sent Stewart's 1st Division to Longido to cut off the German lines of communication, while the South African 3rd Infantry Brigade under Brigadier-General Jacob van Deventer and the South African Mounted Brigade were to attack the Chala Heights. Tighe's 2nd Division was to make another assault on Salaita.

The advance did not go as Smuts had hoped. Stewart proved reluctant to advance at any great speed, and despite Smuts sending him a series of blunt signals telling him to hurry up, little was achieved. The Germans fell back in good order, without having to become engaged in heavy fighting. An encounter with a small German force took a day to deal with, and it was not until 14 March 1916 that Stewart's troops joined up with the rest of the force. The Germans had fallen back onto Taveta, while van Deventer reached Chala on 8 March, before advancing onto Salaita, which he found to have been abandoned by Lettow-Vorbeck's forces some time before. Lettow-Vorbeck had fallen back onto a defensive position along the Latema–Reata line, and intended to defeat any British attack before pulling further back, again aiming to minimize casualties to his forces. On 11 March, two Rhodesian regiments were tasked with seizing the position, but the daylight attack went badly. The battalion commander of 3rd KAR was killed by a burst of machine-gun fire as his troops advanced, and the Germans were not evicted from their position. An attack that evening was marginally more successful in that it killed a number of Germans. However, when daylight broke on 12 March, it became clear that Lettow-Vorbeck's men had skilfully withdrawn while still in contact with the enemy, and had left the hills after inflicting over 250 fatalities on the attacking troops.

Smuts was unimpressed with the results of this operation, since although the Germans had ceded territory, they had done so of their own volition, and were far from defeated. He considered the plodding performance of Stewart's 1st Division to have been a major factor in the disappointment, and a debriefing between Smuts and Stewart ended with the latter resigning and being sent to India to await a new position. Brigadier-General Malleson, who had led the initial attack on Salaita, had also incurred an unfavourable assessment from Smuts, who bluntly told him that he had no confidence in him; Malleson also, therefore, departed. General Tighe was the third commander to leave for India, but he did so with Smuts's thanks and a clear expression that he was leaving with his honour intact. These changes allowed Smuts to impose himself upon the theatre of

operations much more firmly than might otherwise have been the case.

On 18 March, a further advance began, this time onto the Ruvu River. Van Deventer was tasked with making a flanking attack from New Moshi towards Kaye. The 1st Division attacked down the Moshi Road, while the 2nd Division attacked from Taveta. Although van Deventer's troops had some difficulty in crossing the Pangani River, they made their way across in reasonably good time – but when the attack was put in, they discovered that Lettow-Vorbeck had once again retired without being drawn into battle. Smuts's men advanced onto Kaye, but were forced to dig in under heavy fire from the German positions. When dawn came, it was clear that Lettow-Vorbeck's men had pulled off another skilful withdrawal during the night. Although the withdrawals meant that the Germans were ceding territory to the British, this did not have deleterious effects upon German morale.

Brigadier-General Edward Northey was appointed to command the British forces on the Rhodesian–German East African border, and proved a formidable opponent for the wily Lettow-Vorbeck. At the end of the war, Northey remained in Africa, and served as governor and commander-in-chief of Kenya between 1919 and 1922.

Lettow-Vorbeck had instilled an understanding amongst his men of what he was attempting to achieve, so his soldiers were proud of the fact that they had managed to thwart the attempts of a much stronger enemy force to bring them into a decisive battle that would probably have culminated in their total defeat.

While the British had not achieved the outright victory they had sought, there was reason for some degree of satisfaction. Smuts had successfully concluded the first stage of operations before the rainy season set in, and the threat to the operation of the Kenya–Uganda railway network had been removed.

German Askari troops undergoing training. The Germans were extremely proficient trainers of their indigenous troops during the African campaign, and the Askaris' military skills made a profound difference to the successful continuation of the German effort in East Africa.

In addition, a position that could be exploited after the rains had been achieved, with the way into German East Africa territory being open. Smuts had also done much to mould the variety of troops that were available to him into an effective fighting force, and took the opportunity to reorganize his command into three divisions: two South African and one British. Each had a mounted brigade for improved mobility, and the size of the forces was to be boosted by the expansion of the KAR and the arrival of West African troops in the area. Thus, as the rainy season of 1916 set in, the British Empire forces were at last in a position to attempt to conquer German East Africa.

ACTION RESUMES

By 1 April 1916, Smuts had finally completed the reorganization of his forces, and embarked upon the last phase of planning the next stage of the campaign in

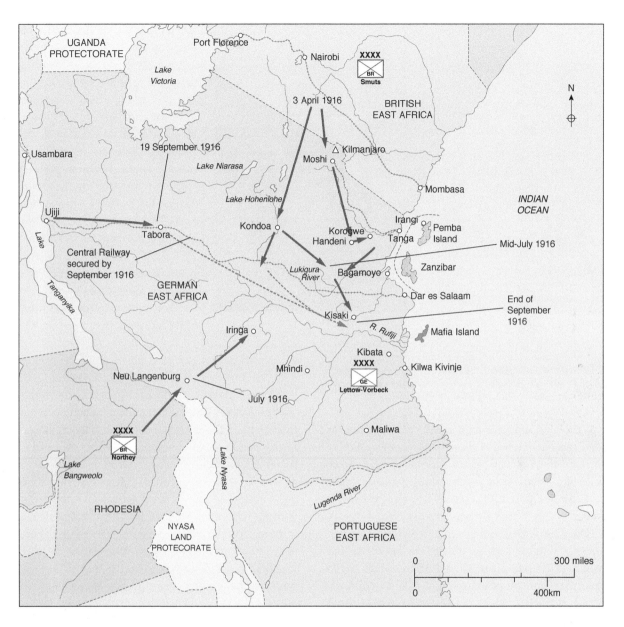

UGANDA PROTECTORATE

Port Florence

Nairobi

XXXX
BR
Smuts

3 April 1916

BRITISH
EAST AFRICA

N

Lake Victoria

19 September 1916

Usambara

Lake Niarasa

Kilmanjaro

Moshi

Mombasa

Lake Hohenlohe

INDIAN OCEAN

Ujiji

Tabora

Kondoa

Korogwe
Handeni

Irangi

Tanga

Pemba Island

Mid-July 1916

Lake Tanganyika

Central Railway secured by September 1916

GERMAN EAST AFRICA

Lukigura River

Bagamoyo

Zanzibar

Dar es Salaam

End of September 1916

Kisaki

R. Rufiji

Mafia Island

Iringa

Mhindi

Kibata

XXXX
GE
Lettow-Vorbeck

Kilwa Kivinje

Neu Langenburg

July 1916

Maliwa

XXXX
BR
Northey

Lake Bangweolo

Lake Nyasa

RHODESIA

NYASA LAND PROTECORATE

Lugenda River

PORTUGUESE EAST AFRICA

0   300 miles

0   400km

East Africa. Smuts appreciated that following Lettow-Vorbeck would be of little utility, and doing so raised the further complication that he might split his forces back into guerrilla bands that would be used to make the occupation of German East Africa impossible. Smuts was left with something of a problem, since his preferred approach of forcing the Germans into a decisive encounter was almost impossible to achieve, given that Lettow-Vorbeck was fully aware that to be

Smuts's invasion of German East Africa, April–September 1916. After early success, bad weather and over-extended supply lines meant that operations lost momentum. Although East Africa had fallen by the end of the year, Lettow-Vorbeck's force evaded capture.

forced into such a situation would mean the end for his troops. Instead of pursuing this approach, Smuts instead decided that he would invade German East Africa from several directions. Smuts decided upon a

A British water supply column. The need for drinking water and other essential supplies was a major concern for the British, particularly during the offensives of 1916, when the speed of advance outpaced the supply chain, leaving several British formations suffering from near starvation.

two-pronged attack: one along the Usambara railway line, the other towards the central railway running through the German colony. Northey would attack from the south, while Belgian units who were now available from the Congo would be employed in the west.

On 3 April 1916, van Deventer's division began to advance towards Kondoa Irangi. The South African Mounted Brigade made a rapid advance and found the first German position on a hill at Lolkisale, which happened to be the only source of fresh water for many miles. The South African troops worked their way up the hill, using the rocks and boulders for cover, and managed to dislodge the Germans after some hours. Van Deventer then sent a squadron of mounted troops to protect the flank as they advanced. Although the Germans had been dislodged, a large number of horses had been killed in the action along with 60 mules. As the rainy season had come late in 1916, the lack of horses and mules meant that it became increasingly difficult for the

troops, who were compelled to carry more weight on their backs as the lack of alternative means of carriage became more noticeable. The rain and mud made it almost impossible to advance, although, through sheer force of will, the Mounted Brigade managed to make it to Kondoa Irangi on 18 April. In the face of the South African forces, the Germans pulled back. The success had been bought at a price, however, since the South African 1st Brigade had suffered heavy losses to the point where it had been rendered ineffective.

The South Africans set about building defensive positions in and around Kondoa Irangi, while Lettow-Vorbeck transferred a number of companies to the area to hold the British back. Once again, Meinertzhagen's intelligence assessment of what had occurred was spot on: he informed Smuts that the Germans had weakened their forces in the Usambara region, but found that his interpretation was not accepted until it was too late to exploit it. Lettow-Vorbeck put in a counterattack against Kondoa Irangi on 9 May, employing some 3000 men. The attack failed to dislodge the South Africans from their position, but this was of little real importance. The South Africans, as well as having to worry about further attacks, had to wait for their supplies to catch up with them before they could push on, the logistics system having been completely outpaced by the rapidity of the advance. By the middle of May, the supplies had arrived, and the rains had begun to ease. Smuts now pushed on to the Usambara railway line, and did so without meeting much resistance. However, his men had started to fall ill as a result of malnourishment (some units had to operate on half rations for a time) and exposure to the harsh weather. Sickness levels increased dramatically in the wet, muddy conditions, and supplies of ammunition had fallen to a critical level. Smuts therefore halted his forces on 31 May at Same.

After a period of regrouping, Smuts was ready to move on. He planned to seize Handeni, splitting Lettow-Vorbeck from the German forces that had been operating in the Usambara area under the command of Major Kraut. Smuts hoped that if he did this, he might trap the forces along the central railway, which might finally force the Germans into a battle from which they could not disengage easily. The advance went well, and was particularly notable for an attack by the 3rd KAR on the Zuganatto Bridge, the capture of which allowed for the taking of Korogwe. Smuts was most impressed and the performance of the KAR confirmed his decision to raise more battalions of this regiment. However, despite the impressive performance of the KAR and other troops during the advance, Lettow-Vorbeck's innate ability to time his withdrawal won through again, and the Germans had left Handeni by the time that Smuts's men arrived there.

Smuts's next course of action was to employ a flying column to attack the flank of German positions on the Lukigura River while Kraut's men were fixed in position by a frontal attack from the 1st Division. This attack was a success but marked the end of the advance. The 1st and 3rd divisions had outrun their

Troops under the command of General Jacob van Deventer on the march during operations in East Africa in 1916. Van Deventer, like Smuts, had fought against the British during the Boer War, but became one of the empire's most respected military commanders.

supply lines again, and were forced to pause. An assessment of operations suggested that both sides had reason to be content. Smuts had taken a large amount of enemy territory in the course of the advance, while Lettow-Vorbeck remained undefeated and could be in little doubt that his actions were tying down a great number of troops who would have otherwise been employed in France and Flanders.

It was not until the third week of July that the British forces were ready to resume their advance, and when they did so, they suffered the same frustrations as before. The German Askaris withdrew with considerable skill on every occasion that they encountered van Deventer's troops, and they could not be fixed in any one place to allow them to be destroyed. The fact that 100 miles of the railway was now firmly under van Deventer's control was

An assortment of German ammunition and ordnance captured during the British attack against Bagamoyo in August 1916. The Germans could ill afford the loss of ammunition, but the extent of British supply dumps in Eastern Africa was such that Lettow-Vorbeck was able to replenish his ammunition by raiding these locations.

consolation for the inability to bring the Germans to a decisive battle. The campaign now began to follow a repetitive pattern, with Smuts's troops advancing and Lettow-Vorbeck always remaining one step ahead, ceding territory to the British force in lieu of being compelled to fight a numerically superior enemy. By 26 August, the British held the central railway, and Smuts declared himself satisfied. He was aware, though, that the advance had stretched his troops to their limit, and that it was time once again to pause.

While Smuts's advance had continued, Northey had enjoyed a similar level of success with his advance into the south of the German colony. His small force of around 3000 men had captured the German district headquarters at Neu Langenburg, and then advanced towards Iringa, with the 1st KAR leading the way. On 24 July 1916, Northey's force encountered a substantial German defensive line at Malangali, but the KAR overcame the resistance with considerable aplomb. However, Northey was painfully aware that his right flank was dangerously exposed to an enemy counterattack. Nonetheless, he pushed on, and by 29 August his force had reached and occupied Iringa.

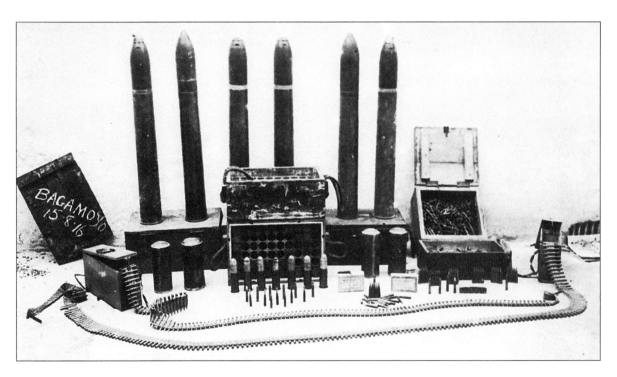

The next phase of the operation saw the capture of the German coastal ports, a move that would be of considerable assistance in overcoming the supply difficulties that had bedevilled the advance since April. Bagamoyo was captured on 15 August, and Dar es Salaam, significant because it was the capital of German East Africa as well as being a major port, fell on 4 September 1916. The attack was supported by the Royal Navy, which somewhat bizarrely decided that the taking of the city had thus been a naval action and that prize money was due to the sailors involved.

Appreciating the value of the ports, Smuts pressed on along the coastline until it was all under British control, and as a final objective, aimed for the Uluguru Mountains and Kisaki. By the end of September, both these objectives had been achieved, but at the cost of rendering the troops incapable of continuing the advance. Supply difficulties were now a serious issue that would take time to resolve, while the troops themselves were worn out by a mixture of the hard

Wounded British and African troops are placed aboard a hospital train for evacuation from the front. The British made considerable use of the lengthy rail network they had built in Africa for this purpose. This not only improved survival rates, but also proved a fillip for troop morale.

conditions and disease. Thus, at the end of September 1916, Smuts brought his campaign to a halt, aware that it had lost momentum. Although he had successfully conquered most of German East Africa, including its capital, and taken all the ports, Smuts could not be completely content, since the wily Lettow-Vorbeck had once again managed to elude him, ensuring that the bulk of his forces remained intact and thus a potential threat.

CHANGE IN COMMAND

Following the conclusion of the offensive, the British forces conducted several mopping-up operations, notably with the capture of Kibata Fort on 18 October, a mission undertaken by the Kilwa Force (so-named after their location) under Brigadier-General Harrington, whose force included a new battalion of the KAR which was involved in its first fighting during the operation. Kilwa Force was tasked with the destruction of German food supply depots, which were becoming increasingly difficult for the Germans to access. Lettow-Vorbeck decided that he could exploit the situation and counterattacked at Kibata between 6 and 9 December 1916, inflicting heavy losses on the KAR and the Gold Coast Regiment. The effect was to force the

'The behaviour of the natives, both during and after the war, clearly shows that they would have preferred the continuance of German dominion to that of the other foreign powers'

Heinrich Schnee, *German Colonization Past and Future*

rest of the Kilwa Force to head towards Kibata, reducing the pressure upon Lettow-Vorbeck's food supply. As the year drew to a close, Lettow-Vorbeck remained undefeated in open battle with the British, and his success at tying down a large number of troops led to his being awarded Germany's highest decoration, the *Pour le Mérite*. He learned of this from a most unusual source, namely Smuts. Smuts heard the news and suspected that Lettow-Vorbeck would not be in a position to receive information, so wrote a fulsome letter of praise to his opponent congratulating him on his award. Lettow-Vorbeck recorded his admiration of Smuts's chivalrous behaviour in his response. Although the war in East Africa had involved hard fighting, Lettow-Vorbeck's observation that the warfare in the area had been conducted with considerable chivalry and mutual respect between the two sides – something which he suspected was lacking elsewhere – was an accurate summation of this peculiar colonial conflict.

A German observation post. The Germans established such positions to warn of approaching British forces, since Lettow-Vorbeck's concept of operations involved avoiding contact with numerically superior enemy forces unless the engagement could be conducted upon German terms.

In response to the Kibata attack, Smuts decided that he needed to cross the rivers Mgeta and Rufiji before the flood season, enabling him to reinforce the Kilwa Force. Smuts formed his main body into four columns with the intention that these should use their ability to manoeuvre to overwhelm the enemy on the bank of the Mgeta, while simultaneously attempting to outflank them to cross the Rufiji at Mkalinzo. The lead force was under Brigadier-General Beves, and he was tasked with carrying out the flanking manoeuvre.

The rainy season made movement towards the river extremely difficult, and it became clear to Smuts that the offensive was going to be a difficult task, since the Germans had strengthened the defences at Kibata considerably after their capture of the fort. The battle that ensued occurred in terrible weather, and Beves briefly managed to surprise the Germans. The columns crossed the river Rufiji and established themselves on the German side of the watercourse, only to discover that, yet again, the Germans had quietly withdrawn so as not to be forced into an open battle with a numerically superior force. Any doubts that Lettow-Vorbeck had complete mastery of the art of withdrawing his forces in the nick of time disappeared for the few remaining sceptics who thought that he was merely lucky.

Smuts was now forced to leave East Africa, not as a result of dissatisfaction with his performance over the course of the preceding year, but because he had to represent South Africa at the Committee of Imperial Defence meeting taking place in London. He left as the rains started in early February 1917. The season

was one marked by the abnormally high amount of rainfall, and it meant that all hopes of defeating Lettow-Vorbeck quickly had to be abandoned. The British had other things to worry about, since the rain made communication links impassable, and severe supply difficulties began to affect their ability to feed and equip their soldiers. Lettow-Vorbeck took the opportunity to pull further away from the Rufiji delta while the rain was falling.

Early 1917 was marked by one notable success for the British Empire forces, against a German force operating independently of Lettow-Vorbeck. A column of men led by Captain Wintgens had successfully evaded the British for more than a year, fighting occasional, sharp engagements with Northey's force. After fighting his way through British positions with considerable skill, his column had become such

A British field gun team advances through flooded ground. The African campaign was punctuated by periods of appalling weather, which seriously hampered offensive operations and allowed German forces to break contact with their pursuers.

Two wireless operators at Beho, January 1917. The rudimentary nature of their equipment can be clearly seen in this photograph, but wireless was a vital communication tool for the British forces during the campaign, in spite of the difficulties in making it work effectively in jungle conditions.

a problem that the British tasked a force under Brigadier-General Edmonds with tracking Wintgens down. Wintgens himself was forced to surrender on 21 May as a result of falling seriously ill, but he handed over command to Oberleutnant Nauman, who contined to fight. Nauman changed his direction of advance on a regular basis, making him almost impossible to track accurately, but on 30 September 1917 his force was surrounded by the 4th KAR near to the British East African border. Nauman attempted to fight his way out, but surrendered the entire force of just over 140 men on 2 October.

Once the rainy season had come to an end, rather later than was normal, fighting flared up again. On 6 July 1917, Lettow-Vorbeck's men ran into Beves's Kilwa Force at Mhindi, and the Germans withdrew to Narungombe. The British columns attacked Narungombe, and ran into serious difficulties. The 3rd KAR attacked on the Germans' left flank and forced them to pull out after some fierce hand-to-hand fighting. The British Empire forces then made preparations to attack the Germans. Lettow-Vorbeck pre-empted them, and attacked the British at Maliwa, inflicting extremely heavy casualties. A German force of around 1500 men defeated a much larger force, and won its most notable victory of the war, with the possible exception of the Battle at

Tanga at the opening of the war. However, even though the Germans lost only 519 men in comparison to the 3000 British casualties, this was a blow that Lettow-Vorbeck's force could ill afford to sustain. Furthermore, the fighting during 1917 had begun to cause ammunition shortages for the Germans, and supply difficulties meant that it, and the vital quinine tablets to prevent malaria, were running low, as was food. Living off the land was starting to become a difficult proposition for Lettow-Vorbeck's men as the area from which they could gather food shrank in the face of the British advance. These considerations led to Lettow-Vorbeck deciding that he should withdraw

his force into Portuguese East Africa. He abandoned Nambindinga on 21 November 1917, and crossed into Portuguese East Africa four days later.

The year ended with the British in a curious position. By one measure of success, they had achieved a great deal, being in almost total control of German East Africa; by another measure, namely that of defeating their enemy in a decisive battle, they had failed. Lettow-Vorbeck's force was still in a position to continue to harry the British, and this meant that he could still achieve his aim of ensuring that British troops would have to remain in the area in some numbers to deal with his operations.

1918 – THE FINALE

Lettow-Vorbeck's move into Portuguese East Africa meant that the Allies still had to attempt to defeat him, and this would require further manoeuvring of troops around eastern Africa. Although Lettow-Vorbeck's efforts were diverting a relatively small amount of Allied effort away from other theatres of war, it was enough to be a source of frustration to the Allies.

The British Empire forces, now under General van Deventer after Smuts's departure, faced a number of challenges in planning the pursuit into Portuguese East Africa. The terrain was particularly challenging, since it consisted of thick brush, which was difficult to traverse. This meant that it would be possible for a small force of skilfully handled troops such as Lettow-Vorbeck's to hold up a much larger opponent as they attempted to close with the main body of the enemy. Van Deventer, however, had made a considered analysis of the situation, and concluded that the main difficulty facing Lettow-Vorbeck was going to be gaining access to sufficient food supplies. Van Deventer reasoned that if the Germans used up all the food that was available to them in Portuguese East Africa, Lettow-Vorbeck might then head back towards German East Africa in search of sustenance for his men.

A group photograph of a unit of the King's African Rifles, September 1917. The KAR was a particularly effective formation during the war, reaching a peak strength of over 30,0000 locally raised troops and another 3000 British officers and NCOs.

Elements of British forces move into Portuguese East Africa, in pursuit of Lettow-Vorbeck's forces, which had successfully overwhelmed the Portuguese troops they had encountered. Bitter fighting between elements of the King's African Rifles and the Germans ensued.

Van Deventer therefore decided that his plan of campaign would not be to conduct a hard march through the heavy brush in pursuit of the Germans, but to carry out operations with the aim of denying Lettow-Vorbeck the opportunity to return to German East Africa. At the same time, Deventer planned to use his forces to bring Lettow-Vorbeck to battle as frequently as possible. This would impose more pressure on the Germans as they attempted to find food and as their ammunition supply decreased because of frequent encounters with the British forces. Van Deventer had a further concern, which was to ensure that he kept Lettow-Vorbeck out of Nyasaland, since if the Germans were able to penetrate there, they would have another supply of food to exploit, which would make bringing about their defeat an even longer process.

Lettow-Vorbeck went onto the offensive as soon as he had crossed into Portuguese East Africa, defeating a force of Portuguese Askaris. The Germans took the Askaris' rifles, ammunition and medical supplies. They did not, though, find any food supplies to help prolong their campaign. This lack of food meant that Lettow-Vorbeck had to change his plans, splitting his force into two and sending a column led by the retired Major-General Wahle (who had joined Lettow-Vorbeck in 1914 as one of his subordinates, despite his rank) off to the west, while Lettow-Vorbeck took the main body of the force along the Lugenda River. The Portuguese forces that were encountered by both columns were soon overcome, and there was little that the Portuguese could do to stop them. A British force landed at Port Amelia and moved inland with the intent of engaging the Germans when they found them. By March 1918, the British had reached Medo where a detachment of Germans had established a defensive position. Bitter fighting ensued between the Germans and the 2nd Battalion of the 2nd KAR, during which both sides ran out of ammunition and were forced to resort to use of the bayonet and hand-to-hand combat. The arrival of the Gold Coast Regiment to support the 2nd Battalion of the 2nd KAR meant that the Germans were now facing a particularly difficult situation, and they broke contact under the cover of darkness.

In keeping with van Deventer's desire to raise the pressure on Lettow-Vorbeck, the British set about harrying the Germans as frequently as possible. The pressure applied was such that the German commander gathered his forces together at Nanungu, with the aim of moving south to break contact with the British if at all possible. Van Deventer now thought that he might have the chance to finally trap the Germans at Korewa, where they could be engaged in a decisive confrontation. However, the countryside around Korewa was easy to defend, consisting of extremely thick bush and, being in a gorge, it was surrounded by cliffs. The Germans took advantage of the terrain and held up the British for a considerable amount of time, but eventually they were forced to retire. They had inflicted heavy casualties on the

attacking forces, and were able to retreat without being caught in a decisive battle. The British had come close to finally gaining a clear victory over Lettow-Vorbeck's force, but they had not concentrated quite enough troops to achieve the level of success they had hoped for. However, the Germans had been forced to leave a considerable amount of their ammunition supply at Korewa, which represented a serious blow.

This setback was shortly forgotten when the town of Malema fell to the Germans, since this offered them access to a plentiful food supply. Having replenished his food stocks, Lettow-Vorbeck then pressed on towards Alto Molocue, which as one of the main Portuguese

British and African troops relax in the aftermath of a successful attack on a German position. Such scenes became more common in 1918 as the British seemed to be on the verge of forcing the Germans into a decisive battle – but the skilled Lettow-Vorbeck always managed to avoid this.

A part cutaway of the Lee Enfield Number 1 Mk.3 rifle, showing the bolt action that made the weapon easy to operate and gave it a high rate of fire. The Mk.3 and its derivative the Mk.3* were the standard British rifles of World War I, and remained in production until 1955.

administrative centres appeared to be a potential source of ammunition and medical supplies. This move forced van Deventer to shift his base camp from Port Amelia to Mozambique. The Germans took Alto Molocue, but found that it did not have the supplies they wanted, so they moved on. An engagement with Portuguese forces at Namacurra led to the seizure of more weapons from the defeated enemy, but the Germans failed to locate the ammunition store that they knew to be somewhere in the area. Lettow-Vorbeck then arrived with the rest of the force, and decided to move on to the industrial area of the town. Near the railway station, the Germans ran into more Portuguese troops, and routed them. This left the station, under the protection of two companies of the KAR. However, they were unable to stop the Germans from forcing them to retreat, and as they tried to escape down the river many were drowned in the fast-flowing waters. When the Germans explored the town, they discovered enormous stocks of food and ammunition, along with a consignment of Lee-Enfield rifles.

Now re-equipped, Lettow-Vorbeck had more freedom of action than before, and decided to march to the northeast on the grounds that the Allies would fear that this presaged an invasion of Mozambique. The British moved to intercept him, and the two sides

A 1918 propaganda poster, depicting Lettow-Vorbeck at the head of his troops. He remained undefeated and only surrendered when news reached him that Germany had capitulated. He was accorded enormous respect by his opponents, especially Jan Smuts.

ran into one another at Namirrue. Lettow-Vorbeck's troops managed to take the British by surprise, and in the fighting that followed, the 3rd Battalion of the 3rd KAR was wiped out. The Germans pressed on to Chalaua, before turning away on news that the British were there in strength. Lettow-Vorbeck then moved his force to the north in the expectation that returning to German East Africa would take the British by surprise and buy an advantage as the British reacted to this. Elements of the 2nd Battalion of the 2nd KAR pursued the Germans and attacked them; however,

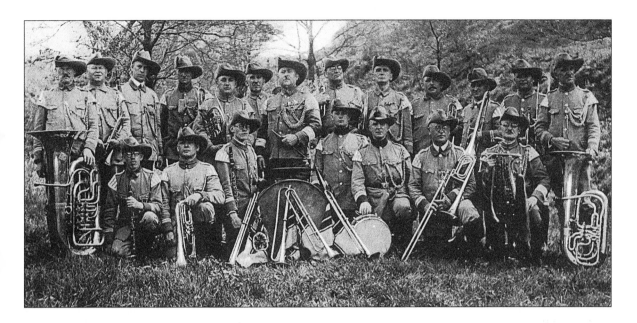

German *Schutztruppe* ('protection troops') band members pose for the camera. They are wearing the standard khaki field uniform and the distinctive Südwester hat. The area of service (South-West or East Africa and Cameroon) was denoted by the colour of the hatband and edging.

the attack went in against the main body rather than the flank force that the KAR had thought they were engaging, and the German counterattack that followed drove the KAR troops off. Lettow-Vorbeck briefly flirted with the idea of pursuing the KAR and inflicting a decisive defeat upon them, but chose not to on the grounds that this risked delaying his force long enough for the British to bring up reinforcements. Instead, he broke away from the surviving KAR troops and headed off towards the Ruvuma River. He crossed the river at Nagwamira on 28 September 1918 and re-entered German East Africa.

Van Deventer was forced to redeploy his entire force to meet this new development; even after fighting for four years at a distinct disadvantage, Lettow-Vorbeck held the initiative. Lettow-Vorbeck continued to move northwards, before turning towards the town of Fife on the border with Northern Rhodesia. Lettow-Vorbeck intended to seize the supplies and ammunition he knew to be stored in the town, but the British had established a strongly defensible position, and after the initial attack failed Lettow-Vorbeck withdrew, rather than risk a pitched battle breaking out. Lettow-Vorbeck then headed towards the town of Kasama, which information from locals suggested might be another potential source of food and ammunition.

SURRENDER

As Lettow-Vorbeck marched towards Kasama on 13 November, he was approached by a truce party, which handed him a signal from van Deventer informing him that the war had ended two days previously. Van Deventer presented his surrender terms, which included a clause that allowed all Lettow-Vorbeck's officers and European troops to retain their arms as a mark of respect for what Van Deventer described as 'the gallant fight which you have made'. Lettow-Vorbeck accepted the terms, and marched his force on to the town of Abercorn, where they surrendered on 25 November. Lettow-Vorbeck led the column of troops into the town to be met by a guard of honour drawn from the KAR. Lettow-Vorbeck formed his men into three ranks, saluted the Union flag and read out his acceptance of the surrender terms to Brigadier-General Edwards, thus bringing the war in the African colonies to an end.

CHAPTER 4

Italy at War 1915–16

According to the terms of the alliance by which the country had bound itself in the later years of the nineteenth century, Italy entered the war on 'the wrong side'. One complicating factor had been Italy's poor relationship with Austria-Hungary over territorial claims that sought to complete the process of Italian unification. As with many other nations, the spirit of nationalism was a main imperative for entering the war.

I taly had allied itself with Germany and Austria-Hungary since 1882, with the signature of the Triple Alliance, but its membership of this group was not a comfortable one. It was in Italy's interests to maintain links not only with Germany and Austria, but also with France, Russia and Britain. To complicate matters the Italians and Austrians had a bitter rivalry over the so-called *Italia Irredenta* ('Unredeemed Italy'), territories on the Dalmatian

Italian troops advancing under fire. With a very limited front to fight on, the Italian Army was forced to attack over difficult terrain and on predictable axes. The resulting heavy casualties eventually drained morale, but the Italian Army remained confident of victory for a surprisingly long time.

coast, most notably the city of Trieste. There were some 750,000 people of Italian descent living in these areas, and by 1914 it appeared that the only thing preventing a war between the Austro-Hungarians and the Italians was the fact that they were bound together by the Triple Alliance.

The Austrian ultimatum to Serbia was regarded with hostility by the Italian populace, and it appeared almost certain that the Italian Government would refuse to break neutrality to fight alongside its supposed ally. Assisting Austria in its attempts to crush the Serbs would have been politically difficult, if not impossible, given the way in which Austria was perceived by the average Italian, and Prime Minister Antonio Salandra's government in Rome had little intention of pitching its forces into a war that would enjoy little, if any, public support. The

Twelve regiments of Bersaglieri troops fought for Italy in World War I. Originally fast-moving skirmishers and mountain troops, they were often deployed as elite shock formations due to their high morale and aggression. The distinctive feathers are still worn as part of dress uniform.

Italians contended that the Austrian ultimatum was an aggressive act, no matter what the circumstances that had led to its being issued, and pointed out that their obligations under the treaty were purely defensive: if Austria or Germany were attacked, then Italy was obliged to assist in repelling the aggressor, but circumstances in which Germany and/or Austria began the conflict were not covered under the terms of the agreement.

A further complication lay in the attitude of the Italian Government to territorial acquisitions in the Balkans, a matter covered by the alliance treaty. The Austrians were obliged by the terms of the agreement to provide Italy with compensation, in the form of more territory, if the Austro-Hungarian armies made conquests in the Balkans. In essence, this meant that a war of conquest that brought Serbia under Austro-Hungarian control would require the government in Vienna to hand over land to Italy – and the Italians hoped that this would be the territory they coveted along the Adriatic and Dalmatian coasts. The Austrians, however, were reluctant at the thought

of giving any land to the Italians, and made it clear that they would not even consider doing so – treaty obligations or not – unless Italy joined the war. Italian efforts to point out that the treaty conditions regarding the handover of territory were not dependent upon participation in a war were rebuffed by the Austrian foreign minister, Leopold von Berchtold, who was known to be amongst those most reluctant to even consider ceding Austrian territory to the Italians.

In this unpromising environment, the Italian Government unsurprisingly remained resolutely neutral. However, this was a position that appeared to be fraught with risk. The Italians were concerned that the Germans and Austro-Hungarians would seek to punish them in some way if they did not participate in the war. The Italians believed that the German Army was likely to achieve victory in any major war in Europe, and this would, in effect, give the Kaiser a free hand to do as he wished. It was well known in Rome that the Chief of the Austrian General Staff, Hötzendorf, was an advocate of a preventative war against Italy, since he thought that a war between the two powers was inevitable at some point. The pretext of punishing Italy for not meeting what the Austrians felt to be a moral obligation of providing support in war might be employed to allow just this course of action to be undertaken.

The border between Italy and Austria-Hungary as it stood in 1915. The Trentino and Istria regions, among others, were the cause of dispute between the two nations, despite the fact that both were part of the Triple Alliance. Italy's entry into the war hinged on being given these territories.

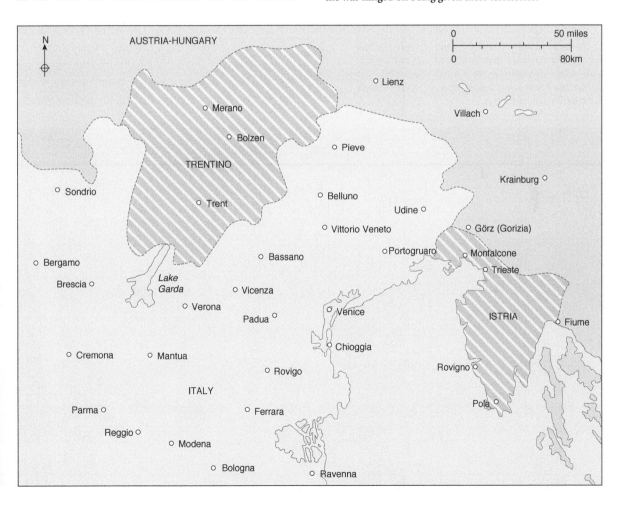

Salandra felt that it would be irresponsible to ignore this possibility, and the Italians embarked upon some very careful diplomacy in an attempt to ensure that any move to stay neutral would not backfire upon them. This was more complicated than it might at first appear, since it was quite clear to the Italian Government that entering a war in which Britain and France were participating (and while there was debate as to whether the British would fight in a major European war, there was little doubt regarding French involvement) would be extremely dangerous, given the ability of these nations' navies to interfere with the vital flow of imports upon which Italy relied. The Italian foreign minister, Antonio di San Giuliano, therefore set about managing the expectations of his allies while seeking to keep the Italian electorate supportive, and not committing

Italy to any precipitate action. He began to outline a policy under which Italy did not explicitly rule out joining in the war. San Giuliano held out the prospect of Italy remaining a non-belligerent at the outset of a war begun by Austria, but coming into the conflict at a later date to assist, as long as Austria reached a fair accommodation over the issue of the allocation of territory as under the articles of the Triple Alliance treaty. By 1 August 1914, it was clear to all involved in negotiations that the Italians would not participate in the war for the time being.

When Germany declared war on France on 3 August 1914, the Italian Government issued its declaration of neutrality, stating that although some of the European powers were now at war, Italy remained at peace and intended to stay out of the conflict that had just started. This rather bland, benign statement concealed the concerns of the Italian Government, which was unable to overcome its fears that this move might prove disastrous in the event of an early victory for the Austrians and Germans. To make matters worse, the war brought an early end to the tourist season,

At the outbreak of World War I, tensions between Italy and Austria-Hungary were high as a result of disputes over Italian territories on the Adriatic coast. This Austrian artillery unit was one of many deployed to the borders between the two nations.

The Italian–Austro-Hungarian border was carefully watched from vantage points high in the mountains. For observers like these Austrian troops, such work was uncomfortable but necessary in order to have early warning of an attack that many officers and government officials felt was inevitable.

causing unemployment, and the ranks of the jobless were swelled by Italians who had been working in the belligerent nations and who had returned home after the outbreak of war. The government therefore had to divide its attention between the possible risks of external powers attacking Italy and the danger of social upheaval caused by the changed economic conditions. An economic crisis, punctuated by runs on several banks and a collapse in confidence in the stock market only added to the difficulties. To make matters worse, the war curtailed imports and there was a shortage of both grain and coal. The unstable economy remained a cause of concern for the rest of the year, but this crisis ebbed in the attention of the government when news of German successes in France and Belgium reached Rome. Rumours that the Germans would soon beat the French and British forces and then turn their attention upon their treacherous former ally caused alarm amongst the Italian ruling elite. King Vittorio Emanuele III, an anxious man at the best of times, became concerned and doubtful about his government's chosen course of action: his nerves became so frayed that he was advised by his doctors to take a relaxing cruise in the Mediterranean, but he refused to do so on the grounds of the increased possible threat from submarines that might mistake the royal yacht for a tempting target.

Franz Conrad von Hotzendorf (1852–1925)

As commander-in-chief of the Austro-Hungarian Army from 1906, Hotzendorf was involved in both political as well as military decision making. He was greatly concerned by the need for rapid modernization of the army, and argued strongly for launching preventative wars against both Italy and Serbia. His stance brought him into conflict with the foreign minister, and at the end of 1911 Conrad was compelled to offer his resignation. However, as the political situation in Europe worsened, the royal family recalled him as Chief of the General Staff in December 1912. Conrad held command of the Army until March 1917. The new emperor Karl saw Conrad as being intimately associated with the outbreak of war, and fully opposed to beginning peace negotiations with the Allies. Conrad was removed as chief of staff, and was sent to command an army group in the Tyrol. His attack on the Italians in June 1918 failed because of poor planning. As a further mark of respect for his service, Karl appointed him as Colonel of the Royal Life Guards and raised him to the rank of count. However, Conrad elected to retire from service.

Salandra feared that the careful diplomacy of the preceding weeks would be for naught, but the air of gloom surrounding the Italian administration rapidly lifted when news of the German defeat at the Battle of the Marne reached them. The idea that the German Army was invincible was shattered, and the parlous situation in which the Austrians found themselves – facing a Russian invasion in Galicia and finding the Serbs a far more difficult prospect than they had ever imagined – only added to the lightening mood in Rome. Indeed, the setbacks for Germany and Austria seem to have changed the atmosphere from one of impending doom to one of considerable confidence. Rather hastily, the Italians appeared to reach a conclusion diametrically opposed to their thoughts at the start of August 1914, namely that the Germans and Austrians were unlikely to win, and that the Allies would triumph. Almost at once, the Italians began to consider whether or not the time was opportune for sacrificing neutrality so as to join the Allied powers. It began to appear that joining the Allied powers would facilitate the realization of Italy's territorial ambitions – the question being one of timing, for if the Italians waited for too long, there would be the danger that they would not be taken seriously when the peace treaty was drawn up, and their neutrality would perhaps be the cause of their aspirations being thwarted permanently. Having begun August firmly convinced that neutrality was the best course of action, by the end of September 1914 the Italian Government was giving serious consideration to entering the war.

THE MOVE TOWARDS THE ENTENTE

As the early fighting on the Western Front became bogged down, the British and French began to make less than subtle overtures to the Italians, albeit in the form of implied threats that prolonged neutrality would be a disadvantage. The Allies made it quite clear that nations that had not participated in the war would be quite unable to expect that they would gain in any way from the conflict in terms of acquiring additional territory. To concentrate Italian minds, the Allies, notably the French, began a propaganda campaign aimed not just at the government, but at Italy as a whole. Tales of German atrocities, particularly against the Belgians, were widely disseminated, achieving exactly the desired effect of creating considerable sympathy amongst the devoutly Catholic Italians for their fellow Catholics, as well as considerable anger towards their supposed oppressors. Belgian politicians were enlisted in the campaign, travelling to Italy and addressing public meetings, where they stressed that it was vital that Italy join the war to help defeat the Germans so as to end the atrocities and to allow the perpetrators to be punished for their crimes. The Belgians were not alone: a group of French writers and artists also headed for Italy and attempted to influence political opinion by meeting with numerous Italian politicians and having an audience with the Pope. Although the precise success of this propaganda effort is hard to quantify, it seems to have had some effect on the Pontiff, who asked a series of stern questions of the leader of the German Catholic movement,

the politician Matthias Erzberger, regarding the appalling behaviour of German troops, who were said to have embarked upon a frenzy of looting and sexual violence against Belgian Catholic nuns. Erzberger – who had no idea what the Pope was talking about, beyond knowledge that the Allies were propagating such stories – was unable to answer, creating an unfavourable impression of the German cause in the eyes of the Vatican.

Allied propaganda notwithstanding, the majority of the Italian population remained unconvinced of the merits of joining the war. However, it appears that there might have been some influence upon opinion other than that of the Pope, since a pro-war faction formed, seeking to pressure the government into participation on the Allied side. The pro-war

Once the decision to join the war had been made, preparations to defend Italy were begun in earnest. These troops are preparing defensive entrenchments based on experience gained by other nations on the Western Front in the early months of the war.

lobby was quite small, but it was vocal and possessed considerable influence; it also benefited from being a cross-party grouping, removing the idea that its formation had come about as an attempt by one of the political parties to drive forward its agenda. The war lobby gained support amongst leading Italian industrialists and the middle classes; more significantly, the most prominent members of the pro-war lobby included those who owned the most successful newspapers, which led to editorials reflecting the pro-war perspective. Some of the newspapers became particularly vitriolic in their calls for war, with a number of journalists and commentators suggesting that Salandra was being too slow in moving towards a declaration of hostilities, and that he ought to be replaced for failing to deliver one in as timely a manner as the pro-war party would have wished.

By the end of October, the Italian Government had reached the view that it would have to enter the war, since it was in the nation's best interests to do so. San Giuliano's contribution to shaping the conditions under which the Italians would join the Allies was cut short when he died on 16 October, finally succumbing to the ill health that had bedevilled him for many years, exacerbated by the tensions of the summer and early autumn. Salandra initially assumed the post of foreign minister himself, but soon came to appreciate that his lack of experience in foreign affairs and the burdens of office facing the Prime Minister meant that it was impractical for him to continue. He therefore appointed Sidney Sonnino as the new foreign minister. Sonnino was a close friend of Salandra, and was an extremely experienced politician. He had initially argued that Italy's best interests in a war would be served by fulfilling its alliance with Germany and Austria, but had shifted his position: by the time Salandra appointed his friend, Sonnino was convinced that Italy would be making a grave error if it did not participate in the war on the side of the Allies. Although there was still time to see what could be achieved by negotiation, it seemed that unless Austria modified its stance, joining the Allies was in the national interest.

Shortly after Sonnino's appointment, Salandra reshuffled his government, sacking a number of ministers who were still unconvinced by the merits of the course of action being pursued. This meant that the only possible obstacle to the plan to join the war was the king. Vittorio Emanuele, however, was an indecisive man, and although he had given tacit approval of the government's policy, he did not want to have to make the final decision. He told Salandra that he felt that it was the government's decision as to whether the country went to war, and that he would support whatever decision was reached. Although unwilling to make the final decision, as a member of the House of Savoy, it was most unlikely that Vittorio Emanuele would set aside years of enmity between the House of Savoy and the Habsburgs, a point that his mother was quick to reinforce. In addition, Vittorio Emanuele's wife, Queen Elena, was a Montenegrin, and her sympathies clearly did not lie with the Austrians.

Although Salandra could count upon the support of the cabinet and the king, he faced a further political challenge before finally setting the country on the path to war. This came in the form of Giovanni Giolitti, the man who had dominated pre-war Italian politics. Giolitti's popularity had declined by 1914, and in the early part of the year he had chosen to retire as Prime Minister, surrendering office in favour of Salandra after elections in early March 1914, despite still leading

'Our neutrality ought to have been, and ought to be, not inert and listless, but active and vigilant, not impotent, and strongly armed and ready for any eventuality.'

Antonio Salandra, addressing the Italian Parliament, 3 December 1914

The border between Italy and Austria-Hungary was characterized by steep Alpine terrain, and it was there that any war would be fought. As a result, training in mountaineering techniques, as demonstrated by these Austro-Hungarian soldiers, was considered vital to success.

the largest party in the Italian Parliament. Giolitti's retirement seems to have been for rather Machiavellian reasons. There are suggestions he thought that Italy would soon be subjected to an economic crisis and accompanying unrest, and preferred that Salandra should take the blame for this; he would then bring down the Salandra administration thanks to his parliamentary position and return to power.

Cavalry were unable to undertake large-scale operations in the steep terrain of the Austrian–Italian border region. However, their mobility was useful in maintaining patrols over a wide area. These Italian cavalrymen, equipped with rifles, would normally dismount to fight in such terrain.

Salandra was fully aware that Giolitti had the power to cause the government difficulties to the point of destroying it, and he had to tread carefully, not least since Giolitti was against intervention. Salandra had one advantage, and this was that Parliament had gone into recess in July, and no date for its meeting again had been set at the time the European crisis broke out. This gave the Prime Minister time to prepare the ground for facing Parliament when the time came, which turned out to be on 3 December 1914.

In his opening address to the Chamber of Deputies, Salandra argued that neutrality alone would not serve Italian interests, since these vital interests would be

The standard infantry small arm of the Italian Army was the bolt-action Model 91 rifle. Introduced in 1891, it was chambered for 6.5 x 52mm ammunition, fed from a six-round internal magazine. It is normally referred to as the Mannlicher-Carcano, though this designation was never officially used.

threatened if Italy remained neutral and left the field open to those who would seek to deny the country its 'just aspirations'. However, he crafted his speech with considerable skill, so that it was not possible to draw the implication from his words that he intended to take Italy into the war.

As a result, many deputies thought that Salandra meant nothing more than to suggest that the status quo was inadequate and that negotiations with Austria were required, while others thought that the speech was designed to raise a degree of uncertainty in Berlin and Vienna, with the possibility of securing concessions. Giolitti, although concerned by Salandra's speech, seems to have believed that the government had no intention of entering the war, and was happy to lead his followers in supporting a motion of confidence in the Cabinet.

THE FINAL CRISIS

Having been given additional political strength by this success, Salandra and Sonnino set about negotiating with Austria in a final attempt to gain something from them without having to embark upon war. On 2 December, the Austrians seized Belgrade, and the Italians promptly opened formal negotiations with Vienna on 11 December, seeking territorial compensation under terms of the treaty that had established the Triple Alliance. There was a different tone to the Italian position now, though: while the

Italians had previously told the Austrians that being given territory was a pre-requisite for their support against the Allies, they now made it clear that territory was required to ensure that Italy would stay neutral. The implication that a refusal would lead to Italian intervention on the Allied side was clear.

Negotiations dragged on, with the Austrians proving most reluctant to move. There appeared to be an opportunity in January 1915, following the success of a Russian offensive in Galicia. The Austrians worried that the Italians might intervene in the war, placing them in an extremely difficult position, since they would be unable to send more troops to fight the Russians if forces were required to fight the Italians. As a result, the Austro-Hungarian Crown Council decided that an offer of the southern Trentino should be made to the Italian delegation. Sonnino suspected that this offer was nothing more than a distraction aimed at keeping the Italians out of the war for a while longer, and was correct to do so: a strong body of opinion in Vienna saw the surrender of territory to Italy as being nothing more than a temporary measure, to be reversed by force of arms once the war was over. He refused to accept, and more concessions were offered, until by May, the Austrians had offered more territory and recognition of disputed border areas. This was still not enough to satisfy the Italians, just as Salandra and Sonnino had expected – which was why, in March 1915, they opened negotiations with the Entente.

The battleship *Erzherzog Karl*, one of three ships forming Austria-Hungary's last pre-Dreadnought class, was already obsolescent when completed. One important innovation was that this was the first class of battleship to mount its secondary armament in electrically powered turrets.

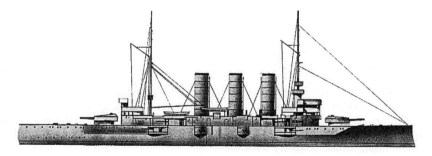

Deducing (correctly) that the Austrian offer of territory to stay out of the war was a temporary measure to be reversed later, Italy declared for the Allies in return for territorial concessions, thus committing her troops to a difficult war.

The initial negotiations went well, and although the result of the bargaining meant that not all Italian aspirations were met, the terms on offer were acceptable to Rome. On 26 April 1915, agreement was reached on all points. Italy would join the war on the Allied side by the end of May, in return for which the Italian territorial aspirations agreed upon in the negotiations would be realized at the conclusion of the war. There remained one obstacle to the Pact of London being implemented, namely opinion in Italy. The Italian public and many legislators were still firmly in favour of peace, and Giolitti remained amongst those who did not wish to see Italy go to war. Although Salandra's speech to the opening of Parliament in December 1914 had given his Cabinet breathing space, the potential for a crisis over Italian intervention in the war remained. To make matters worse, the Russians suffered a major setback on 3 May when the Gorlice offensive drove them back all along the front, suggesting that Italian intervention

would not be as easy as had been anticipated by the government. By 13 May, it appeared that the crisis was insurmountable: Salandra's government had agreed to join the Allies, but it appeared that political pressure in Italy would make it impossible for them to carry the declaration of war in Parliament. At a difficult Cabinet meeting, Salandra decided that the only answer to the problem was for the government to resign so that a new administration could solve the crisis.

However, when Salandra went to Vittorio Emanuele to offer his resignation, the monarch was not minded to accept it, and said he would take time to consider the position. He did so in the knowledge that Giolitti was not prepared to assume the premiership again. In an audience with the king on 10 May, Giolitti had told the monarch that he could not possibly become Prime Minister once more since he was regarded by many Italians as being pro-Austrian, which would compromise his position in negotiations with Vienna. Also, he noted that rumours were sweeping the capital suggesting that he was in the pay of Berlin (a false accusation) and this was a further reason for Vittorio Emanuele not to consider asking him to resume the highest political office.

Furthermore, as news of the government's resignation spread, the pro-war lobby organized demonstrations throughout the country, and as these gathered momentum, it seemed that the crisis was on the verge of being defused. On 16 May, Vittorio Emanuele recalled Salandra's Cabinet and announced that he would not accept the resignation. The following day Giolitti left Rome, aware that there was nothing he could do to prevent Italian entry into the war: if he brought the government down over the issue, he would precipitate another crisis, and this was now undesirable. With Giolitti's departure, the anti-war party lost its leader, and the clear sign that the king was in favour of entry into the war led to a number of prominent anti-war figures switching their position: they informed the press that, while they had been in favour of neutrality, it was now quite clear that their duty as loyal Italian patriots was to support the king's decision. On 20 May, the Chamber of Deputies assembled once more, to vote on whether to go to war. Salandra and Sonnino were cheered as they went to their seats, and Salandra opened proceedings by introducing a bill granting the government the powers that would be necessary if Italy was to go to war. In support of this, Sonnino then presented a document that outlined the series of negotiations with the Austrians, and after a recess to allow the parliamentarians to read the contents, a vote was called, which was carried in the government's favour by 407 votes to 74, a far greater majority than Salandra could have dared hope for a few days previously. Following this parliamentary success, mobilization was declared on 22 May, and the next day saw

Where to deploy forces to contain an Italian attack was a considerable problem for the Austro-Hungarian high command. However, geographical and political considerations made the Isonzo Valley the most likely target. This analysis was soon proved correct.

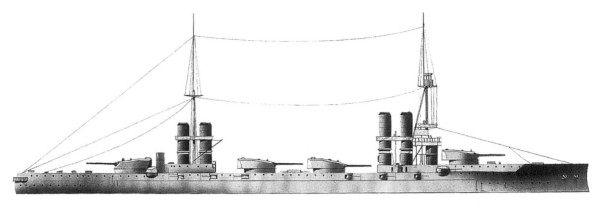

Laid down in 1909, the battleship *Dante Alighieri* was Italy's first Dreadnought and the first capital ship in the world to mount triple turrets on the centreline. She served as a flagship throughout the war, blockading the Adriatic coast to keep Austro-Hungarian naval assets contained.

the Italian ambassador to Vienna, a long-standing opponent of war with Austria, called upon to deliver the formal declaration of war to the Austro-Hungarian foreign ministry. Early on the morning of 24 May, the Austrians opened the fighting when elements of the navy bombarded a number of coastal towns, while Venice was attacked by a small formation of Austrian aircraft.

THE OPENING ROUNDS

The Italian declaration of war left the Austro-Hungarians facing a dilemma, since they could not be sure of the direction from which any offensive against Austria would be launched. The long frontier between the two countries possessed several points that appeared to be tempting targets for the Italians, a matter which complicated the Austrians' deployment of forces.

However, a careful consideration of the terrain in which the fighting would occur left the Austrians convinced that the only place along the frontier from which the Italians could conduct a major offensive was in the Isonzo Valley. In addition to being the only area where the movement of forces on a large scale would be possible, the Austrians noted that many of the inhabitants were Italian-speaking, something that would make an attack in the valley an attractive proposition, since it could be portrayed as the first

step in liberating Italians from the rule of the Austro-Hungarian Empire. This appreciation of the situation persuaded the Austrians to place the bulk of their forces to defend the Isonzo Valley, a move that proved to be perceptive given the considerations the Italians applied to their military planning.

The Italian plan of attack had dismissed much of the hard mountain terrain between Austria and Italy, which made it impossible to envisage large-scale operations being conducted there with any degree of success at all. Only on the Isonzo, between the Krn Mountain and the Adriatic Sea, was the terrain adequate for a large offensive, and even here it was problematic. It would be difficult for any attacker to cross along the entire front of the Isonzo, given that the area between Görz (known to the Italians as Gorizia) and Tolmin would compel the assaulting forces into high plains at Bainsizza, an unpromising location for a decisive battle. Even in the more favourable location of the Isonzo Valley, there was only a relatively small area in which meaningful combat operations could be carried out by the massing forces.

The Italians thus intended to seize Görz and the much longed for city of Trieste, one of the places that Italian nationalists were determined to see incorporated into the Italian state. The Austrians, on the other hand, wanted to retain the ability to control the Adriatic, something that would be challenged if they allowed the Italians to gain control of Trieste. Also, there were good reasons for putting up a determined fight against the Italians: by mid-1915, Austrian losses on the Eastern Front had been significant, and losing yet more men in an Italian offensive would be a disaster, leaving Austria-Hungary vulnerable on two fronts.

The Italian Chief of the General Staff, Luigi Cadorna, organized the forces available to him on the Isonzo front into two armies, the Second and Third, respectively commanded by General Pietro Frugoni and General Vittorio Emanuele, the Duke of Aosta. These armies would lead the way. Meanwhile, the First and Fourth Italian armies were to secure the South Tyrol at Verona and Belluno to allow them to press into Austrian territory over the mountain ranges at the earliest possible opportunity.

The Austrians, however, were more than ready for such a plan of action: their forces, under Prince Eugen, had already begun work on a defensive line in April 1915. Eugen gave command of the Austrian Fifth Army to General Svetozar Boroevich von Bojna four days after the outbreak of war, based upon Boroevich's outstanding performance in defending the Carpathian Mountains and then the success of the Gorlice–Tarnow offensive earlier in the month. Boroevich had a simple conception for the defence along the Isonzo, issuing succinct and clear orders: 'The troops should construct positions, place obstacles in front of them and remain there.'

While this may seem like a gross oversimplification of conducting a defence of a crucial position, it was

'We entered this, the greatest war in history, to safeguard the highest and most ancient aspirations, the most vital interests of our country. Italians of all classes must have a reasoned conviction of the justice of our cause.'

Antonio Salandra, June 1915

the clearest articulation of Boroevich's approach to what would become a long and drawn out series of offensive operations by the Italians on this front. Boroevich was presented with a series of options for trapping the Italians on the Doberdo Plateau, plans that involved grandiose counterattacks along the bridgeheads at Görz, but he rejected them in favour of a straightforward and robust defence instead.

THE FIRST BATTLE OF THE ISONZO

The Italian attack did not come at once, as the Austrians had expected, and they were able to use the time profitably, improving the readiness and strength of their fortifications and destroying the railway bridges that the Italians would need to move forwards if the opening phase of the offensive was a success and could be exploited. On 25 May, the first Italian troops arrived at the Isonzo, and Brado was occupied the next day. Following these preliminary moves, Cadorna issued orders for a general offensive to be launched on 27 May, which began with five surprise attacks against Monte Sabotino and Görz. The defending troops rebuffed the first attack, and a second assault on 28 May met with a similar lack of success as the Austrians followed the simple instructions issued by Boroevich regarding staying in their positions.

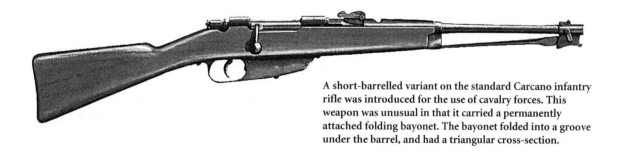

A short-barrelled variant on the standard Carcano infantry rifle was introduced for the use of cavalry forces. This weapon was unusual in that it carried a permanently attached folding bayonet. The bayonet folded into a groove under the barrel, and had a triangular cross-section.

General Luigi Cadorna (1850–1928)

Cadorna was the son of the Piedemontese general Raffaele Cadorna, a hero of the Italian wars of unification and of the Seven Weeks War against the Austrians. In 1914 Cadorna agreed to become chief of staff of the Italian Army, a position he had already once rejected. Cadorna was openly contemptuous of Italian politicians, and his uneasy relationship with the government was mirrored by those with his subordinates. During the war, he sacked over 200 of his generals, and developed a reputation as a harsh disciplinarian, which included the execution of officers whose units withdrew. Cadorna did not, however, not prove himself to be a great general, largely thanks to his lack of real success in any of the multiple Isonzo offensives, which were conducted in terrain that was ill suited to such operations. The final straw for the Italian Government came with the disaster at Caporetto in 1917; Cardona was replaced by Armando Diaz, and sent to serve as the Italian representative on the Allied Military Council at Versailles.

The Italians changed tack with a new assault at Krn, but this also failed to break through. A renewed effort on 5 June by the Italian VII and IX corps against the Doberdo Plateau was combined with simultaneous attacks on Görz by the Italian VI Corps and on Monte Kuk by the Italian II Corps. Unfortunately for the Italians, these attacks were uncoordinated, and it became obvious that the planning for the fire support for the assaults had been somewhat haphazard, as the attacking troops did not receive anything like the weight of supporting artillery fire that was required to dislodge the Austrians from their posts. After three days of confused fighting, the Italians regrouped and put in an attack on the Görz bridgehead, but were repulsed with heavy casualties over the course of 8, 9 and 10 June.

Despite Boroevich's general conception of how the war should be fought on the Isonzo, the Austrians had not simply sat back and allowed the Italians to attack. On 2 June, the Austrian XV Corps had carried out a counterattack against the Italians advancing between Tolmin and Karfreit, but a lack of artillery and mutual fire support from neighbouring units meant that they suffered heavy casualties and were unable to do much more than slow down the Italians. Boroevich issued instructions that the counterattack was to be stopped on 4 June, anxious to ensure that he suffered as few casualties as possible.

On 11 June, the Italians launched another attack near Plava on the position known as Hill 383. The intention was to create a bridgehead between Görz and Tomlin, and the Italians attacked with much courage and vigour. However, their opponents, in the form of Major-General Guido Novak von Arienti's 1st Mountain Brigade, put up fierce resistance. Although the Italians briefly gained control of Hill 383 on 16 June, they were evicted the next day by Novak's troops, and it became clear to General Frugoni that the attack had lost momentum and needed to be called off.

The main Italian effort came on 23 June 1915, when a major offensive began with a large-scale artillery bombardment of Austrian positions. Ultimately, the VII and X corps from Italian Third Army were to attack with the aim of reaching the edge of the Doberdo plateau. While they conducted this attack, XI Corps was to distract the defenders with a dummy attack near Sagrado and the mouth of the Wippach River, and II Corps would cross the Isonzo to seize the Kuk heights. This was the first large-scale battle between the Austrians and the Italians, and saw 40 Austrian battalions confronting 75 Italian battalions; the Italians enjoyed a similar superiority in artillery. After seven days of intense shelling of the Austrian lines, the Italian infantry attacked on 30 June, mainly along the edge of the Carso (Karst) Plateau. Despite the numerical supremacy and the

preparatory bombardment, the Italians found the offensive extremely hard going. The Austrians inflicted fearful casualties on the attackers, and the Italians took only a small amount of ground on the left bank of the Isonzo at Sagrado. Cadorna threw more men into the battle, dispatching attacks against the Görz bridgehead, the Podgora heights and Monte Sabotino, but each of these was driven back by the outnumbered Austrians. Cadorna reorganized his forces so that the entire Italian Second Army could attack Görz, and in the light of this threat Boroevich felt compelled to send all his reserves into the front line. His gamble was successful, and once again the Italians were repulsed with heavy casualties after some bitter fighting.

There were similar stories from all along the front: Monte Sabotino and the positions at hills 205 and 240

The Isonzo Valley was one of the few places where large-scale troop movements were possible, but it was not an easy place in which to operate, and was easy to defend. The river itself provided a significant obstacle that required a variety of measures to overcome.

remained firmly under Austrian ownership despite heavy attacks from Cadorna's men, and Italian casualties around Görz were estimated in the region of 4000. It was clear that the Italian offensive had ground to a halt in the face of stiff opposition, gaining little more than a mile of enemy territory for the loss of almost 2000 dead and 11,500 wounded. The Austrians also took another 1500 men prisoner. In contrast, Austrian casualties (dead and wounded) were no more than 8800, with a similar number of men taken captive. As the offensive petered out, Cadorna pulled his forces back to in

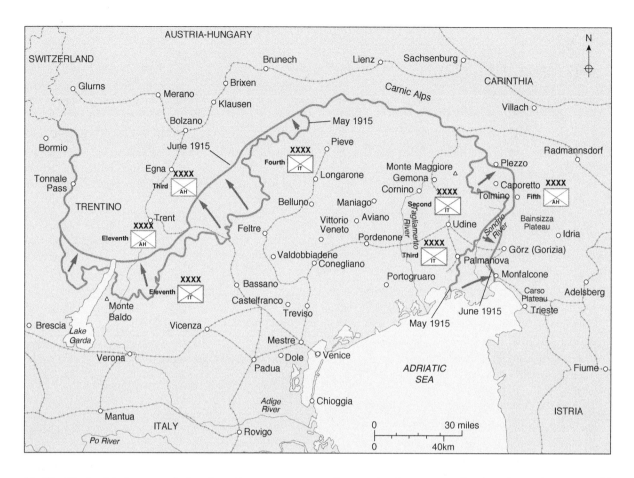

AUSTRIA-HUNGARY

SWITZERLAND

CARINTHIA

The First Battle of the Isonzo took place from May to June 1915. It resulted in small gains for the Italians and no major breakthrough that might yield long-term results. However, the Austrians were hard pressed and the prospects for an eventual Italian victory seemed good.

order to allow them to regroup. The Austrians, despite suffering a higher ratio of dead to wounded than the Italians, were left in good spirits, aware of the fact that they had been considerably outnumbered and yet had managed to hold off their opponents. It would not be long before the Italians tried again.

THE SECOND OFFENSIVE

After the failure of the first attempt to drive the Austrians back on the Isonzo, Cadorna made plans for a renewed assault. It seemed that he was convinced that the way to achieve a breakthrough was to simply hurl his troops against the outnumbered Austrians on

the premise that, eventually, Austrian resistance would crumble. It was a somewhat optimistic interpretation of the likely outcome of an attack.

This perspective was not shared by General Boroevich, who used the lull in the fighting to bring in fresh troops to replace those who were still recovering from the ferocity of the earlier engagements, and brought up reinforcements for use as a reserve in future fighting. The Austrians still faced the problem that their defensive positions were rudimentary, despite the great effort put into building them, thanks to the unforgiving nature of the terrain which made it all but impossible to dig proper fire positions; rather, a small amount of rock was hacked out of the mountainous terrain, the rubble piled around the hole that had been created, and sandbags were placed on top of this second layer to provide some sort of cover. The problem facing the defenders was simply that

Archduke Eugen von Habsburg-Lothringen (1863–1954)

Unlike many of his relatives, Eugen took his military profession seriously, attending the War School in Vienna and serving on the general staff. After the outbreak of war, Eugen was appointed to command the Southern Front, but – perhaps unfairly – other senior commanders viewed him as no different to the other royal generals, who had not received any meaningful staff and command training and thus were unsuited to command. Conrad, the chief of staff, frequently interfered in his decisions as a result. Despite these frustrations, Eugen commanded two armies in the Trentino offensive of 1916, and on the accession of his cousin Karl to the throne, he was promoted to field marshal. After Caporetto, the Italian front was reorganized, and Eugen was left without a job as a result. After the armistice, he was expelled from Austria and forced to live in exile for 15 years before being allowed to return to his homeland.

the heavy Italian artillery fire invariably blasted the sandbags and rubble layers of the defensive positions into oblivion, exposing the defenders to incoming fire.

Although Cadorna's belief in a renewed assault may have contained a tinge of optimism, he was not so foolish as to ignore the lessons of the first one. The preparatory bombardment was to be much shorter, but more concentrated against the key objectives, rather than spread out along the front, with the aim of causing much greater damage to the Austrian positions. Thus, the Italians began their shelling on 18 July 1915 paying specific attention to the Carso plateau, which was to be the objective for the leading troops of their IX and IX corps. Unfortunately for the Italians, they broke through in only one place, despite the fact that the pressure of the assault forced the Austrian VII Corps to send almost all of its reserves forward within the first few hours of the attack. The opening assault of the first day was followed on 19 July by an attack on the southern section of the line. Once again, despite the concentrated bombardment, the Austrians were able to repel the majority of the Italian troops, and only minor territorial gains were made. The Austrians suffered yet more heavy casualties, and Boroevich was compelled to ask for the swift dispatch of reinforcements from the Balkan front.

While Boroevich was awaiting the arrival of the fresh units, he had to deal with another attack on 20 July, this time carried out by the Italian XI Corps from the Duke of Aosta's Third Army. XI Corps was given the task of attacking Monte San Michele, in conjunction with VI Corps. By 5.30pm that day, Monte San Michele was in Italian hands, and it appeared that, at last, success was in the offing. However, the Austrian VII Corps spent the early hours of 21 July preparing a counterattack, which was put in at 4am after a short, sharp two-hour bombardment. After vicious hand-to-hand fighting, the Austrians drove the Italians from their positions, and were back in control of the mountain by 5.15am. This presaged an outbreak of hard fighting all through the battle area over the course of the next two days. Cadorna misinterpreted the situation, thinking that the Austrian Fifth Army had become ineffective, and decided to continue with the attack. This was a mistake, since he threw in his last reserves in the form of XIII Corps. While this meant that the Duke of Aosta's Third Army was able to continue the attack, it also meant that when it became clear that Austrian Fifth Army was far from finished, the Italian attack had, in effect shot its bolt, since there were no more troops to put into the battle to remove the Austrians from their positions. The Italian attack began to lose momentum, and within a matter of days, the Second Battle of the Isonzo had degenerated into a series of desultory skirmishes. The opposing armies broke contact on 10 August 1915, bringing the second battle to an end. Losses had been high: the Italians suffered

ABOVE Despite the severe difficulties faced by the Italian Army on the Isonzo front, some attacks were successful. Here Italian troops storm an Austro-Hungarian dugout. Although some ground was gained, it was never possible to make a general breakthrough and achieve lasting strategic results.

BELOW A field hospital behind the lines on the Isonzo front. This was an era in which defence was much easier than attack over any ground. Casualties were inevitably heavy in any offensive operation, especially against an enemy dug in overlooking difficult terrain.

almost 42,000 casualties, while the Austrians lost over 46,000. Many of the latter were a direct result of the inadequate robustness of the Austrian defensive positions, caused by the difficult ground.

THE THIRD AND FOURTH OFFENSIVES

Despite the setbacks of the second Italian offensive, Cadorna remained optimistic. However, along with the rest of the Italian high command, he was concerned about the prospect of the Austrians launching an attack during September, since there were conflicting notions of the intended use of the Austro-Hungarian units that had not been sent to the Eastern Front. When it became clear that these troops were to be used for the combined German–Austrian attack on Serbia, Cadorna decided that he would definitely renew his offensive, which he did on 21 October. Following the pattern of the previous battles of the Isonzo, a preliminary artillery bombardment, this time lasting for three days, was conducted against the Austrian positions, and infantry advanced early on the morning of the 21st. Once again, though, the Italians were unable to do anything more than break into the Austrian line at a number of discrete points. Although the Austrians were again at a numerical disadvantage, and once more had to throw all their reserves into the fight, they held firm and there seemed to be no prospect of the Italians converting the few local successes into a general breakthrough.

On 25 October 1915, Cadorna extended the attack to take in the Görz bridgehead again, and this looked as though it might overrun the Austrian positions. However, the determined defence for which the Austrian forces on the Isonzo were becoming renowned held out once more, and on 3 and 4 November the fighting began to peter out. Despite heavy casualties on both sides, the position on the Isonzo remained much as it had been before.

Yet still Cadorna was undismayed, and began planning for another assault. He hoped that by keeping the tempo of operations high with short periods between the assaults he would manage to wear the Austro-Hungarians down to a point where they could no longer hold out against the weight of

the Italian attacks. He was also aware that the Italian parliament was due to meet shortly, and that the government would face political pressure over the fact that the expected swift victory against the Austrians had not been achieved.

Cadorna therefore set out to begin another offensive, taking care to ensure that the units that had suffered casualties in the previous fighting were brought back to strength and that he had a ready supply of reserves for use as the battle went on. He also chose to alter the way his guns were used,

Svetozar Boroevich von Bojna (1856–1920)

The son of a Croatian non-commissioned officer who was granted a commission in the Austro-Hungarian Army, Boroevich was destined to be a soldier. He attended the War School in Vienna, and rose steadily through the ranks. He was raised to the nobility in 1905, adding the suffix 'von Bojna' to his surname. At the outbreak of war, he was commander of VI Corps, which he led with distinction during the Galician campaign, notably at the Battle of Komarów. Boroevich was given command of Third Army in early September 1914, and defended the Carpathian passes throughout the winter before launching the initial phase of the Gorlice-Tarnow offensive in May 1915. He was then posted to the Isonzo front as commander of Fifth Army. Promotion to Generaloberst (colonel-general) came in May 1916, followed by the distinction of having command of his own Army group (Army Group Boroevich) from August 1917. He was in command for all of the Isonzo battles and the fighting on the Piave. A final promotion to field marshal ensued in 1918. Following the collapse of Austria-Hungary, Boroevich retired in December 1918.

Italian troops moving into position to attack. The early Italian offensives on the Isonzo put heavy pressure on the Austro-Hungarian defenders, forcing them to cut short the rest periods allocated to troops rotated out of the combat zone and draining manpower away from the Russian Front.

since it had become clear that the way in which the artillery had been employed lacked tactical flexibility; however, although he sought advice from the French, it would take too much time for any alterations to artillery procedures to be fully implemented. On the Austrian side, the heavy fighting of the past five months had taken its toll. The troops were worn out, and this meant that the rotation of units in and out of the front line occurred before those regiments that had been sent for a period of rest were able to fully recuperate and be at maximum readiness. Morale was problematic, although the fierce determination of Boroevich to fight on appears to have had some effect in influencing the willingness of his troops to follow a man whom most of them respected.

Once again, the Görz bridgehead was the main objective, with fighting taking place in all the areas where the past three offensives had occurred. And yet again, Monte San Michele, the Carso Plateau and Piave remained in Austrian hands despite the best efforts of the Italians to dislodge them. The importance of gaining the Görz bridgehead increased, not least because Cadorna recognized that finally taking it would be a considerable boost to Italian morale. Thus, on 18 November 1915, after leaflets were dropped on the town to warn civilians that fighting would once more break out, the Italians launched a four-hour bombardment, which destroyed

The Italian battleship *Benedetto Brin,* belonging to a class of two ships that were more akin to battlecruisers than line-of-battle ships. Their armament was good but armour protection was reduced to improve their speed. *Benedetto Brin* was lost to sabotage in September 1915.

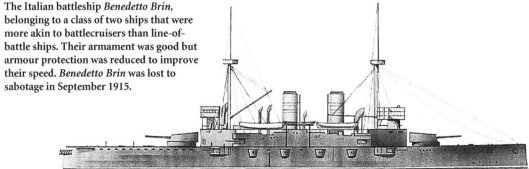

much of the town. It did not, however, manage to destroy the Austrian defences, and during the weeks that followed, the fighting between the Austrian and Italian troops accounted for most of the remaining buildings in Görz, but it still remained firmly under Austrian control. Finally, on 29 November, the Italian Second Army, now under the command of Lieutenant-General Luigi Capello, managed to take the Oslavija Ridge, which at least gave the Italians direct sight into the now-ruined Görz. Once again,

however, the Italians had begun to lose momentum in the face of the Austrians' resistance, and although the fighting continued until 15 December around Monte Sante Michele, and at various locations around the Görz bridgehead, there was no prospect of the battle reaching a successful conclusion, and Cadorna called it off. This meant that despite launching four offensives, the Italians were no nearer to achieving their objectives than they had been at the outset of the Second Battle of the Isonzo.

ON TO THE FIFTH BATTLE

Despite the conspicuous lack of success achieved on the Isonzo, the Italian high command remained committed to seeking a breakthrough on this front. Although this might appear ill advised with the benefit of 90 years of hindsight, it must be recalled that the difficulties of the terrain on the border between Italy and Austria-Hungary meant that launching a major attack anywhere else along the front line would stand little chance of success. Therefore, the Italian plans for operations in 1916 retained the aim of keeping pressure on the Austrian forces in the hope that they would eventually break under the strain. Also, the Italians appreciated that they had been carrying out operations at something of a disadvantage during 1915, since they were not fully prepared for war when they joined the Allies. There had been a lack of trained reserves and shortages of equipment, and it appeared that rectifying these problems might present the solution by which the Isonzo offensives would succeed. As part of maintaining the pressure, Cadorna laid plans for a fifth Isonzo offensive for the early part of 1916. The planning challenges were compounded in January 1916 when the Austrians launched a counterattack on the Oslavija Ridge and succeeded in wresting it back from Italian control on 24 January.

The Italians were also now becoming alarmed by reports of Austrian preparations for an offensive of their own, to be launched in the southern Tyrol. This threat to Italian territory meant that Cadorna was now rather more reluctant to commit his forces to a major offensive on the Isonzo, but in keeping with the decisions of the Second Allied War Council (which had met at Chantilly in December 1915) for simultaneous Allied offensives in France, Russia, the Balkans and Italy, Cadorna felt it his duty to attack.

There was little that he could do to overcome the limiting geography of the battle area that had constrained the previous offensives, and the target

Movement in the mountains is always slow going, as travelling between two points that are close together as the crow flies may require a long descent and an arduous climb back up. A force that can occupy the best high ground before the enemy has a huge advantage.

Using artillery in the mountains poses a number of unique challenges. Light guns that can be dismantled, like this Austro-Hungarian piece, are often the only effective weapons. It is sometimes possible to position heavy guns at great altitude, but it inevitably requires a great feat of mountaineering to emplace them.

of the attack was a familiar one in the form of the Podgora Ridge; however, unlike the previous four offensives, the intention behind this battle was not to take ground, merely to inflict attrition on the enemy while seeking to gauge their strength.

On 11 March 1916, the Fifth Battle of the Isonzo opened with a preparatory bombardment, followed 48 hours later by the infantry attack. A combination of bad weather and insufficient forces to push the Austrians back meant that the battle began to peter out almost immediately. Cadorna's attention was distracted by the increasing threat of an Austrian attack in the Tyrol, despite the best efforts of the Austrians to conceal their preparations. Thus, as the battle came to an end on 17 March, it had achieved little beyond demonstrating Italian solidarity with their Allies. However, the pressing need to address the potential threat presented by the Austrian forces apparently massing for an attack on the Trentino now required Cadorna's full attention, and it would be some time before fighting on the Isonzo would be renewed.

CHAPTER 5

The Italian Front 1916–17

In the wake of the five failed Italian offensives, the Austrians moved to the offensive in the Trentino in April 1916. The fighting saw only a small tract of territory changing hands, at the cost of 28,000 Austrian casualties, before the focus shifted once again to the Isonzo front in August 1916. Fighting would continue there into 1917 without breakthrough until the major powers became involved later in the year.

General Cadorna was forced to delay plans for any further Italian efforts in the Isonzo area by the clear signs that the Austrians planned to launch an offensive of their own in the Trentino. General Conrad had made plans for an attack into Italy that he hoped would strike a decisive blow and knock Italy out of the war. He proposed a joint Austro-Hungarian–German offensive that would start as soon as the conquest of Serbia was completed, with the aim of driving out the Italians from positions in the

The narrow front available meant that Italian offensives were limited to predictable axes of attack. The Austro-Hungarian Army had ample time to prepare the defence of these avenues. These Italian troops are moving up to make a renewed attack across the Isonzo River.

Lessini Alps and forcing back the front line towards the southeastern foothills of the Alps. From here, Conrad proposed launching an attack to drive deep into Italian territory and to threaten Venice. The campaign would culminate with the Austrian Army reaching the Adriatic coast, compelling the Italians to surrender.

Unfortunately for Conrad, when he put his proposals to Erich von Falkenhayn, the German chief of staff, he was rebuffed. Falkenhayn thought that Conrad seriously underestimated the number of troops that would be required to achieve the offensive he was proposing, and furthermore, he was far from convinced that this would bring about the great victory that Conrad foresaw. Falkenhayn noted that the Italians were dependent upon Britain and France for financial assistance, foodstuffs and coal, and the chances of the Italians risking these to sign a separate peace treaty with the Central Powers was, in Falkenhayn's opinion, somewhat fanciful.

Artillery offered a means to strike at troops dug in on nearby mountains, but in order to be of any use it had to be moved into position. Mountain troops on both sides became adept at hauling dismantled guns into firing positions.

Conrad was not dissuaded by Falkenhayn's rejection of his plan and continued to push it forward until the end of January 1916, by which point the Austrian foreign minister had joined in the effort to persuade the Germans that the offensive was a good idea. The Germans were reluctant for reasons other than those of the perceived lack of troops in Conrad's plan. Falkenhayn was planning a major operation against the French at Verdun and could not countenance the thought of weakening the forces assigned for the purposes of that attack to support Conrad's plan, since to do so would have risked fatally undermining the Verdun operation. When the German attack at Verdun began, Conrad was outraged at the fact that the details had been kept from him, and he regarded this as a grave insult by the Germans. In retrospect, alliance politics meant that it would probably have been better if Falkenhayn had at least given some intimation as to his plans and explained that this was the cause of his reluctance, rather than just turning down Conrad's proposal. An infuriated Conrad was determined to demonstrate to the Germans that his plan was viable, even if this

meant acting unilaterally. Conrad's conviction that he could strike a blow that would knock Italy out of the war was utterly unshakeable, and on 6 February 1916 he issued instructions for the offensive.

Archduke Eugen was appointed as commander-in-chief of the offensive, and was tasked with creating an invasion force made up of 14 divisions along with five dozen heavy artillery batteries to support operations. Two months were set aside for preparation, and the offensive was to begin on 6 April 1916. The main body of the attacking force was to consist of the Austrian Eleventh Army under General Viktor Dankl, drawing upon troops who were currently stationed on the Isonzo front. Other troops would come from III Corps, part of Austrian Fifth Army, while a further

division would be provided by the Austrian Tenth Army. VIII Corps was brought back to Austria from the Balkan front, and three further divisions were withdrawn from the Eastern Front to bring Dankl's recently created force up to strength.

General Hermann Kövess von Kövesshaza's Austrian Third Army was to be the other army employed, and its task would be to follow up the opening attack by Dankl's troops. This army was given the Austrian I Commando Corps and three infantry divisions to boost its strength. By removing units from

Mountain troops have always been considered an elite formation in most armies, as they need the same infantry skill as other soldiers but in addition must live and fight in a harsh environment where others might struggle to survive.

the Eastern and Balkan fronts, Conrad managed to assemble his 14-division force for the attack on Italy. Conrad also envisaged a naval attack being carried out alongside the offensive, but his request for the bombardment of coastal towns was turned down by the senior naval officer, Admiral Haus, as being impractical. Conrad instead had to accept a fleet of small gunboats and armed launches, which would force their way into the Venetian Lagoon and open the way inland to the rivers if the need arose.

Conrad's grand plan began to take shape as the Austrian Eleventh Army formed up in the Lessini Alps. This was no small feat, since the area was perhaps the most challenging part of the Alpine range in which an army commander might find himself operating. The

General Viktor Dankl (1854–1941)

Dankl was the son of an army officer. He attended a military academy, and graduated into the 3rd Dragoon Regiment in 1874. Joining the general staff in 1880, Dankl enjoyed steady promotion, culminating with command of the First Austro-Hungarian Army when war broke out in 1914. He defeated the Russians at the Battle of Krasnik in August 1914, but was forced to retreat after a Russian counterattack. Despite this setback, Dankl's success made him a national hero. He was posted to the Italian front in 1915, and took command of the Eleventh Army in March 1916. The failure of the Asiago offensive, combined with serious ill health, led to Dankl resigning his command in June. Having recuperated, he commanded a formation of the Imperial Guards until his retirement in December 1918. After the war, he was a prominent advocate of veterans' rights and campaigned for the restoration of the Habsburg monarchy.

Italians had established a line of fortifications that presented a major obstacle to an attacking army. This challenging scenario for striking into Italy was made even more taxing by Conrad's decision to attack on 6 April. He had chosen this date because of intelligence that suggested the Allies intended to attack on all fronts during the summer: Conrad wished to forestall this by launching his attack first. This meant that the date that had originally been considered was abandoned, but this decision to bring the attack forward appeared to overlook the fact that the weather in Alpine areas during April, particularly on plateaux over approximately 1000m (3000ft) high, tended to consist of heavy snowfall that would seriously compromise movement of forces, even if they were trained mountain troops. It appeared that Conrad's eagerness to attack – both to forestall the Allies and to give a demonstration of capability to the Germans – led to him overlooking this simple consideration. The marching up of the attacking force was indeed delayed, and bringing heavy artillery batteries into position was utterly impossible, as they were unable to traverse the snow-covered ground.

A change in the weather in the middle of March helped to improve conditions for mobility, but the deep snowdrifts that lay in the mountains made progress incredibly slow. Although the two Austrian armies were in position by 25 March, there was no way that they could launch an attack. Archduke Karl Franz Josef, the heir to the dual monarchy, had been appointed as a corps commander in the Austrian Eleventh Army (largely for publicity reasons – Conrad had made certain that the corps had an unusually high number of highly trained and intelligent staff officers to assist the Archduke in his decision making), and sent reports to Conrad suggesting that his troops were having some difficulty with the conditions. Troops carrying anything more than light packs on their backs were sinking waist-deep into the snow, and Karl Franz Josef suggested that there was no chance of making a successful attack – and possibly not even beginning an attack – in such conditions. Dankl agreed and delayed the offensive, because of the need to increase the amount of time spent preparing for it.

The Austrians faced a further major difficulty. As alluded to previously, the Italians were fully aware of the fact that Austrian troops were massing for an attack thanks to their intelligence services, and General Cadorna had been given an intimation that an attack was likely as early as December 1915. By 22 March 1916, the Italian high command had received detailed reports that gave an accurate picture of the build-up of the Austrian forces around Trent, and identified the two plateaux over which the attack would be launched. The Italians reinforced units based in the Lessini Alps, and brought up reserve troops for the First Army, which was in the line of the assault. A number of recently formed infantry regiments were also brought up, while artillery batteries were sent from the Isonzo front to help meet the threat. In addition to these measures, the Italians sent their troops out on raids, and in a series of skirmishes managed to cause considerable disruption to the preparations of a number of Austrian units.

General Cadorna planned to contain the Austrian attack, and to concentrate forces along the Calassa Valley and in the Sette Communi area. Unlike Conrad, who seemed to assume that, having given direction, the offensive would run smoothly if he communicated by letter and telegram with Archduke Eugen's command, Cadorna took the trouble to visit his units to inspect the defences. This enabled him to consider differing opinions as to how best to defend the area when the attack came, so that there was no lack of clarity over what had to be done, and by whom. In contrast, Conrad's 'hands off' approach to giving direction took delegation too far. Cadorna's approach meant that when it became clear that the commander of Italian First Army, Lieutenant-General Brusati, did not agree with the defensive plan, he was able to address the issue: finding that Brusati was

> 'Cadorna is the most humorous of all the generals in the great war … liked, feared and respected by every Italian soldier and civilian with whom I have conversed.'
>
> Alfred Harmsworth (Lord Northcliffe), 1916

The support weapons of the time were heavy and bulky, making them unsuited for close support in mobile operations. This Fiat-Rivelli Modello 14 machine gun was one of the most modern designs available, but still lacked mobility, especially in mountain terrain. Such weapons were best suited to defensive operations.

Getting artillery such as these Italian weapons into the high peaks represented a major feat of engineering and mountaineering skills. The tactical benefit was the ability to bombard enemy troops who had previously been invulnerable to such attacks.

immoveable in his opinion that the defence should be concentrated on the first and second lines of defence in the Lessini Alps, Cadorna demonstrated that Brusati was not immoveable in another sense by sacking him and bringing in Lieutenant-General Count Pecori-Giraldi. Cadorna's careful approach meant that he had a large number of troops in the area in which the offensive was to fall, to the point that he had perhaps been over-cautious by having militia and customs battalions sent to the front to assist in manning the defences.

Conrad's willingness to allow his commanders to operate with an almost free hand was to prove a serious problem. During the build-up period, Archduke Eugen decided that he did not like the plan of attack as constituted and decided that, instead of having

the Austrian Eleventh Army begin the assault to be followed by Austrian Third Army, it would be better to start the advance of both armies at the same time. Eugen did so because he had been given intelligence information that suggested the Italians were building up their strength in front of the Austrian XX Corps. Eugen was concerned that this might prevent the Archduke Karl Franz Josef from leading his corps – known informally as the 'Crown Prince Corps' rather than by its correct numerical designator – to victory. Because it was essential for reasons of prestige that Karl Franz Josef was seen to gain a great victory over the Italians, Eugen began to tinker with the disposition of the two armies to ensure that XX Corps had sufficient troop numbers to carry the day. He did so with little reference to Conrad's

These Austrian troops have emplaced their machine guns in shallow, temporary trenches. While troops on all fronts dug in wherever they could, the massive and more or less permanent trench systems of the Western Front were, as a general rule, not seen in other theatres of the war.

plan, or with any real thought about the implications for the parts of the line from which the reinforcements for Karl Franz Josef's corps had originated.

To compound the errors of judgement still further, Karl Franz Josef had expressed the optimistic point of view that he wished to achieve a great victory with as little cost as possible. While this was an admirably sensible and humane objective, it was perhaps unwise for the Crown Prince's wishes to be translated into direct orders to officers under his command urging them to ensure that they lost as few men as possible. Further orders were issued towards the end of April that ordered infantry units to attack only after a full preparatory bombardment, and even then only if they had constant artillery support. Conrad became aware of these changes, but expressed his irritation only via telegram when the situation was such that it really

Despite initial successes, the Austrian Trentino offensive bogged down and then collapsed. One reason for this was the breakdown in command and control caused by a sudden and badly handled reorganization among the advancing forces. Already struggling with logistical problems, senior Austrian officers gradually lost control of the situation.

The Italian Supreme Command were well aware of the Austrian build-up for an attack in the Trentino region and made preparations to defeat it. Meanwhile Austrian planning was derailed by political considerations and excessive tinkering. As a result, the offensive failed.

required him to go to the front and to impose some order on proceedings. His original plan for the attack was all but unrecognizable.

THE TRENTINO OFFENSIVE

The offensive began at 6am on 15 May 1916, with a heavy artillery bombardment that reached its peak between 9 and 10am, at which point the infantry moved forwards to attack. The artillery bombardment inflicted considerable damage on the Italian defensive positions, and these locations succumbed easily to the attacking infantry. By 5pm, XX Corps had gained the major success that had been hoped of it when it captured the defensive positions on Costa d'Agra, while Monte Coston fell later in the day. On 16 May there was further success, when the Austrians broke into the Italian lines on Soglio d'Aspio, meaning that XX Corps had breached the first line of defence.

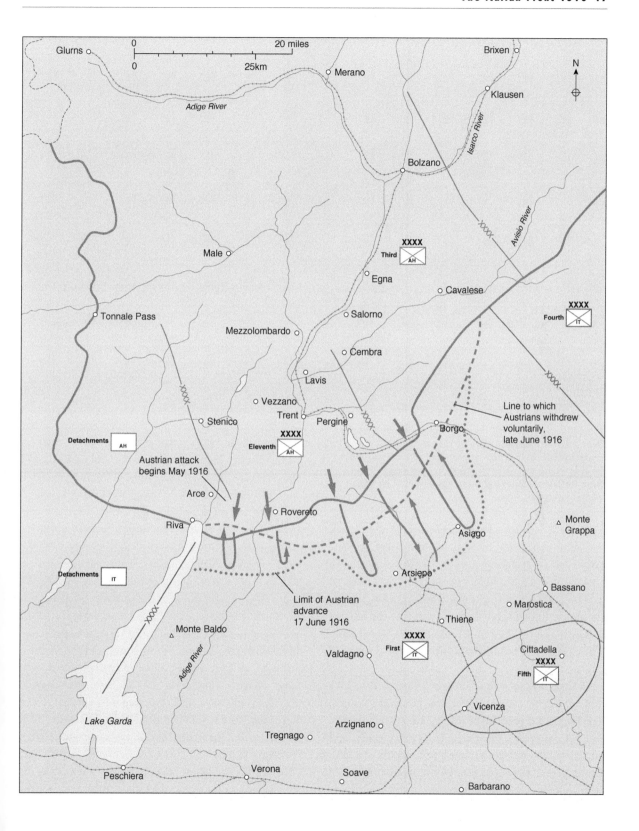

Glurns

0 | 20 miles
0 | 25km

Merano

Brixen

Klausen

Adige River

Isarco River

N

Bolzano

Avisio River

Male

XXXX
Third | AH

Egna

Cavalese

XXXX
Fourth | IT

Tonnale Pass

Salorno

Mezzolombardo

Cembra

Lavis

Vezzano

Line to which
Austrians withdrew
voluntarily,
late June 1916

Stenico

Trent

Pergine

Borgo

Detachments | AH

XXXX
Eleventh | AH

Austrian attack
begins May 1916

Arce

Rovereto

Asiago

Monte
Grappa

Riva

Detachments | IT

Arsiepo

Bassano

Marostica

Limit of Austrian
advance
17 June 1916

Thiene

Monte Baldo

Adige River

Valdagno

XXXX
First | IT

Cittadella

XXXX
Fifth | IT

Vicenza

Lake Garda

Arzignano

Tregnago

Peschiera

Verona

Soave

Barbarano

The war in the mountains shared one characteristic with trench warfare, in that high-angle heavy artillery was often the only way to hit enemy positions in such steep terrain. These Austrian troops have taken possession of an Italian 280mm mortar position.

While XX Corps had succeeded from the outset, the same could not be said for the Austrian VIII Corps, which had been unable to take any ground because of a lack of artillery support and as a result of the Italian troops of the Roma Brigade putting up stiff resistance. It took three days to overcome the Italians at Piazza as a result, and it took until 18 May before VIII Corps achieved its first objective, the capture of Zugna Torta.

Despite the fierce resistance, by the end of 17 May it appeared that the offensive was going as planned. Karl Franz Josef was able to inform army headquarters that his corps had completed its breakthrough, and the Austrian commanders were particularly satisfied, thinking that they had clearly shattered the Italian defences, which would make for a relatively easy breakout into the Venetian plains. As they waited for the artillery to be brought up so that the next phase of the advance could continue, none of them appreciated that this was ultimately to prove an illusory hope.

Cadorna's careful preparation of the defensive plan meant that he was able to send his reserves up to the front, and this proved vital in the fighting over the next two days. Although the Italians had a hard time, not least because of confusion over exactly where the main effort of this phase of the Austrian offensive was directed, leading to some units being deployed to the wrong area, they managed to do enough to prevent a breakthrough. Cadorna, though, was deeply worried, since by 20 May almost all of his reserves had been used up. In a conference with General Frugoni and the Duke of Aosta, the three generals agreed that, if necessary, they would withdraw from the Isonzo front to ensure that the Austrians did not break out onto the Venetian plains.

Cadorna had also made contingency plans for the creation of a new army (the Italian Fifth Army) if the need arose, forming it out of all available reserves that had not been committed to the initial defence of the front. On 21 May, the Italian Fifth Army came into being, with the aim of regrouping in the area around Vicenza, Padua and Citadella. The second defence zone in the Lessini Alps was abandoned, and yet more troops were drawn in from other fronts. Cadorna also sent a request to the Russians that they begin diversionary attacks on their southwestern front to draw the attention of the Austrians. Although they were hard pressed, the Italians had at least created a clear plan as to what to do next. This was more than could be said for their opponents.

COMMAND DYSFUNCTION

The Austrians, by contrast, had begun to sink into a state of confusion. On 20 May, Archduke Eugen had issued orders for a complete regrouping of the forces under his command. No one appeared to have any idea as to why he had done this, and the orders that followed for the reorganized forces only added to the state of confusion, with command of the most advanced Austrian forces, those best placed to continue the momentum of the attack, suddenly being vested in the hands of three different commanders, none of whom was entirely certain as to what their neighbouring officers had been told to do next. This meant that there was a certain lack of coordination in the next phase of the attack, which served to slow it down. By the end of May, the Italians had started to impede the offensive. By June, most of the Austrian attack had become bogged down.

Although the Austrians had now pitched their reserves into the battle, and despite the fact that they achieved some minor successes, it was clear that the offensive had begun to run into difficulties. Austrian supply lines had become over-extended, and there was a growing shortage of ammunition, something that affected the Austrians' artillery particularly badly. The Italians, who had begun the offensive at a distinct disadvantage as far as artillery support was concerned, were surprised to discover that they now had the upper hand, something that had the added effect of boosting the morale of the defending troops.

General Hermann Kövess von Kövesshaza (1854–1924)

Born into a military family, Kövesshaza was educated at military academy before joining the Austro-Hungarian Army. A promising young officer, he was given accelerated promotion, and by 1914 was a general officer, albeit on the verge of retirement. The war changed his plans, and he was appointed to command the Austrian XII Corps. This was swiftly followed by command of the Austrian Third Army. His reputation enhanced after capturing Belgrade, Kövesshaza then served briefly on the Italian front before taking over the Seventh Army on the Russian front. When Seventh Army took Czernowitz in August 1917, Kövesshaza was promoted to field marshal and given command of his own army front. The end of the war with Russia left him without a command appointment until he was handed the poisoned chalice of commander-in-chief of the Austro-Hungarian Army, overseeing its disintegration in 1918.

Hermann Kövess von Kövesshaza inspects officers from his army, June 1916.

The final blow to the offensive came on 4 June 1916. News reached Eugen's headquarters that the Russian General Brusilov had launched a major offensive on the Eastern Front, and four days later two divisions were diverted from Italy to support the defence against that attack. Still Conrad thought that his offensive against the Italians could succeed, and he urged one last effort. On 15 June, the Austrian I Corps made an attempt to break through the forest at Monte Lemerle so that it could attack towards Monte Pau. However, within a day the weight of Italian defensive fire had been such that the attack was brought to a sudden halt. On 17 June, Conrad succumbed to the inevitable and called off the offensive. He told General Dankl that much of the reason for failure was caused by his poor leadership – a most unfair charge, given that a lot of the damage had been done by Conrad's lack of 'grip' over Archduke Eugen – and the furious Dankl insisted that he be relieved of command immediately. As well as costing the career of an army commander, the 'butcher's bill' for the Trentino offensive had been heavy: 12,000 Italians died and another 40,000 had been taken prisoner, but the Austrians had gained only a small tract of territory, and at the cost of 28,000 casualties (5000 of which were fatalities) and another 2000 who had fallen ill.

THE ITALIAN RIPOSTE

As soon as it became clear that the Austrian offensive had run out of momentum, the Italians planned a two-stage counterattack, aiming to consolidate their positions on the Asiago Plateau before pushing further forward to drive the Austrians out of their recently occupied positions. The Italians had mustered a total of 177 battalions against the Austrians' 168, while they also had an advantage in terms of the number of artillery pieces available, outnumbering the enemy by 800 guns to 680. However, this numerical advantage was offset by the fact that the Austrians were in strong defensive positions. Also, the number of men deemed necessary for the offensive required the withdrawal of resources from elsewhere on the Italian front, precluding further operations in other areas. Thanks to alliance politics, this imposed certain demands upon

> 'From the Adige to the Brenta, the commanding positions and strongly organized defences which the enemy previously captured have aided his resistance to our advance. Nevertheless, we have made significant progress.'
>
> Italian War Office communiqué, 28 June 1916

the Italian counter-offensive: at the conferences held in Chantilly in December 1915 and mid-March 1916, the Italians had agreed to coordinated action with their alliance partners, with the Italian contribution being another offensive on the Isonzo. The obligation for the attack to take place at the same time as the planned Anglo-French efforts meant that it was imperative for the Italians to conclude their efforts on the Asiago Plateau in good time for a redeployment of forces back to the Isonzo area to begin preparations for the offensive on that front.

The plan for the Asiago Plateau was straight-forward: the attacking forces would advance simultaneously on both flanks, and this would be followed by an advance in the centre, with the ultimate objective being to establish a position on a line running from Cima Portule to Monte Meata. The plan for achieving this position involved breaking through the front line and then wrapping up the Austrian flanks and forcing them to fall back.

The assault began on the right flank on 18 June 1916, and succeeded in taking the first line of Austrian defences on the southern edge of the plateau. However, the attack then came to a standstill as the Austrians managed to block any further penetration of their lines. The attack on the left took place four days later, but despite two days of hard fighting, the Italians were unable to break though the enemy lines.

However, the Austrians decided that it was necessary to withdraw, since this would permit them to shorten their front line and send the forces released to the Russian front, where they were urgently required.

Italian mountain troops moving through the Adamello Mountains. Movement in this terrain was slow and arduous at best. Ammunition and supplies had to be carried over the same terrain, and when forward supplies ran out it severely limited the achievements of any offensive.

They started to retreat on the evening of 25 June, heading for positions that had already been prepared to meet such an eventuality. The Italians lost contact with the Austrians as they headed to their new line, and it took until 27 June until they caught up with them once more. The Italians put in a series of new attacks, aiming to capture a number of key objectives. These attacks did not achieve their desired aim, and the intensity of fighting increased as the Austrians made a counterattack of their own. The Italians fought off the Austrian attacks, and then resumed their offensive on the left-hand flank at Vallarsa. However, on 9 July the Italian Supreme Command issued a warning order to the Italian First Army that they should be prepared to end the offensive by 21 July, since the

Italian troops, advancing on the Isonzo front, make best use of the available cover. The presence of occupied high ground all around made offensive operations even more costly than usual. Gains tended to be limited by the presence of natural fallback positions for the defenders.

artillery and reserves on the Asiago front would start to be withdrawn for the forthcoming operations on the Isonzo. After a few days, it became obvious that the Asiago offensive had lost momentum, and it was halted. The Italians then set about attempting to straighten the line that they held, albeit without the benefit of the reserves, who were being removed from the line to be fed into the Isonzo front instead. By 24 July 1916, the offensive had come to a halt, and the fighting that followed took the form of limited attacks on the Austro-Hungarians, who remained secure in their new positions.

BACK TO THE ISONZO

With the Asiago counter-offensive at an end, the Italians began the process of moving elements of the First Army over towards the Isonzo so that the forces there were of the required strength. They conducted this redeployment with considerable skill, without the Austrians managing to detect the movements. The Italian attack on the Isonzo was to take the form of an assault on Görz, which was to begin on 4 August 1916. The plan behind this attack was to take the right bank of the Isonzo, which would prevent the Austrians from making an attack into the Venetian plain; however, as the fighting on the Asiago went on, the Italian Supreme Command modified the plan so that the objective was slightly less ambitious, with positions between Monte Podgora and Monte Sabotino to be seized as a precursor to surrounding San Michele.

The Italians had learned from their previous experiences on the Isonzo, and made sure that they had the necessary forces in place, particularly in the form of artillery. They also took care to make certain that they had established a robust logistics chain so as to avoid some of the difficulties that had occurred in the previous fighting. The Italians still faced a major problem, however, and, as on previous occasions, this was the strength of the Austrian defences, particularly on the bridgeheads at Görz and Tolmino, and on the left bank of the river. These areas were covered with obstacles and a sophisticated trench network, bolstered by a heavy concentration of machine guns to break up an offensive.

Emperor Karl I (1887–1922)

The last Habsburg emperor, Karl attempted to open peace negotiations with the French within days of taking the throne. The failure of the negotiations, followed by the disastrous revelation that they had taken place, left Karl in the worst possible situation – still at war and now deeply mistrusted by his German allies. Karl did not help himself with his ill judged interference in military operations, notably the failed 1918 offensive on the Piave. As the various nationalities within the empire started to proclaim their independence, Karl announced that he was withdrawing from affairs of state on 11 November. Karl's attempts to regain the throne in Hungary in 1921 led to him being exiled to the island of Madeira, where he and his wife, Queen Zita, were forced to live in greatly reduced circumstances, until his death from pneumonia aged 35 in April 1922. He was beatified by the Roman Catholic Church in 2004, in recognition of his attempts to bring the war to an end.

Operations began with a feint attack in the Monfalcone sector by the Italian Third Army, with the aim of drawing in the Austrian forces. Beginning on 4 August, this attack succeeded in gaining positions to the east of Monfalcone on 10 August, but it did so without achieving the desired effect of pulling Austrian units away from Görz.

The main attack went in on the left wing against the bridgehead at Görz, the plan being that the Austrians should be forced back over the river, leaving the Italians in control of the outskirts of the town. Monte Sabotino was taken quickly, the Austrians being driven out of their positions in under an hour, while Podgora was taken by the end of the afternoon. The Austrians

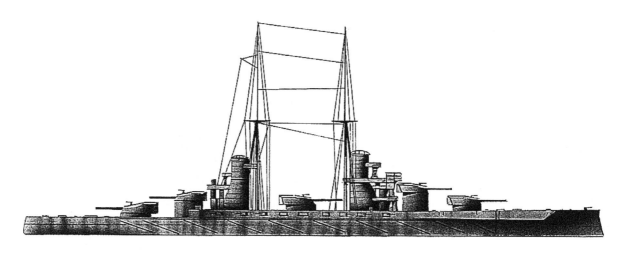

The presence of Italian battleships in the Adriatic was both a symbol of power and a means of controlling the sea lanes. The balance was somewhat redressed by the sabotage of the battleship _Leonardo da Vinci_ (show here) by Austrian forces at Taranto on 2 August 1916.

delivered a series of fierce counterattacks, but they failed to dislodge the Italians. In the centre, the Italians ran into stiff opposition, but had managed to get some patrols onto the bank of the Isonzo itself by nightfall. Further Austrian attempts to counterattack on 6 and 7 August were repulsed, and on 8 August the Italian 12th Division made its way into Görz.

This success tempted the Italian Supreme Command to modify its plan, and orders were given to pursue the Austrians, so that they could not retire in good order and to dig themselves in just to the east of Görz. The fierce fighting in the opening phase of the offensive had left the Italian troops weary and in need of rest, so there was some delay as they were organized for the pursuit. They followed the Austrians doggedly, and finally re-established contact on 9 August, only to discover that the Austrians had blown the bridges behind them, placing them out of contact.

A further attack was made along the whole front on 14 August, but the Austrians had fallen back onto prepared positions and inflicted heavy losses upon the Italians. Since it was clear that a properly prepared assault would be required to remove the Austrians from these positions, the offensive was called off, bringing the Sixth Battle of the Isonzo to a conclusion.

The Italians had reason to be satisfied with the results, since they had compelled the Austrians to withdraw a large number of troops from other fronts to meet the attack. On a broader strategic level, the success enjoyed by the Italians helped to encourage the Romanians to declare war on the Central Powers on 27 August 1916. The Italians, still only at war with Austria-Hungary up to this point, made their declaration of war on Germany two days later, but there was little immediate obvious effect: the implications of making the Germans their enemy were only to be fully appreciated in 1917.

The Italian Supreme Command now set about planning further offensive action, this time aiming to threaten Trieste. The Isonzo offensive was to resume (to prevent Austrian troops from being sent to the east to crush Romania), aiming to capture Monte Rombon. The attack began with a massive artillery bombardment at dawn on 14 September 1916, and the infantry went in at 3pm that afternoon. The attack began promisingly, since it broke through enemy lines to a depth of two kilometres (1.25 miles), and San Grado di Merna and the feature known as Hill 144 were both captured. This, though, was the limit of success. On the Italian Second Army's front, Monte Rombon was captured on 16 September, but the Italians could not consolidate their position in the face of enemy counterattacks and withdrew.

Unfortunately for the Italians, the weather turned at this point, just as the Supreme Command was

ABOVE Italy launched three major attacks on the Isonzo in late 1916. The first (the Seventh Battle of the Isonzo) was in September but resulted in such high casualties that the offensive could not be resumed until October. By early November some gains had been made, but at great cost.

BELOW Both battleships of the Italian *Regina Margherita* class were lost during the war. The name ship of the class (shown here) struck mines laid by a U-boat and her sister, *Benedetto Brin*, was sabotaged in 1915. The light armour of both ships may have contributed to their loss.

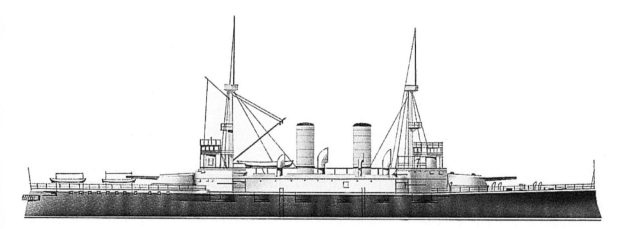

becoming worried about the losses being taken. The high command took the sensible view that it was not prepared to take huge losses for little gain, and the strength of the Austrian resistance was increasing. It was highly probable that the poor weather would only make attacking more difficult, and the fact that the enemy was in well founded positions meant that Italian casualties were likely to increase, while the probability of success declined. This prompted the Italians to conclude that prosecuting the offensive any further was pointless, and the Seventh Battle of the Isonzo came to an abrupt halt.

The Supreme Command, however, fully intended to resume operations later. This occurred on 10 October 1916, and the objectives were the same as they had been for the previous attack. The Eighth Battle of the Isonzo differed only in that the front upon which the attack would take place had been extended slightly, to allow for an attack on the high ground east of Görz. The Italian artillery opened fire on 9 October, and the barrage lasted until the afternoon of the next day. Although the Italians made some limited gains of territory, they were unable to exploit this, and the offensive again ended as a result of a combination of lack of success in the face of the enemy defences, and the appalling weather conditions. Remarkably, the tenacious Italian Supreme Command wished to continue operations, and a ninth battle was planned. This opened with an artillery bombardment on 25 October, lasting for three days. After a lull, the barrage resumed again on 1 November, and the infantry attack started at 11am. The Italian Second Army attacked east of Görz, while two corps from the Italian Third Army attempted to advance on the Carso Plateau. The results of the offensive proved disappointing, and it was called off on 4 November, largely because the Austrians were inflicting heavy casualties upon the attacking troops, and the weather

> 'On the lower Isonzo, our artillery and trench mortars were active against the enemy lines. We repulsed an attack on the Carso, taking 100 prisoners.'
>
> Italian War Office communiqué, 17 August 1916

had once again become appalling. The Italian soldiers were now exhausted after carrying out three offensives within the space of six weeks (even if each attack had been of limited duration), and it made sense to stop.

Italian casualties from the Seventh, Eighth and Ninth Isonzo battles ran to around 9000 killed in action, with over 40,000 wounded. Another 23,500 were reported as missing in action, with the total losses being estimated at over 75,000 men left for relatively little gain. The Austrians suffered losses of around 63,000, a testament to the ferocity of the fighting. Assessing the results of these battles, the Austrians concluded that they had, perhaps, been a little fortunate in holding on to most of the ground they occupied; they attributed the lack of any greater Italian success to a reluctance to deploy reserves in a prompt manner. The Austrians were painfully aware that they did not have many reserves of their own now that they were fighting a multi-front war, but in 1917, they were able to exploit a new source of troops: Germany. There was a further new factor in the equation, in that Emperor Franz Josef I died on 21 November 1916. He had been on the throne for 68 years, and by the time of his death was one of the few commonalities that bound the disparate Habsburg empire together. Many of the differing nationalities within the Austro-Hungarian Empire respected Franz Josef and held real affection for him; they did not hold the same feelings for his successor, his great-nephew Karl.

While Franz Josef had considered the war to be a necessary evil, Karl – particularly as a result of his front line command noted previously – held very different views and was determined to find an honourable peace settlement as soon as possible, realizing with perhaps greater clarity than any of his ministers that defeat would mean the end of the empire. Thus Austria-Hungary entered 1917 led by an emperor who was eager to see the war come to an end, and whose clear-cut lack of enthusiasm for the war was to have serious implications for the Habsburg–German relationship. Karl also made a change in his high command. General Conrad did not impress the new monarch, so he sacked him and appointed General Artur Arz von Straussenberg as chief of staff of the Austro-Hungarian forces.

1917: ON THE ROAD TO DISASTER

General Cadorna was painfully aware of the prospect of a German intervention in the Italian theatre of operations, and this curbed his enthusiasm for future offensive action. The situation in Italy also changed because of a number of alterations that occurred in the Allied nations. First, General Joseph Joffre was replaced as the French commander-in-chief by General Robert Nivelle, who gained this position largely because of the confident manner in which he informed French politicians – whose support he enjoyed in a way that Joffre did not – of his plan to end the war before 1917 was out. Nivelle's 1917 offensives nearly destroyed the French Army rather than the Germans, and he had been sacked by June. In Britain, there was a change of government, with David Lloyd George succeeding Herbert Asquith as Prime Minister following Asquith's resignation. Lloyd George, who believed that it was possible to win the war somewhere other than on the Western Front, and with fewer (specifically British) casualties, called an inter-Allied

British troops and artillery were sent to Italy in an effort to bypass the Western Front stalemate and defeat Germany by knocking Austria out of the war. However, the Italians were demoralized and worried about German intervention, and were thus reluctant to make any major attack.

conference, which met in Rome in the first week of January 1917. Lloyd George proposed that the Italians be reinforced by British and French artillery. He also advocated a further offensive, claiming that if the Austrians were defeated, the Germans would be as good as defeated too – an argument that had much to commend it on a superficial level, but which did not entirely take account of the realities of the strategic context of the war. The French, however, were reluctant to concur with this view. Cadorna complicated the discussions further with a request for eight French and British divisions to be sent to support any attack. It was decided that the British and French governments would send military advisers to investigate further the potential for operations on the Italian front.

The first adviser to arrive was Nivelle himself. He discussed the possibility of a German attack on Italy with Cadorna, and although he did not rule out such an eventuality, he argued that it was unlikely to take place before the summer at the earliest. Cadorna was not reassured. He had been further concerned by the fact that Romania's declaration of war had not, in fact, done much to help divert forces from the Italian

front: by 6 December 1916, the country had been forced to surrender following a combined Austro-German invasion. Cadorna was now concerned that the success of the operations against Romania might persuade the new German chief of staff, General Erich von Ludendorff, that a combined assault on Italy might be a worthwhile next step.

Italian reluctance to launch another offensive became a source of some irritation for the British and French, and further military missions followed. The British Chief of the Imperial General Staff, Sir William Robertson, visited Italy along with the French general Maxime Weygand at the invitation of Cadorna, and it began to dawn on the two men that the Italian forces would probably be in need of considerable assistance if the Germans did participate in an attack on the country. Robertson reached the view that in addition to sending heavy artillery, it would be necessary to send infantry divisions to help out as well.

The result of this visit was the signature of a convention between the British and Italians on 7 May 1917, in which it was agreed that if the need arose, six British divisions would be sent to Italy. The French did not conclude a formal agreement, but laid down their plans for the swift conveyance of troops if they were required. To increase Cadorna's confidence, the British decided that it was necessary to send 10 howitzer batteries to Italy, and the leading elements of this force set off for the country on 7 April 1917. The 10 British batteries were joined by another sent

Aerial reconnaissance was an important factor in making artillery bombardment effective, especially in terrain where the guns were essentially firing blind. Among the aircraft used for this task were the Dorand Ar.1 biplane shown here. The observer could be required to man the plane's machine guns in addition to spotting the fall of shot.

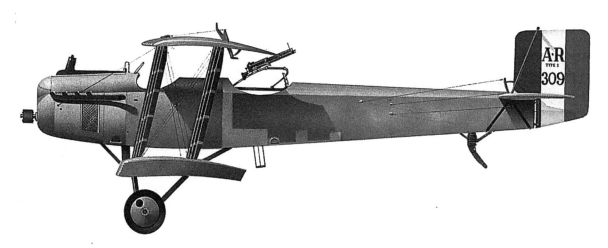

in July, and then by French artillery in the form of a dozen more batteries of heavy artillery.

THE TENTH BATTLE OF THE ISONZO

The progress made during Robertson and Weygand's visit to Italy helped to allay some of the concerns Cadorna expressed, and he began to plan another offensive in the Isonzo Valley. It was due to commence on 7 May, to coincide with the signature of the Anglo-Italian convention on the supply of British troops, but appalling weather meant that it had to be put back by a week. When the attack opened on 12 May, part of it went particularly well, with units from the Duke of Aosta's Italian Third Army making some gains, including the seizure of part of the Monte Kuk Ridge. However, the attempt to take Görz failed, and to make matters worse, the Austrians, fearing for the safety of Trieste, sent reinforcements to General Boroevich. He used them with considerable skill to inflict an extremely sharp reverse on the Italians on 4 June: in a sweeping counterattack, Boroevich regained ground and took large numbers of prisoners as he went. After three weeks of fighting, both sides began to run short of ammunition, and the battle petered out.

Casualties had been high on both sides: the Italians suffered over 35,000 killed and 96,000 wounded, while over 25,000 men had been taken prisoner. The Austrians had suffered far fewer fatalities, with 7300 dead, another 45,000 wounded and some 23,000 prisoners of war. The heavy Italian casualties began to raise the faintest murmurs of defeatism amongst the Italian troops, who began to ask whether the fact that 10 offensives on the Isonzo, which had achieved very little other than the shedding of much blood, meant that it was time for Cadorna to turn his attention elsewhere. Whilst not abandoning the Isonzo front completely, Cadorna had indeed decided to attack elsewhere, and this came in the form of the Battle of Ortigara in the Trentino sector.

ORTIGARA

Cadorna's plan was that an attack should be launched north of the Asiago, with the intention of turning the Austrians out of the positions they held in the area.

Heavy mortars of this sort, in 240mm and 280mm calibres, had a short range but fired in a high arc that could clear most obstacles. Their shells were powerful and arrived almost vertically. However, shells often buried themselves in soft ground before detonating.

There were sound military reasons for doing so, since the positions gave the Austrians the ability to drive into the Italian rear if they chose to attack in this area and managed to break through the Italian defences.

Ten Italian divisions were massed on the Asiago Plateau over a very short line of less than 14.4km (nine miles) width. The Italians intended to attack the right of the Austrian Sixth Army in the area Ortigara–Monte Forno, with the Italian XX Corps breaking through the Austrian positions and taking control of the whole of the northern edge of the plateau between Asiago and Cima Portule. As the day of the attack approached, it became painfully clear to Cadorna that some of the material support promised by the British and French was not going to arrive in the area in time. Also, the Austrians had become aware of the fact that an attack was in preparation and began to take steps to ensure that their defences held. Cadorna, therefore, had good reason to postpone the attack, but chose not to. When the offensive began on 10 June 1917, the area was shrouded in heavy fog, but the Italian artillery and mortars inflicted serious damage upon the Austrian defences, while the liberal use of gas in the bombardment ensured that gun crews who still had weapons to use would have to do so encumbered by their gas masks, making their work far more laborious as they tried to load and fire their artillery pieces.

This promising opening could not be exploited, though. When the Italian infantry attacked, they discovered that they were facing determined resistance, and were unable to break through the Austrian lines. After heavy losses, they finally managed to advance in dead ground, but this meant that the sole penetration of any note achieved by the Italians came from the two Alpini groups that had been positioned in the dead zone where the Austrian artillery was most unlikely to fall. They attacked the defences while the Austrians were in the process of reinforcing them, and some bitter fighting broke out. The Austrians managed to retain control of

Height 6906 of the Ortigara position, but the Italians seized Height 6585 and then took Height 6794. This appeared to offer the opportunity for an attack into the Austrian rear, but this was not to be. The Italian command had lost control of the attack at this point, and it proved impossible to regain it so that a combined effort could be put in. The fighting had broken down into localized actions, and this meant that by the end of 10 June the Italians had made gains in several key areas, but had been unable to exploit them. General Mambretti, commanding the Italian Sixth Army, realized that, now the element of surprise had been lost, the Austrians would be able

to put in a fierce defence all along the front, with a risk of heavy casualties. He urged that the offensive be called off. Cadorna was most reluctant to agree, and all that he would concede was a period of 48 hours for the troops to recuperate before the attack resumed again, although individual units were to conduct local attacks to harry the defences. This was a serious misjudgement, guaranteed only to increase Italian losses. In fact, if Cadorna had held to his opinions and attacked again the next morning, the Austrians would probably have been forced to fall back in the face of superior numbers.

The two-day pause gave the Austrians time to reinforce, which they duly did. A counterattack was planned for 15 June, and it achieved surprise. A rapid bombardment at 2.30am preceded the attack, and the Austrians immediately broke into the Italian positions. After bitter fighting, the Austrians were finally repulsed, and an Italian counterattack then followed. However, despite launching a series of assaults, the Italians were unable to break the Austrian line, and the day turned into a litany of failed attacks. By the time the attacks stopped in the evening, each side had lost over 6000 men.

The Italians planned a further attack, along the entire front, and this began on 18 June, at 8am with the customary artillery bombardment. The Austrians' defensive positions were completely destroyed in a four-hour barrage, and the Italians then advanced with the aim of taking the summits of the Ortigara and the positions at Lepozze. It took until the middle of 19 June before the main summit of the Ortigara (Height 6906) fell, again with heavy casualties.

THE BATTLE ENDS

Although the Italians had successfully driven the Austrians off the Ortigara, they had not done so permanently. The Austrians prepared to make an attack of their own, and they did so in the early

After 10 offensives on the Isonzo had achieved little at very high cost, the Italian Army attacked on a different front, hoping to turn the Austrian flank. Austrian gunnery was effectively suppressed by a combined explosive and gas bombardment, but, despite gains, this offensive also failed.

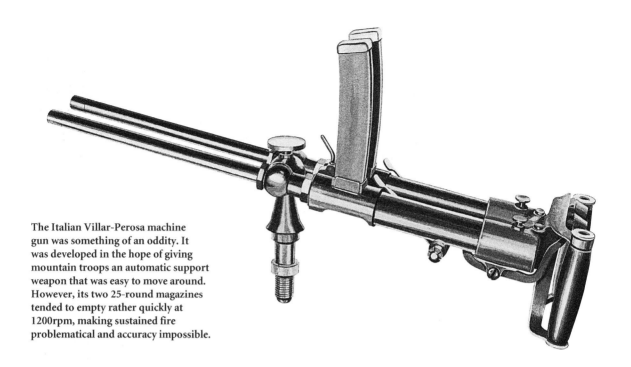

The Italian Villar-Perosa machine gun was something of an oddity. It was developed in the hope of giving mountain troops an automatic support weapon that was easy to move around. However, its two 25-round magazines tended to empty rather quickly at 1200rpm, making sustained fire problematical and accuracy impossible.

morning of 25 June 1917. The Austrian attack broke into the Italian positions on Monte Ortigara and began driving them back. The Italians, who had suffered heavy casualties in the preliminary bombardment, now found that a number of their positions were facing the Austrians to their front, while the advancing barrage had moved beyond their positions and made it impossible for them to retreat. Units in this position had little option other than to surrender immediately. Italian artillery caused considerable casualties amongst the Austrians as they dug in to their newly reoccupied positions, but it became clear that the Italians were not going to be able to dislodge them, as several attempts at counterattacks failed. On 26 June, Cadorna called off the offensive and withdrew to Porta Maora.

The end of the battle came as a bitter blow to the Italians, since much careful planning had achieved very little. The morale of the soldiers had suffered from a further instance of an offensive bringing heavy casualties and little to show for the sacrifice, and Cadorna and his subordinates began to become increasingly concerned at the depressed attitude of

many of their troops. Their next attempt on the Isonzo front did little to improve matters.

THE ELEVENTH BATTLE OF THE ISONZO
Despite the failure of the Ortigara offensive, Cadorna was undaunted. He fully intended to respect the inter-Allied agreement to launch offensives that occurred in close proximity to one another, appreciating the importance of ensuring that the enemy was faced with the dilemma of how to withdraw troops from one front to another without fatally weakening his position in the location from which the units had been redeployed. When the Russians began their summer offensive on 29 June 1917, the British passed news to Cadorna that they intended to begin their own attack (which would be at Ypres in Belgium) on 31 July. Cadorna therefore set about planning for another offensive on the Isonzo, with the aim of it beginning in early to mid-August. He had been boosted by the provision of more artillery and six fresh divisions, and to take account of his additional strength, restructured his forces. The Gorizia (Görz) Command was abolished, and General Capello was

promoted to take command of the Italian Second Army. Second Army was to be reconstituted 16km (10 miles) north of Tolmino, with a strength of 17 divisions and 850 heavy guns at its disposal. A specially constituted force, in the form of the Italian VIII Corps was given the task of holding the line at the Görz bridgehead. The Italian Third Army was given an uplift in strength, increasing to 18 divisions.

The Austrians, on the other hand, had only 18 divisions against the 35 Italian ones. Although reinforcements had been sent after the Tenth Battle of the Isonzo, the prevailing circumstances meant that three of the divisions that had participated in that fighting had to be sent to the Russian front, leaving the Austrians only one division better off than they had been. To make matters worse for the Austrians,

Italian casualties on the Isonzo depleted the morale of the fighting units and eventually led to the Caporetto disaster, but it was not all one-sided. This Austrian officer was wounded in the same area while leading a patrol.

they had stripped the Trentino front of troops to bolster the position at the Isonzo, leaving that area only lightly held, while no further reinforcements could be sent unless the Germans were able to provide forces.

While the Austrians were numerically inferior to the Italians, there was one comfort: their defensive positions remained strong and difficult to break into. The Italians appreciated this, and at the Allied conference held in London on 7 and 8 August 1917, Foreign Minister Sonnino requested that the French and British provide 400 heavy guns before

Various innovations were tried in the hope of gaining an advantage, including primitive body armour. While of some use to snipers and artillery observers, for assault troops such as this Italian soldier the weight of metal offset its protective value to the point where it was a hindrance.

the offensive started. This appeared to be a difficult request to fulfil, since these guns would have to come from the French and British front lines, something that was highly unwelcome to the British during their offensive at Ypres. Sir William Robertson told the British War Cabinet that if the guns were sent to the Italians, the offensive in Flanders would have to be called off, and that in his view, the best means of aiding the Italians would be to continue the offensive at Ypres, thus preventing the Germans from releasing forces to aid their Austrian allies. The French, who were recovering from the widespread mutinies that had afflicted the army in the aftermath of Nivelle's ill conceived offensive, did not appear in a position to help either, but the work undertaken by the new commander-in-chief of the French armies of the

North and Northeast, General Philippe Pétain, meant that he might be able to reconstitute his forces so that artillery units could be sent at a later date. The artillery question therefore remained unresolved for the moment, and the Italians had to plan to operate with what they had, even though Cadorna may have feared that the number of heavy artillery pieces was insufficient to help force victory against the Austrian lines on the Isonzo.

Cadorna's plans for the latest battle were drawn up in such a way as to ensure that the army commanders had rather more freedom of action than had previously been the case: Cadorna recognized that this ought to allow for faster decision making on the part of the commanders, and to allow them to adapt as the battle unfolded. The Italian Third Army was given the Carso Plateau and Trieste as objectives, while the Second Army was to take the Bainsizza Plateau before moving on to capture the Selva di Ternova. VIII Corps was to wait in the Görz bridgehead and exploit any opportunities to advance that emerged as the battle went on. A diversionary attack would be made against Tolmino to complete the opening element of the offensive. General Capello, given freedom to choose how he would conduct his operation, decided that the Italian Second Army would make a flanking attack between Plava and Selo, despite the fact that this was a risky manoeuvre that required his force to cross the Isonzo gorge under the nose of the enemy.

The preliminary bombardment that opened the offensive began at 6am on 18 August, and was followed up by the infantry some hours later. Although the Austrians had some success in destroying the temporary bridges thrown across the Isonzo by the Italian Second Army, Capello's troops managed to carry out the risky task of crossing the river under the direct view of the enemy in the early hours of the morning of 19 August. Elsewhere, though, the attack did not go so well. The Tolmino diversion failed to achieve anything other than heavy casualties for the Italians, while the Italian Third Army's initial attack made very little progress. In the absence of heavy guns from the French and British, the Italians had decided to provide some fire support from ships close to the coast, but even this amplification of the amount of firepower available was insufficient to enable the Third Army to resist an Austrian counterattack which threw them back almost to their start line.

On 20 August the Second Army continued its advance, and broke through the enemy lines at Auzza on a 1830m (2000-yard) frontage the next day. The Italian Third Army had not managed to make any notable gains, and Cadorna reassigned a number of its units and artillery pieces to the Italian Second Army in the hope that this would maintain the momentum of the attack. The Austrians continued to fall back, leaving General Boroevich facing a dilemma as to how to stem the enemy advance. He was visited on 23 August by Emperor Karl and General Arz. Boroevich was informed that there was now a plan for an Austrian offensive on the Tolmino-Caporetto front. The Germans would be providing six divisions to assist, following careful negotiations

between Berlin and Vienna. Boroevich suggested that it would make sense for him to break contact with the Italians rather than continue to suffer casualties to no obvious purpose, now that he would not be called upon to launch a large counterattack on the Isonzo. His suggestion found favour with Arz and the commander of the Southwest Front, Archduke Eugen, which led to him withdrawing from the Bainsizza Plateau on the night of 23/24 August 1917. The Italians first learned of the withdrawal from the sound of Austrian engineers destroying various bridges to make pursuit more difficult. The Italians attempted to follow the Austrians, but the terrain in the Bainsizza militated against this: already a rocky area, the lack of bridges and the shell-holed ground made pursuit

These Italian assault pioneers are using a portable metal shield, like the pavise of the medieval period and for much the same purpose. The shield provided a mobile form of cover for wire-cutting parties.

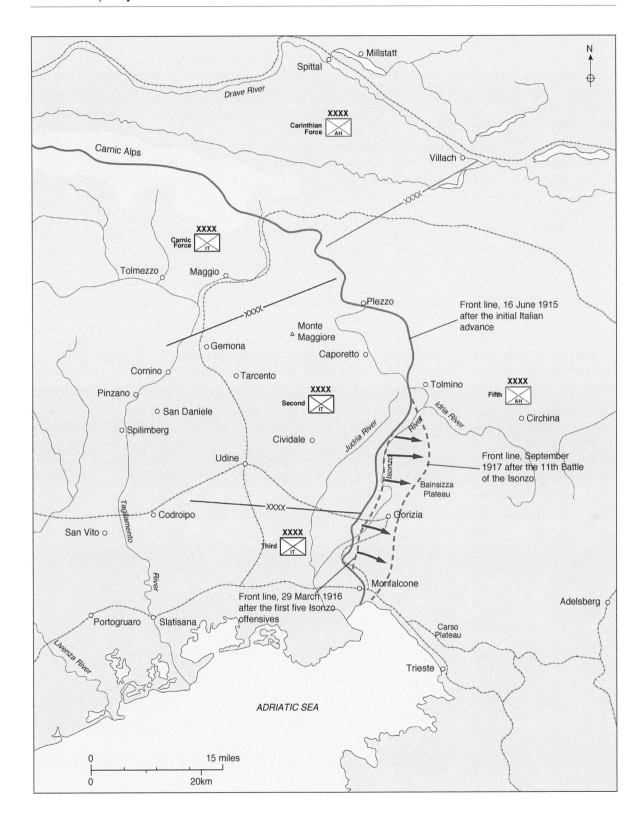

N

Millstatt

Spittal

Drave River

Carinthian
Force
XXXX
AH

Carnic Alps

Villach

XXXX

Carnic
Force
XXXX
IT

Tolmezzo   Maggio

Plezzo

Front line, 16 June 1915
after the initial Italian
advance

XXXX

Monte
△ Maggiore

Gemona

Caporetto

Tolmino

Idria River

XXXX
Fifth   AH

Cornino

Tarcento

Pinzano

Second
XXXX
IT

Judria River

Isonzo

River

Circhina

San Daniele

Spilimberg

Cividale

Udine

Bainsizza
Plateau

Front line, September
1917 after the 11th Battle
of the Isonzo

Tagliamento

Codroipo

XXXX

Gorizia

San Vito

Third
XXXX
IT

River

Monfalcone

Adelsberg

Front line, 29 March 1916
after the first five Isonzo
offensives

Portogruaro   Slatisana

Carso
Plateau

Livenza River

Trieste

ADRIATIC SEA

0   15 miles

0   20km

a slow business. Over the course of the next few days, Cadorna began to doubt the wisdom of prosecuting the pursuit any further. Once the Austrians stopped and dug in, his infantry would have to make use of artillery to stand any chance of breaching a hole in the enemy line, and the guns were still in the process of attempting to catch up with the infantry. Cadorna therefore ended the pursuit on 29 August, although the operation to capture Monte San Gabriele was to continue, along with the attempt to break through the Austrian defences to the north and east of Görz. These two small continuations of the offensive both failed: the attacks around Görz made no difference to the position and were abandoned, while Monte San Gabriele changed hands several times before the Austrians gained the upper hand and drove the Italians back. The fighting stopped on 13 September. Cadorna had already announced that it was his intention to conduct another offensive before the end of the month.

At this point, the French decided that it would be opportune to provide Cadorna with artillery. They did so because, on 31 March 1917, they had been approached by Prince Sixte of Bourbon-Parma

After the initial gains of the first months, the Italians made very little progress on the Isonzo front. This was not for lack of trying; the Italian Army suffered over 300,000 casualties in this region – about half of its total for the entire war. Some 200,000 Austro-Hungarian troops also became casualties.

An Italian Caproni Ca3 bomber, a distinctly primitive looking aircraft whose three engines allowed it to carry a respectable bomb load for the time. The central gunner had to stand in a cage on top of the engine. Several squadrons equipped with this aircraft operated on the Italian front.

regarding the possibility of peace negotiations between the Allies and Austria-Hungary. Sixte's approach was at the behest of his brother-in-law: Emperor Karl. Karl was keen that his approach should remain secret, which the French honoured.

However, they felt no inclination to see the pressure on the Austrian forces reduced, reasoning that the worse the situation became for Austria-Hungary, the more likely Karl would be to make firm his tentative suggestions for a separate peace settlement. It seemed eminently sensible to help increase the pressure by seeing an Italian success, and the French Government therefore gave Pétain permission to send 18 artillery batteries to join the Italian forces. While not the heavy guns that Cadorna really wanted, they represented a welcome addition to the battlefield firepower available to the Italians.

Cadorna's confidence in the validity of an offensive was to be shaken, however, when intelligence information began to reach him suggesting that the Austrians were planning an offensive of their own. On 14 September, the Swiss–German border was closed, and there were rumours that Austrian divisions were beginning to concentrate in the Trentino area. More alarmingly, the rumours suggested that some of the units that had been seen were not Austro-Hungarian, but German. Cadorna immediately ordered a series of raids to be carried out in the area to see if there was any substance to the gossip, but the raiding parties returned with no evidence of anything out of the ordinary.

The British and French attempted to reassure Cadorna that the rumours were just that, arguing that it would not be possible for the railway lines in the Trentino area to bring up the necessary number of troops for a major offensive. Cadorna initially reached the same conclusion, but on 20 September, surprised his allies by announcing that he was temporarily abandoning his plan for a new offensive. He cited a lack of ammunition, but the French and British suspected that there was more to it than this: indeed, Cadorna later admitted to the British military mission in Italy that he was also concerned

Although there were many signs of an imminent attack, the Italian Supreme Command was not willing to believe there was a real danger. Troops in front-line positions such as these were unprepared when the offensive began.

about the heavy losses sustained to date, along with a lack of reinforcements, a shortage of officers and concerns about the possible implications that another costly offensive on the Isonzo would have on public opinion, which appeared to be moving in favour of an early peace. At this news, the French decided to recall their artillery batteries, assuming that they would be far better used back in France, where operations were ongoing.

Little did they realize that in just over a month Cadorna would need all the artillery and additional manpower that could be supplied, for the Austrians and Germans were about to launch a devastating offensive that would profoundly alter the nature of the war on the Italian front.

General Artur Arz von Straussenberg (1857–1935)

Straussenburg was a brilliant student set for a career in law, but enjoyed his year's service in the Austrian Army so much that he applied for, and received, a commission in 1878. A successful career as a junior officer followed, and he joined the general staff in 1888. Promotion ensued, and by 1908 Straussenburg was a major-general, commanding an infantry brigade. When war broke out he was given command of an infantry division. His successful handling of the formation brought further promotion, and he was appointed to lead the First Army in 1915. Highly regarded by his colleagues, Straussenburg was appointed Chief of the General Staff after Conrad was sacked. When the spring 1918 offensive failed, Straussenburg offered his resignation, which was refused. Retiring at the end of the war, Straussenburg lived in Vienna, supplementing his meagre income by writing his memoirs and a history of the war.

CHAPTER 6

From Disaster to the Brink of Victory

By late 1917, planning for an Austro-German offensive against the Italians had been under way for some time. The first suggestion of an offensive to knock Italy out of the war had been raised by General Conrad over a year earlier, when he proposed an attack in the Tyrol and on the Isonzo. This time, though, the strategic situation suggested that Conrad's idea had far greater merit.

T he proposal for a joint offensive was examined in some detail by the Germans, at the behest of General Ludendorff. His staff conducted a thorough appraisal and informed him that removing the Italians from the war would be of considerable assistance to operations on the Western Front. It appeared likely that the Italians would receive assistance from their allies, particularly from the French. If this were the case, then the Allies would be weaker on the Western Front. If, however, the Allies

As morale in the Italian Army plummeted, the Central Powers were preparing for a major offensive. This achieved surprise and triggered a collapse all along the front, resulting in the loss of over 300,000 Italian troops, most of them as prisoners such as those seen here.

chose not to intervene, the results of a successful offensive would shorten the Austrian front, which would in turn allow a redeployment of Austro-Hungarian units to either the Eastern or Western fronts. Also, the occupation of northern Italy would make it possible to threaten French territory from the Alpine front, which would require a redeployment of Allied troops to meet it, thus weakening their forces in the main area of fighting. Although the plan was tempting, Ludendorff rejected it, on the grounds that ammunition was in short supply, and because

When Emperor Karl I assumed the throne in 1916 he set about trying to reform the Austro-Hungarian Army. He was, among other things, opposed to the use of poison gas in warfare. His plans came to naught, however, and he is chiefly remembered for presiding over the dissolution of his empire.

The participation of Germany in the war against Italy brought additional men and *matériel* to bear. Artillery observation using static tethered balloons was useful in some areas, though the balloons themselves were often targeted by fighter aircraft and were unable to retaliate.

he suspected that the Allies would continue offensive operations in 1917, which would in turn require the German forces on the Western Front to remain at maximum possible strength.

Conrad was not to be deterred; he was well known for his desire to defeat the Italians, and his advocacy of an attack on the country dated to before the war, fuelled predominantly by a dislike of Austria's southern neighbours and mistrust of their intentions. At a command conference between the Germans and Austrians on 23 January 1917, he expressed serious

doubts about the German proposals to win the war through the use of unrestricted submarine warfare. He proposed that victory would most likely be achieved through a land offensive, and again suggested an attack on Italy. Once more, the attack would be in the form of an offensive on two fronts, first along the Isonzo, which would fall on the Caporetto sector, to be followed a week later by the main thrust in the Tyrol. Once again, though, he was to be disappointed. The Germans had already decided that they needed to pull back from the Hindenburg Line on the Western Front (perversely, withdrawal here represented something of an operational coup for the Germans since it compelled the Allies to occupy ground that was extremely difficult to defend), and suspicions that the new French commander, Nivelle, was planning an offensive meant that it was unwise to plan to attack on another front by stripping troops away from the front

This image gives some idea of the difficulties inherent in attacking across the Isonzo. With its bridges destroyed and overlooked by high ground, the river was a significant obstacle to any advance by either side.

line in France. Conrad was therefore advised that an attack in Italy would simply not be possible until after Nivelle's offensive had been dealt with. Conrad's idea was not rejected for reasons of impracticality, but its timing was not right. By the time it came to reconsidering the possibility of an attack in the Caporetto sector, Conrad had been removed from command by Emperor Karl, and the planning for the Austrian contribution would be made by his successor, General Arz von Straussenburg.

THE DECISION FOR THE OFFENSIVE

After the rejection of Cadorna's proposals in January 1917, circumstances began to moderate Ludendorff's opinions of the viability of a joint offensive against the Italians. First, political tension between Vienna and Berlin began to increase. The Austro-Hungarians began to appreciate that one of their worst fears was being realized: before long, the only means of gaining success in battle on any of the active fronts upon which they were fighting was to operate in conjunction with the Germans, since Austro-Hungarian forces would no

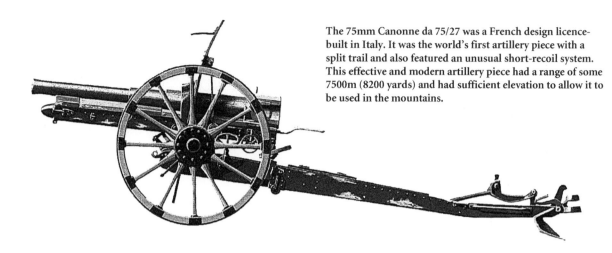

The 75mm Canonne da 75/27 was a French design licence-built in Italy. It was the world's first artillery piece with a split trail and also featured an unusual short-recoil system. This effective and modern artillery piece had a range of some 7500m (8200 yards) and had sufficient elevation to allow it to be used in the mountains.

longer be strong enough to win clear victories on their own, particularly given the attrition they were suffering on the Eastern Front against the Russians. The thought that they would need to involve the Germans was a painful one for the Habsburgs, since they had always regarded the Balkans as being purely within their sphere of influence, and did not wish to see the Germans interfering. Now, though, it appeared that they had no other choice. This in turn risked the possibility that the Germans would dominate any peace settlement in the Balkans and southern Europe, and there was a danger that the hard-won peace would not be the one that Vienna had aspired to on the outbreak of war. The emperor protested to his advisers that any peace dominated by the Germans would represent nothing less than the end of the Dual Monarchy. Kaiser Wilhelm, meanwhile, made rude remarks about the value of the alliance, claiming that maintaining a relationship with the Habsburgs was not worth sacrificing any of the gains made in northern Europe. General Hindenburg, meanwhile, expressed the view that leading German troops into Bohemia would represent the peak of his military achievements – blissfully ignoring the fact that Bohemia was very much an Austro-Hungarian possession, and that Germany's allies would be most unimpressed with his comments.

These diplomatic tensions gave rise in some quarters to the belief that a joint operation between the Germans and the Austro-Hungarians might be the only means of maintaining the alliance, although this was not a view widely held. However, the events of spring and summer 1917 began to make the idea of a joint assault against the Italians more attractive to both parties. In August, Karl informed Berlin that it was his view that the current nature of operations in Italy would not bring about a decision and that it was necessary to launch an overwhelming offensive on the Italian front. He asked Kaiser Wilhelm to ensure that German troops were sent to relieve Austrian troops on the Eastern Front, enabling him to undertake an attack against what

> 'Ludendorff was not at first enthusiastic over a joint offensive against Italy. He preferred to overthrow Romania by advancing into Moldavia. However, he finally gave his consent, and Kaiser Wilhelm and Hindenburg also agreed.'
>
> General von Cramon,
> German liaison officer to the Austro-Hungarian Army

An Austrian 305mm mortar. While effective from static positions over fairly short ranges, such weapons were unwieldy and could not keep up with the infantry during an advance or retreat. The Italians lost many such weapons during the retreat after the defeat at Caporetto.

he called 'the hereditary enemy'. As an indication of his determination to attack, Karl authorized the conscription of all young men aged 18 to 20.

The Austro-Hungarian Director of Military Operations, General von Walstätten, was sent to German headquarters to seek the support of Hindenburg and Ludendorff for the proposed attack. Ludendorff was concerned at the thought of an Austro-Hungarian offensive against the Italians. The question of what the results of a decisive victory

would be troubled him. Although Karl's attempt to open negotiations with the French had remained secret, the Germans strongly suspected that the new Austro-Hungarian emperor was intent on seeking a peace settlement as expeditiously as possible, even if this meant peace at the price of abandoning the German Empire to its fate. The alternative possibilities also preyed upon Ludendorff's thinking. He had little confidence in the ability of the Austro-Hungarian troops, and was concerned that Karl's bid for decisive victory might lead to decisive defeat – with the concomitant effect of pushing him towards a separate negotiated peace with the French, Russians and British. An appraisal of the Austro-Hungarian political–military situation carried out in spring 1917 by Hans von Seeckt, provided by the Germans to act as chief of staff to Archduke Josef's army group, suggested that the situation was grim, with the emperor being deeply concerned about the prospect of a revolution breaking out amongst the varying nationalities that made up the Dual Monarchy and destroying it. Seeckt also suggested that the emperor was concerned about the growing desire for peace being expressed throughout Austria-Hungary, and intimated that there was a danger that he might seek to recognize the concerns of his subjects by attempting to gain a separate peace settlement – which, of course, was exactly what he was attempting to do, unbeknown to the Germans.

These political considerations combined with military circumstances to make Ludendorff change his mind: he had no desire to see the German Army on the defensive on every front of the war during 1917, and the prospect of an offensive in Italy thus became more attractive. When the concerns over Emperor Karl's possible actions after a unilateral Austrian offensive were also taken into account, the case for joining with the Austrians became highly persuasive.

PREPARATIONS FOR THE ATTACK

To settle the debate without further ado, the Germans decided to send Lieutenant-General Krafft von Dellmensingen to reconnoitre the front, since he was a highly experienced mountaineer and commander of German Alpine troops. Dellmensingen's report was mixed. He informed the German high command (the OHL) that an operation in the area would be difficult, but that it was feasible. Furthermore, he expressed the opinion that the Austrians would probably be unable to resist another Italian attack on the scale of the Eleventh Battle of the Isonzo, and this made a joint operation against the Italians not only desirable but necessary. Although Cadorna had moved onto the defensive, there was no guarantee that this would be for long, and all the information available, along with the precedent of earlier operations, suggested that Cadorna would look to launch a new offensive in fairly short order. Taken with Dellmensingen's

view that the Italians would finally manage to break Austrian resistance with a further attack, the OHL decided that the risks inherent in an offensive over difficult ground were of lesser importance than seeing the Italians knocked out of the war. Consequently, the decision to conduct a joint attack was made, although Dellmensingen rejected following Cadorna's standard mode of attack, which involved storming the ridges and then moving along them. He instead made a recommendation that the forthcoming offensive should take the form of wide-fronted sweeps down the mountain valleys, since this appeared to offer a better chance of success.

The German Fourteenth Army under General Otto von Below was given the task of providing the main elements of the offensive force. Below had two Austrian and two German corps under his command, and these were joined by a number of elite light

Lieutenant-General Krafft von Dellmensingen (right), pictured with Prince Rupprecht of Bavaria (left), was an expert on mountain warfare. He recommended the site for the planned offensive, choosing a region on the north flank of the Isonzo front centred on the village of Caporetto.

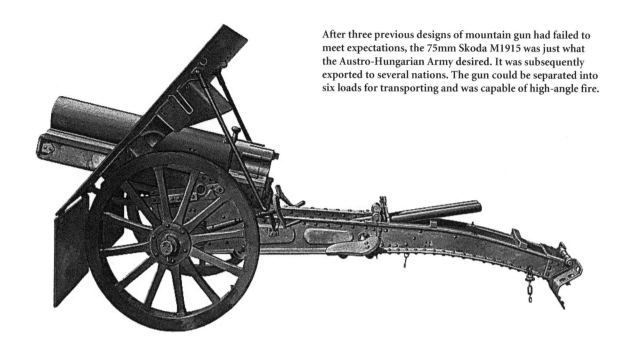

After three previous designs of mountain gun had failed to meet expectations, the 75mm Skoda M1915 was just what the Austro-Hungarian Army desired. It was subsequently exported to several nations. The gun could be separated into six loads for transporting and was capable of high-angle fire.

infantry and stormtroop battalions to bolster the strength of the attack by adding their considerable expertise in leading an offensive to the overall effort. Although the offensive was nominally under the command of Archduke Eugen, in reality this was little more than a political nicety, since Below was given total control over the conduct of the operation, as was common when the Germans provided forces for a joint operation.

On 20 September 1917, Below began the process of moving his heavy guns to the front. This was a major operation, since they had to move from Riga in the Baltic down to the south. Some 1800 guns and 420 howitzers, along with over a million artillery shells, were duly transported to positions that had been prepared while the weapons journeyed south. The assembly of the attacking army took up over 30 per cent of the entire rail capacity of the Austro-Hungarian Empire, and the moving of equipment and manpower took up nearly 2500 trains. Thousands of horses were assembled to provide onward movement of supplies and guns once they reached the railhead. The entire operation to put

together Below's attacking force took a month. In addition to the units already assigned, the Austrians provided a further five divisions to the German Fourteenth Army.

Below had ensured that the arriving troops would be able to assemble with relative ease once they were in the Alps, and carefully camouflaged positions were waiting to receive them just behind their start points for the offensive. Below intended to maximize the benefit of surprise as far as possible, and almost all troop movements took place at night. To confuse the Italians further, an array of spurious wireless messages were transmitted by signals units, seeking to give the impression that all was normal on the Isonzo, and attempting to point Italian attention in other directions. Finally, Below decided that he would employ a massive but short opening artillery bombardment, and the troops would advance behind the protection of a creeping artillery barrage. The method that had characterized previous Isonzo offensives by the Italians, where preparatory fire, warning the defenders that an attack was likely to materialize within a matter of hours, was abandoned

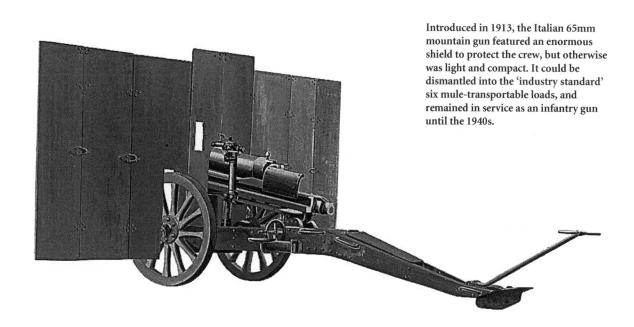

Introduced in 1913, the Italian 65mm mountain gun featured an enormous shield to protect the crew, but otherwise was light and compact. It could be dismantled into the 'industry standard' six mule-transportable loads, and remained in service as an infantry gun until the 1940s.

to achieve the maximum amount of shock and surprise amongst the defending troops.

Below's plan for the offensive called for four divisions – three Austrian and one German – to make the attack in the northern sector, which would be the responsibility of General Alfred Krauss. The centre would be controlled by generals Hermann Stein and Albrecht von Berrer at the head of divisions made up almost entirely of German troops, with just a few Austrians in support. To the south of these generals, a force composed of German and Austrian troops under the command of Austrian General Karl Scotti would attack the Italians opposite this sector, while the Austrian Tenth Army had responsibility in the Carnolian Alps. Boroevich's army group was given the task of fixing Italian forces on the Isonzo front, while Conrad, handed the political fig leaf of a front line command after his removal as chief of staff, was to oversee the Tyrolean Army Group's efforts to prevent the Italians from conducting meaningful resistance against the offensive in the western sector.

Although the Italians enjoyed numerical superiority overall, in the vital Flitsch-Tolmino-Caporetto sector,

they were decisively outnumbered by the enemy. Although there was intelligence from enemy deserters to point to the dangers facing them, the Italian high command remained confident in their ability to hold back any prospective attack. They were confident in the extent of their preparations and their preconceptions of the strength and viability of their defences; thus, from an Italian perspective it appeared that, no matter what the Germans and Austrians attempted, they would be unable to enjoy any success, not least since it appeared to Cadorna and his subordinates that they knew what the Germans and Austrians were going to attempt to do. This was a dangerous assumption, as events were to show.

THE ITALIANS PREPARE

As noted in the previous chapter, concerns about the prospects of an enemy offensive led to Cadorna abandoning his plans for yet another offensive on the Isonzo and moving over to the defensive. However, it soon became clear to the Italians that any offensive would occur only on the Isonzo, given the apparent movement of troops into the area behind the enemy front. By 6 October, the Italians had intelligence suggesting that there were at least 29 enemy divisions located on the Isonzo, and there were more German and Austrian troops on the way: Italian intelligence had established that two Austrian divisions were moving in towards the enemy troop concentration, while a German division and the German Alpine Corps were also approaching. By the second week in October, Italian intelligence had sufficient information to conclude that German forces were concentrating in the Save Valley to the east of Caporetto. Further reports came in of German units being identified as gathering in the vicinity of Tolmino. On 9 October 1917, the Italian intelligence organization reported

Italian troops manning a machine-gun emplacement built of sandbags. The gun is firing through a loophole and care has been taken to conceal it as much as possible. Such a position would be hard to eliminate without artillery.

The Caporetto offensive should not have achieved surprise. Deserters had warned the Italians that an offensive was about to be launched, but these reports were discounted by Italian commanders. Meanwhile the German troops pictured here at Tolmino were preparing for the attack.

that it appeared that there would be an enemy attack by the end of October. More information materialized to support this conclusion; on 20 October, the interrogation of an Austrian defector revealed that bad weather had interfered with the preparations for the offensive, with the result that it had been postponed. The new start date would be 26 October, and the attack would start in the Tolmino area. A group of Hungarian deserters who surrendered on 21 October added more details of the offensive, indicating that it would take place along the entire length of the Isonzo front, with the main weight of the attack falling on the Italian positions around Tolmino. The deserters even

provided details of the nature of the planned artillery barrage, which would, they said, include the use of poison gas.

By 21 October 1917, then, the Italians were in possession of a considerable amount of information regarding the forthcoming offensive that would fall upon their troops in the Isonzo area, thanks to the efforts of their intelligence services. There was one difficulty facing the intelligence staff: none of the senior commanders could bring themselves to believe that the information being provided represented anything other than wishful thinking on the part of the enemy. Although there was little doubt that the enemy attack would fall on the Isonzo front, the idea that the Austrians and Germans would be able to launch an attack on the scale being predicted over the mountainous terrain that had frustrated Italian efforts over the past two years appeared quite implausible. As a result, while Cadorna fully expected an attack, he had little doubt that it would be possible to hold the Austrians back. He informed his subordinates that the difficult terrain around the Tolmino sector would make holding off an attack there a relatively simple task. In fact, Cadorna was so confident that he had given instructions that the sector should be held lightly.

Cadorna failed to appreciate that the Germans and Austrians were just as aware of the difficult nature of the broken, rocky terrain around Tolmino and the difficulties that it presented for an attacking force. Contrary to Cadorna's opinion, the Austrian and German assessment of where to attack had been based upon the fact that the Italians had left the area vulnerable; this was a result of over-confidence in the perceived impossibility of the enemy being able to conduct an effective offensive in the difficult landscape. If they could break through in the area,

> 'The enemy has concentrated strong forces on our front for offensive purposes. A large proportion of these troops and material are German. However, the blow of the enemy will find us steady and prepared.'
>
> Italian War Office communiqué, 24 October 1917

the Germans were confident that they would be able to roll up the Italian positions and then advance into their rear. From here, the Austrians and Germans aimed to set about destroying the entire Italian hold on the Isonzo front, aiming to drive them back across the Tagliamento River.

THE OFFENSIVE BEGINS

The Germans and Austrians had chosen their start points for the offensive well, and had correctly identified the correct place to situate the main body of their offensive at the Tolmino bridgehead. The Italians had positioned two infantry divisions – the 19th and 65th – to defend this sector, little realizing that they were opposed by four enemy divisions, with a further three German divisions in reserve to push the momentum of the attack onwards. This was not all, since there were another three Austrian divisions to the east of Caporetto, again intended to provide the reserve. In contrast, the Italian 50th Division holding the Flitsch basin had nothing standing behind it, making that area of the front particularly vulnerable to an enemy breakthrough; Italian reserves were positioned well to the south, and the task of moving them up to the line quickly in the face of a concerted enemy attack would prove difficult. However, given the confidence of the Italian high command in the inability of the enemy to launch an offensive on the scale necessary to inflict a major reverse on their defences, the location of the reserves seemed both reasonable and sensible.

The Italians had also failed to take into account the continuing supremacy in artillery that the Austrians enjoyed, while the Germans had taken the further step of sending a gas battery to the Flitsch sector, where it was to open the offensive by creating a corridor across the road connecting Flitsch to Saga, denying

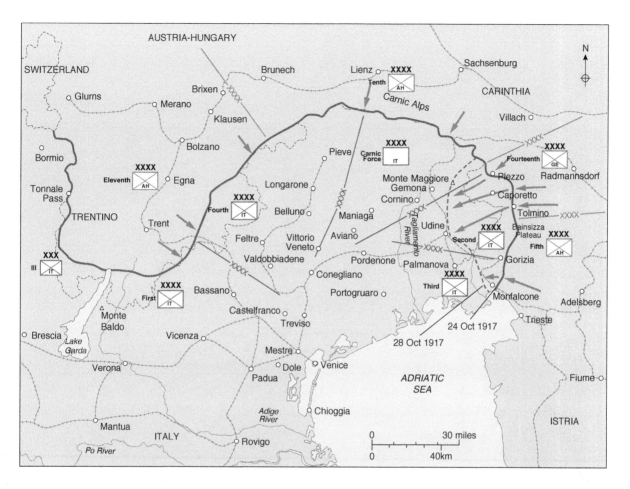

The opening moves of the Battle of Caporetto, up to the Italian collapse, 28 October 1917. The arrival of superior German troops, the use of poison gas and a mistake by General Capello all contributed to the initial breakthrough.

it to defending troops. The Germans would use two types of gas, code-named Blue Cross and Green Cross, against which the Italians' respirators were ineffectual.

The bad weather that punctuated early October 1917 meant that the offensive had to be postponed several times. Finally, Below decided that he would have to attack even though the weather was far from perfect, and the start was fixed for 24 October. As the attacking troops were making their final preparations, the Italians were beset by a disagreement between Cadorna and one of his subordinates over the method of defence that the Italian Second Army should pursue. Cadorna maintained that the defence of the Second Army's front should take the form of a series of small-scale counterattacks.

However, the commander of the Italian Second Army, General Luigi Capello, disagreed. He argued

that it was possible to maintain a flexible defence, which would take the form of a series of attacks against the left flank of the Austrian positions. He therefore placed his three reserve corps in the area between Plava and Monte Kuk, to the south of Caporetto, but in so doing left his own flank in the Flitsch basin dangerously exposed and much weakened. Cadorna realized that this represented a serious danger, and on 20 October issued orders that Second Army was to make a counterattack to restore the position. Unfortunately, Capello had been taken ill, succumbing to an attack of influenza at what proved to be the worst possible occasion; his

German troops in Belluno. The Royal Navy blockade of Germany was starting to tell and many units were short of food. As a result, troops were often more concerned with getting something to eat than pursuing their retreating foes.

second-in-command, General Montouri, chose to ignore the instruction to counterattack, and instead gave instructions to the corps commanders to make small adjustments to the positions of their troops. Failing to see the point, the corps commanders ignored the instructions. It was only when Cadorna made a personal visit to Second Army's left wing that he appreciated that his orders had been ignored, and made hurried arrangements for 34th Infantry Division to be brought into the line. The division was moving into place at 2am on 24 October, just as the Austro-German attack began with a massive bombardment all along the Isonzo front.

The artillery was answered by counterbattery fire from the Italians, but the effect of gas shells soon began to affect the Italian gunners, and their fire slackened considerably. The bombardment then paused briefly, before being switched from the Italian gun positions onto the Italian lines. By 7am, the Austrian and German guns had been joined by heavy mortar fire, aimed at the known locations of Italian headquarters and ammunition dumps in addition to front line positions and the artillery positions. As the mortars began their fire, the Austrian and German infantry surged forwards toward the Italian positions.

The preliminary bombardment had considerable effect. The gas caused havoc in the Italian lines, and added to the effect of the high-explosive shells, which had destroyed most of the communications links between the Italian command positions and the front line. In the confusion, a number of Italian units began to disintegrate as panic set in amongst the troops. This was exacerbated when two mines were detonated beneath the Italian lines at Monte Rosso and Monte Mrzli as precursors to the infantry attack.

After 90 minutes, it became obvious that Group Krauss in the northern sector had routed the Italians, who put up almost no resistance of note. The Austrians reached Flitsch and had to pause to allow their artillery to catch up. A breakthrough had been obtained at the junction of the Italian IV and XXVII corps, and it became apparent that the failure to follow Cadorna's instructions had left most of XXVII Corps stuck on the Bainsizza Plateau, leaving the Italian positions at Caporetto exceptionally vulnerable. The German 12th Infantry Division swiftly forced its way into the Italian front line and broke through the Napoli Brigade, which had only recently arrived in the area in an attempt to reinforce the sector. The Germans pushed on over the Isonzo, and drove to the north and west, aiming for Monte Matajur and the foot of the Kolovrat Ridge. Italian positions on the left bank of the Isonzo collapsed in the late morning of 24 October, and by the early evening the town of Caporetto had fallen into German hands.

When Cadorna made an attempt to assess the position in the late afternoon, the position was chaotic, and ascertaining exactly what had occurred was difficult. It was painfully obvious that the Germans and Austrians had successfully forced a gap in the Italian positions that was 25km (15 miles) wide between Flitsch and Tolmino. If this was not a big enough problem, reports suggested that the realization that German troops were involved in the attack in addition to the Austrians had caused panic in some Italian units, which had lost all discipline and simply broken and run in the face of the enemy.

Although air warfare was still in its infancy, ground attack by aircraft was taken seriously enough that specialist anti-aircraft units were formed. Guns mounted on light trucks, as shown here, could also be pressed into service.

General Luigi Capello (1859–1941)

A somewhat unpredictable field commander, Capello's habit during wartime of allowing journalists to accompany him on the Italian front infuriated Cadorna; however, it guaranteed Capello favourable coverage, particularly following the Italian success at Görz in August 1916. Subsequently, Capello found himself transferred to the less glamorous Trentino sector, before he was moved back to the Isonzo at the head of Second Army in early 1917. Its limited success at the Eleventh Battle of the Isonzo that summer was entirely wiped out by the calamitous events at Caporetto in October. Warned of the possibility of an attack in the sector, Capello ignored Cadorna's orders to withdraw his artillery to safety west of the river and instead issued orders to prepare his best units for a pre-emptive Italian offensive. He was then struck down by illness, and when he returned to his post on 24 October it was too late to save the Italian position. Capello's part in the fiasco brought him official disgrace in a parliamentary report published in 1919, which also blamed Cadorna.

The panic had become contagious in some areas; a number of units of the Italian 19th Division had been badly affected, and the enemy troops in this area had been able to break through and gain a foothold on the left bank of the Isonzo.

In the Tolmino–Selo sector, the resistance had been more effective, and the Germans had been unable to gain as much territory as elsewhere. Nevertheless, they had reached the east of Monte Jessu by the early evening, giving them a commanding view over the Kolovrat, and further south they had taken the bottom of the Globacek Valley. Only as the attacks slowed down in the early evening was Cadorna able to gain some idea of the situation confronting him. Realizing the dire state of affairs on the Italian Second Army's front, he gave orders to the Duke of Aosta to send two divisions to the area, and similar orders were handed to the Italian First Army. The two reserve divisions behind Second Army were moved up towards Monte Globacek in an attempt to strengthen the position there. As the evening drew on, the scale of the disaster facing the Italian IV Corps became apparent. Cadorna immediately issued orders to II and XXIV corps to fall back from the Bainsizza Plateau and to join up with VII Corps on the southern slopes of Monte Kolovrat. Cadorna then gave instructions to Lieutenant-General

It was not immediately apparent just how serious the defeat at Caporetto actually was. The retreat of shattered front-line Italian units infected those behind them with panic, allowing these German troops to move largely unopposed down the Isonzo River valley.

Tassoni, the commanding officer or the Carnian Zone, that he was to hold Monte Maggiore, so that if a general retirement from the Isonzo was required it could be carried out in reasonable order. Having done this, Cadorna sent orders to the Duke of Aosta and Capello, outlining plans to prepare defensive positions on the Tagliamento, where he intended to stop the Austro-German offensive if forced to retreat further.

By the end of 24 October, Cadorna recognized that his forces had suffered a major reverse, but it was not until the early morning of 25 October that he began to understand the scale of the disaster that had befallen the Italians. During the middle of the morning, Capello informed Cadorna that the Second Army had been driven out of all its positions east of the Isonzo, and that his troops on Monte Stol were under severe pressure from the advancing enemy. By midday, Monte Stol had fallen to the enemy, despite fierce resistance from the Alpini troops who had held on until they had run out of ammunition and been forced to pull back. It was at this point that Cadorna realized

that he would have to give serious consideration to a full withdrawal of forces from the Isonzo. He had issued further orders to the Duke of Aosta, giving instructions for the withdrawal of artillery to the other side of the Piave River, while the obviously unwell Capello had arrived at headquarters and in an emotional meeting urged Cadorna to withdraw behind the Tagliamento; Cadorna agreed.

Although the Italians were beginning to re-establish some semblance of order in their defensive efforts, the situation was to decline further as Capello set about attempting to implement his orders. He became so unwell that he was left with no option other than to hand over command to General Montouri. As Montouri assumed control, he was contacted by Cadorna, who consulted him over the wisdom of the general retreat that he had ordered. Montouri proved

The Italian Army adapted this 305mm gun from its intended role as a coast defence weapon into a super-heavy field piece. The weapon had to be dismantled in order to be moved, and putting it back together took a whole day.

Kaiser Wilhelm of Germany (right) and Emperor Karl I of Austria-Hungary (left) visiting the Isonzo front. Although the offensive was a joint one, as was customary the Germans insisted on one of their officers being in overall command.

quite unable to offer his own advice and instead insisted on consulting with his corps commanders to ascertain their opinions and to see if some form of consensus could be arrived at. Seeking consensus in the midst of a reverse that was already teetering on the verge of disaster was deeply unhelpful.

Having consulted the corps commanders, the advice that Montouri gave to Cadorna was utterly disastrous. Taking the reports of his corps commanders into account, Montouri contacted Cadorna at around 9pm on 25 October and told him that it was his view that the defensive positions currently held by his troops were quite defensible, and that a general retirement was not required. This was an absolutely remarkable recommendation, given that some of these supposedly defensible positions had already collapsed when he gave his suggestion, while many others were on the brink of being abandoned. Unsurprisingly, Cadorna accepted the views of the man on the spot, little realizing just how ill conceived the advice was. The truth became apparent throughout the course of the next day, as the Austro-German advance continued with apparently inexorable momentum. Monte Maggiore fell during the course of the day. Cadorna had intended to use this position as the foundation of the Italian defence, and its loss was a bitter blow.

The position fell in the midst of a blizzard, and 10 regiments simply laid down their arms as soon as the enemy arrived.

As the Germans advanced on 27 October, it soon became apparent that it was impossible to hold the positions on the Torre River, which left Udine, the location of the Italian high command, under severe threat. That evening, news reached Cadorna that the Austrians had reached Porte di Montemaggiore, and he decided that there was no option other than to fall back on the Tagliamento. The Isonzo army had been completely routed in the face of the Austro-German offensive, and over a million men retreated towards their new positions. Cadorna had been forced to abandon all the territory that he had taken over the past two-and-a-half years in little

more than four days, with the defensive position that he had established along a 160km (100-mile) front being completely annihilated. Over a quarter of a million men had been lost in the course of the Austro-German offensive; around 200,000 of these had surrendered. Over 1000 artillery pieces had to be abandoned in the headlong retreat. The scale of the Austro-German victory had been immense, and could have been even more substantial if sufficient resources had been available to allow Boroevich's forces to have been fully provisioned: forced to live off the land as

The Italian retreat after Caporetto was a confused affair in which the high command lost control of most of the army. Units that could have covered the withdrawal of others were gripped by panic or fell back themselves in the absence of clear orders to do something more constructive.

a result of the lack of supplies, Boroevich had been unable to advance from the lower Isonzo to destroy the Italian Third Army. Even as the Italians reached the Tagliamento, they remained in danger, pursued by Krauss's forces. In the face of the crushing defeat, Cadorna was left with little alternative other than to issue a desperate plea to the British and French for military aid. It seemed that without it, the entire front could collapse and Italy would be out of the war.

THE AFTERMATH

The collapse of the Italian front on the Isonzo was a matter of deep concern in both London and Paris, and the source of political upheaval in Rome. In the operational area itself, the Duke of Aosta, who had managed to keep the Italian Third Army in good order, in contrast to the panic that had spread through the ranks of the Italian Second Army, was in no doubt that the sudden collapse of the neighbouring force would have serious implications for his men. He was proved correct as soon as it became clear that the position on the Isonzo was untenable and that a withdrawal to the Tagliamento was required.

Within minutes of the decision being made on 27 October, the Italian Third Army headquarters was in receipt of its first orders, followed by another set – parts of which contradicted the first – moments later. This established a pattern, as the headquarters staff were overwhelmed with a flood of orders and detail regarding the disposition of Third Army's units as they withdrew. The end result was a complete breakdown in traffic control along the lines of retreat, which soon became clogged with thousands of troops. To make matters worse, as soon as the local civilian population became aware of the general retreat, they decided to leave before the Germans and Austro-Hungarians arrived. Thousands of them collected together their belongings and flooded out onto the roads, mingling with the retreating soldiers. The combination of the refugees and pouring rain meant that the retreating troops found it extremely difficult to move, and the roads rapidly became clogged as a result.

Fortunately for the Italians, the enemy was not in a position to attack, since Boroevich's forces, which were the nearest Austrian troops to the Italian Third

A private of the Wurttemberg Mountain Rifles, c. 1917. It was as a company commander in this unit that the future Field Marshal Erwin Rommel won the Pour le Mérite, Germany's highest military honour, and established his reputation as a daring and highly aggressive commander.

Army, made no attempt to embark upon a pursuit of the retreating soldiers.

The Italian Second Army, having borne the brunt of the enemy assault, was in a much worse position when retreating, since the order to retreat had arrived when the situation in its lines was already chaotic. General Montuori had been instructed to fall back over the Torre River, but the weight of the German attack on the Italian XXVII Corps had forced it to fall back to the river far more quickly than Cadorna had envisaged, and as the Germans pursued XXVII Corps,

The disorganized retreat of Italian forces after Caporetto resulted in jammed roads and trapped units. A more aggressive exploitation of the situation might have yielded tremendous results. Fortunately for the Italian Army there was no large-scale pursuit.

they drove a gap between the two wings of the Italian Second Army. Further immediate disaster was avoided only by luck, since the Germans lost momentum on 28 October, and this eased the pressure. However, within a matter of hours the sense of crisis had returned, since Italian VII Corps had been attacked by a small German force and their line had been breached. This made falling back to the Torre more complicated, and with it the prospect of Second Army holding the line until 29 October, so as to allow the Italian Third Army the opportunity to cross the river with as much equipment as it could save. As a result of the breaking of the Italian VII Corps' line, the German 200th Division, part of General Berrer's army group, managed to cross the Torre early in the morning, and then swung around towards Udine, widening the gap between the elements of the Italian Second Army as it fell back. Udine was the hub of the Italian command effort, since it housed the headquarters of

both the high command and of Second Army. News that the German 200th Division was approaching sparked consternation, and the two headquarters made hurried preparations to depart. They managed to flee the town about two hours ahead of the arrival of the German troops. The unfortunate Berrer arrived before all the Italians had left, and was shot dead as he was driven into the town.

The Italians were saved from further disasters thanks to the fact that their opponents were suffering difficulties of their own. Many of the German troops were recent arrivals to the area and had not fully acclimatized to operating at high altitudes, meaning they inevitably lost effectiveness as fatigue set in. The Austrians, meanwhile, had suffered from food shortages for some time before the opening of the offensive, and as they advanced they discovered large amounts of food in the villages they passed through.

Vast numbers of Italian troops were taken prisoner by the advancing Austrian and German forces. Here, the crew of an Austrian heavy mortar crew watch the seemingly endless line of Italians being escorted to the rear. Many of them were dispirited after months of bloody but fruitless combat.

Cadorna's Official Communiqué of 28 October 1917

'A violent attack and the feeble resistance of detachments of the Second Army permitted Austro-German forces to pierce our left wing on the Julian front. The valiant efforts of other troops were not successful in preventing the enemy from penetrating to the sacred soil of our Fatherland. The bravery displayed by our soldiers in so many memorable battles fought and won in the past two and a half years gives our Supreme Command a pledge that this time, too, the army to which the honour and safety of the country are entrusted will know how to fulfil its duty.'

(From Source Records of the Great War, *Vol. V, ed. Charles F. Horne, National Alumni 1923)*

The Austrian troops therefore paused to collect provisions, or in some cases, stopped their advance entirely so that they could eat properly for the first time in months. This inevitably slowed the pursuit, giving the Italians the opportunity to break contact.

A further obstacle to a complete rout of the Italians came, ironically, as the Germans and Austrians fell victim to their own success. Initially, orders had been given to the German Fourteenth Army that the limit of their advance was to be the Tagliamento. However, on 29 October Below decided that it would be appropriate to seize the bridges over the river to prevent them from being blown, thus giving him the opportunity to push his men across in a continuing pursuit of the Italians.

Italian losses involved more than men and guns. Supplies and equipment of all sorts had to be abandoned in the retreat. This worked to the Italians' advantage in some ways, as hungry German and Austro-Hungarian troops stopped to loot all the food they could find.

The Austrians agreed with this perspective, and when Ludendorff requested the return of five divisions from German Fourteenth Army to the Western Front, they supported Below's contention that he should retain them until the Tagliamento had been crossed and the Italians driven further back. The Austrians went as far as telegraphing Hindenburg, urging the German commander-in-chief to allow Below to retain the five divisions until the offensive had reached the Piave, since it appeared that there was a good chance that the Italians would be on the brink of defeat if this eventuality occurred.

This all appeared perfectly reasonable, but in fact highlighted a problem facing the Austrians and Germans. The scale of their success took them by surprise, and attempting to exploit the chaos amongst the Italians generated considerable confusion. New sets of orders were issued, countermanded and re-issued, as Below and his divisional commanders attempted to deal with the developing situation, a position compounded by incoming orders from the German high command.

At midnight on 31 October, Below gave orders that the pursuit was to be continued until the Italians were 'annihilated', but carrying out these instructions involved Fourteenth Army's units swinging across in front of Boroevich's Austrian Second Army. This caused considerable confusion as parts of the Fourteenth Army collided with elements of the Austrian Second Army. There was little or no coordination between Below and Boroevich, which resulted in delays as the confusion was sorted out. This led to army groups Krauss and Stein being halted by the Italians, while Hofacker, the unfortunate Berrer's successor as army group commander, compounded the confusion by initially attempting to swing his army to the south in contravention of Below's orders, and then continuing the pursuit across the river

> 'The failure to resist on the part of some units of our Second Army, which retired in cowardice without fighting or surrendered to the enemy, allowed the Austro-German forces to break into our left wing on the Julian front.'
>
> Italian War Office communiqué, 28 October 1917

at Codroipo. As soon as the Italians became aware that they were under threat from Hofacker's force, they blew the bridges over the river, even though 12,000 of their own men, along with large amounts of equipment were still on the other side. Nearby, at Pozzuoli, the Italian XXIV Corps managed to hold off the remainder of Hofacker's force and three Austrian divisions, enabling it to cross the Tagliamento in good order. The confusion that surrounded the Austro-German attempt to overwhelm the Italians meant that they were unable to achieve their aim, and by 1am on 31 October all of the intact bridges across the Tagliamento were still in Italian hands, and the three Italian armies were across the river. Cadorna ordered a pause in the withdrawal to allow his commanders the opportunity to restore some order amongst their troops, and to begin the construction of defences along the Piave River.

The Italians were able to carry out Cadorna's orders, since confusion now dominated the Austro-German efforts on the other side of the Tagliamento. As noted, the move of Below's Fourteenth Army across the front of the Austrian Second Army caused chaos as the troops from the two forces ran into one another. The situation became so confused that one of Boroevich's corps commanders took matters into his own hands and informed Below that he was going to take command of all the troops in his area of responsibility, whether they had been assigned to him or not, since this was the only way that the mess that had been created would be overcome. Having almost imposed some degree of order through this action, the situation was thrown into confusion again as troops strayed into the area of responsibility belonging to Army Group Scotti, which was part of Fourteenth Army. The question of whether this meant that the Fourteenth Army troops had come back under Below's command, or whether they should take their orders from the Austrian Second Army, meant that the pursuit completely lost momentum as the respective commanders paused to regroup and sort out the chaos. By the time this was done, the Germans and Austrians were still on the wrong side of the Tagliamento, since the arrival of the pontoon bridges necessary to get them over the river after the Italians had blown the bridges had been delayed while order was re-imposed. It appeared that the delay might have saved the Italians, but there was still much to worry about, as it became clear that the Austrians and Germans had no intention of allowing the setbacks of 31 October to end their pursuit.

THE NEXT PHASE

On 1 November, the Italians had safely made their way behind the Tagliamento, which enabled them to establish firmer defensive positions. During the course of the day, they fought off a number of attacks by German units aiming to seize the passages across the river. The Germans renewed their assault the next day, with similar results. The failure to cross the river led Below to conceive a plan which involved cooperation with the Austrian Tenth Army, aiming to launch an attack from the north which would drive behind the Italian positions, and aim for Longarone on the Piave River. If this attack succeeded, it would turn the Italian positions, offering the possibility of trapping them between the forces attempting to cross the Tagliamento, and those who had outmanoeuvred them from the north. Below was putting the finishing

Until this point in the war, Italian forces had been attempting to grind their way into Austria, fighting on foreign soil. Finally, the war had entered Italy. These buildings facing onto the Grand Canal in Venice have been damaged by Austrian artillery fire.

touches to this plan on 2 November when he learned that the Austrian 55th Division had managed to force a crossing over the Tagliamento, as had the German 12th Division. 55th Division had captured a railway bridge at Cornino, and discovered that the Italian attempt at demolishing it had only been partly successful: enough of the bridge remained intact to allow the passage of infantry over it. 12th Division had launched a frontal attack on one of the

The threat to Venice and other Italian cities came as a shock to both the authorities and the civilian population. Suddenly the war was no longer distant, and large numbers of civilians took to the roads to escape danger.

few surviving footbridges over the river at Pinzano, and had managed to dislodge the Italian defenders, while they had also succeeded in fording the river further to the south. These successes had a profound effect on the Italian Second Army, which had ceased to exist as a cohesive fighting force by the end of the day to the extent that the Germans encountered no organized resistance in most areas. On receipt of this information, Below decided to abandon his plan for a drive on Longarone, and to resume the pursuit.

The breakthrough caused another crisis for Cadorna. The Italian XII Corps was placed under threat, with two of its three divisions cut off in the

mountains and in danger of being trapped between Army Group Krauss and the Austrian Tenth Army. Despite desperate attempts to escape from their situation, during the course of 4 and 5 November, the two trapped divisions were enveloped by the enemy and destroyed, with over 10,000 men surrendering. Only the third division of XII Corps, which had been in a more favourable position, was able to escape.

Well before XII Corps was destroyed, Cadorna had sent a frank appreciation of the situation on the Isonzo to the government in Rome during the afternoon of 3 November, which was understandably alarmed at the news. Concern increased as to whether the British and French would be able to arrive in time. The British and French had agreed that they would provide support following a request made on 27 October, and readiness orders for the units that were to be sent had been issued within 24 hours. However, organizing the movement of the units from the Western Front to Italy was a more complicated business, and it took a full 48 hours to arrive at a suitably detailed set of movement orders to ensure the smooth dispatch of the forces and all their equipment and supplies. The problem facing the Italian Government now was that it would take until 6 November at the earliest for the

Paul Painlevé (1863–1933)

In 1910, Painlevé gave up being a university lecturer to become a full-time politician. In 1915, he was appointed as French education minister, and became well known for his support of the strategy of seeking victory in Salonika advocated by General Sarrail. Ironically, despite his confirmed status as an 'Easterner', he was to be the man responsible for overseeing the Nivelle offensives of 1917, having been appointed war minister in March that year. His misgivings over Nivelle's grandiose plans were realized in full, and led him to sack Nivelle and replace him with General Pétain. In early September 1917, the Ribot government fell when the socialists withdrew their support, and Painlevé was tasked with forming the replacement administration. Attending the War Council in Rapello, Italy, in November 1917 in the aftermath of the disaster at Caporetto, Painlevé played a significant part in the deployment of the Anglo-French forces that steadied the Italians. On returning to Paris, however, his government was defeated, and he was forced to resign.

Anglo-French force to arrive, and there seemed to be a real danger that the Austro-German offensive would destroy significant parts of the Italian Army before the French and British troops would reach the front. Cadorna's plan to avert such a disaster was to withdraw the Italian Third and Fourth armies back to the Piave River, since he considered that this could be achieved while maintaining the cohesion of the increasingly demoralized troops under his command. Cadorna aimed to hold a line behind the Piave that would stretch from the sea to the river bend around the fortifications on the hill at

The Italian retreat in the wake of Caporetto, to 12 November 1917. Capello had recommended an immediate withdrawal, but was overruled by Cadorna. Eventually Cadorna realized the hopelessness of the situation, and a retreat to the Piave River was begun.

Montello. Third Army fell back to its designated position without difficulty, but Fourth Army had a nerve-wracking transit from its positions on the Tagliamento down to the Piave, since it had to file down a valley, potentially vulnerable to attack as they went. The remnants of the Italian Second Army, finally returned to some semblance of order, went with Third Army and then into reserve, where it was to be rebuilt. The situation on the front remained in doubt, and by the time that Cadorna's planned withdrawal appeared to be working successfully, the whole command situation had altered.

On 30 October, Prime Minister Lloyd George had sent a message to his counterpart in Paris, Paul Painlevé, suggesting that it would be useful to establish a tri-partite War Council with the Italians. Lloyd George had made this suggestion some weeks before,

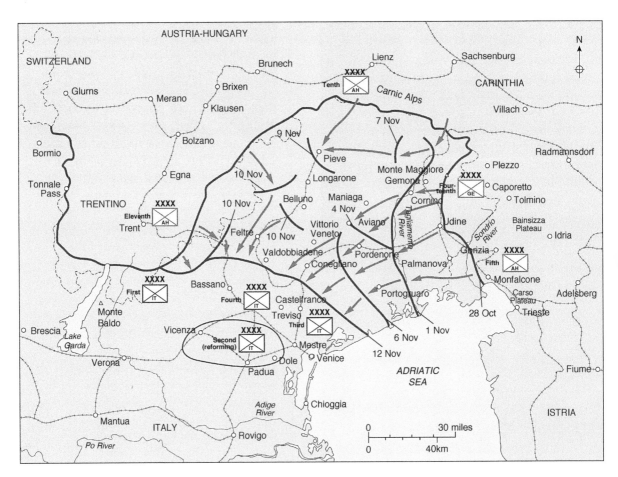

but the situation on the Italian front did not appear to merit such a step; it now appeared vital to hold such a meeting, and a date was arranged for 5 November. At the meeting, the Italians requested the dispatch of 15 French and British divisions to hold the position on the Piave, but found that their allies disagreed; in the eyes of the British and French, this was almost twice the size of the force that was required to assist the Italians. After some discussion, it was agreed that a force of eight divisions would be provided. The British promised to send two divisions immediately, and offered to send more if required. Their assistance came at a price, however, since both Lloyd George, and the British Chief of Imperial General Staff, General Sir William Robertson, had agreed (an increasingly rare outcome to their discussions by the end of 1917) that they had no confidence in General Cadorna. Their opinion was perhaps coloured to some degree by the fact that both men had taken a personal dislike to Cadorna during earlier meetings with him, but the fact that elements of the Italian Army appeared to have collapsed without putting up much of a fight, coupled with the chaos of the retreat and the destruction of the Italian Second Army, suggested that Cadorna could no longer be entrusted with leading the Italian forces. The French and British put their point of view to King Vittorio Emanuele on the third morning of the War Council on 8 November. To the slight surprise of the French and British leaders, the king replied that the decision to remove Cadorna from command had already been reached, although it was his opinion that some of the criticisms levelled about Cadorna's leadership during the recent crisis had been unfair.

News of his dismissal reached Cadorna the next morning, shortly after he had issued a resounding order of the day to his troops, in which he urged them to defend the honour of Italy along the Piave. He was replaced by one of his corps commanders, General Armando Diaz. As if to support the king's point that some of the criticism of Cadorna's handling of the battle had been misplaced, Diaz reported that he felt that bar a minor amendment to the positioning of the Italian Fourth and Fifth armies, there was no need to alter any of the defensive dispositions that had been

General Armando Diaz (1861–1928)

Diaz gained a considerable reputation as an effective officer during the 1911–12 war between Italy and Turkey, leading to his promotion to major-general in 1914 and appointment to General Luigi Cadorna's staff. When Italy joined the war in 1915, Diaz became chief of operations, and enhanced his reputation, despite the generally disappointing outcomes of the Isonzo offensives and the defeat at Caporetto; Diaz was commended for his efforts during the latter, and appointed as Cadorna's successor. He set about rebuilding his shattered forces and the morale of his troops, electing to remain on the defensive along the Piave. However, with the war drawing to a close, Prime Minister Orlando became concerned that Italian claims at any post-war peace conference would be undermined if he could not point to Italian forces playing a notable role in victory. Diaz was persuaded to carry out an offensive at Vittorio Veneto, and won a decisive victory there.

established by the recently ousted commander, and he intended to follow the defensive plan Cadorna had laid down.

Diaz's confidence was strengthened by the fact that Fourth Army had made a successful withdrawal, the risks attached to it notwithstanding, while the weather had turned. Heavy rain and snow meant that it was most unlikely that Below would attempt to launch a new attack against the positions on the Piave, and the British and French were at last beginning to arrive in numbers. The Italians began to hope that the crisis was over and that their situation might, finally, be stabilizing and the prospect of utter disaster at last receding.

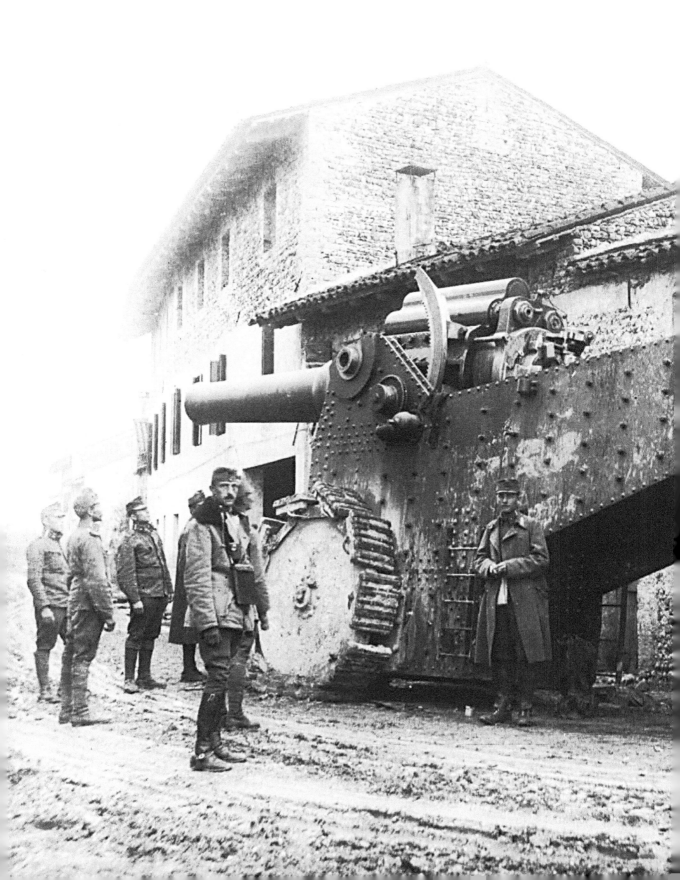

CHAPTER 7

The Defeat of the Central Powers

As 1917 drew to a close, the war in Italy and the Balkans appeared no nearer to resolution than in 1914. The Italian Army had suffered an enormous setback at Caporetto, and Serbia was no nearer to being liberated. However, within six months, the Central Powers would be firmly on the back foot, and, despite their last efforts to rescue the situation, the Austro-Hungarian and Bulgarian war efforts would begin to crumble.

For the Allies, the collapse of the Russian Provisional Government after the October 1917 Revolution appeared to raise the terrible prospect that the Central Powers could soon divert large numbers of troops from the Eastern Front to the west, Italy and the Balkans, since the Bolsheviks had made it quite clear that they intended to seek peace. The Allies hoped that the Central Powers would make demands that the Bolsheviks would find intolerable

Lack of mobility meant that the heavy guns, such as this Italian 305mm howitzer, had to be abandoned by an army forced to retreat suddenly. This particular weapon was a coast defence gun mounted on a mobile carriage to allow it to participate in land actions.

General Otto von Below advocated infiltration tactics to break the strong positions of an entrenched enemy. Ironically, his reputation worked against him. The British held him in such high regard that as soon as he was appointed to a region, they prepared to receive an assault.

and that, somehow, an accommodation could be reached which would see peace negotiations break down and a resumption of fighting in the east.

The Allies did, however, have reason for hope, since the United States had joined the war – although careful to class itself as a co-belligerent rather than an ally – and this promised to bring large numbers of fresh troops to the Western Front. The Germans were particularly concerned by this development, predicting that the sheer weight of numbers and potential industrial output of the United States would make their defeat inevitable. They therefore planned to launch a major offensive on the Western Front in the hope of bringing the war to a conclusion before the Americans could arrive in any great strength. The British and French were aware of the likelihood of such an attack, and began making preparations to meet it – a move that had implications for the withdrawal of troops from other fronts should the need arise. It was now clear that the Western Front was almost certain to be the decisive area of battle, and the prospects for the 'lesser' theatres appeared unclear.

By the second week in November 1917, the Italians had completed their withdrawal to their new positions on the Piave; poor weather had compelled Below to abandon any hope of renewing his attacks against the Italian defences. Diaz was generally content with the position of his forces, but concluded that the Italian Fourth Army was overstretched, and filled its ranks with all the spare manpower that could be found in second-line units. While this meant that the Fourth Army contained a large number of undertrained and inexperienced troops whose behaviour in battle could not be predicted, Diaz felt it safe to assume that the increased numbers of men in Fourth Army's line could only be beneficial; furthermore, he knew that he would be able to rely upon the British and French troops who had been sent to assist.

The first British troops began to arrive in early November as the British 23rd and 41st divisions began their move from France to Italy. They were all in place by 17 November. The British commander, Lieutenant-General the Earl of Cavan, had already agreed to seek permission to bring his forces closer to the front line than had been agreed in the inter-governmental discussions, but Diaz hoped that it would be possible to position them even further forward than Mantua (where it was anticipated that they would link up with the French on Lake Garda), and made strong representations to Cavan that he should attempt to do this. Cavan was not inclined to agree to this request, but felt that it would be expedient to send some British units to join Italian troops since it was thought that this would build confidence amongst the Italians, whose morale was regarded as being rather 'shaky' in the aftermath of their recent experiences.

However, the refusal to send the main body of troops further forward was the source of some tension. General Foch, the French Chief of the General Staff, met with Diaz on 11 November, and the pair had a heated debate over the positioning of French troops. Diaz demanded that French troops take over the whole of the Piave line from Nervesa to the Montello, but Foch refused. At one point in the argument, Diaz theatrically produced a telegram from Prime Minister Orlando in which he implored the British and French to take over parts of the front line. Eventually, Foch came to appreciate that a gesture was necessary for political reasons and gave orders that four French divisions should be moved to the Vicenza area, with Cavan's XIV Corps advancing to protect the right flank.

Two days later, the designated British commander, General Sir Herbert Plumer, arrived and after a meeting with Foch and the Italians decided that he would move the 23rd and 41st divisions forward to the Vicenza line as soon as appropriate logistical arrangements had been put in place. Plumer subsequently cabled the War Office in London, stating confidently that the Germans and Austrians would be unable to break through the Vicenza line once British and French troops were in position, and further advising that two more British infantry divisions should be sent, along with a brigade of cavalry. Plumer, one of the most thoughtful and skilled British generals of World War I, had concluded that not only would the presence of his troops permit a successful defence, but that it would be possible to launch a counter-offensive in due course, with the prospect of driving the Austrians back.

While Plumer was making his dispositions, Foch was busy moving the French XXXI Corps forward, and would be joined shortly by the French XII Corps. One small problem remained for inter-Allied cooperation: the lack of unified command. Foch maintained that the designated commander of French forces in Italy, General Marie-Emile Fayolle, should have complete control over the Anglo-French force, but Robertson demurred, refusing to contemplate the idea that a general of Plumer's standing should be forced into a subordinate position. The end result was a split Allied command, with Plumer being firmly in charge of his own national contingent.

As the British and French moved forward, improving weather gave the Austrians and Germans one final opportunity for an attack, which fell on the Piave line on 16 November. Little progress was made, and although Monte Tomba fell on 22 November, a follow-up attack all along the front launched the next day enjoyed little success. Indeed, Foch felt so confident that the situation was under control that he left for France the same day. The Austrian troops were exhausted, and the intensity of the fighting had reduced the number of men available, shifting the

Frederick Lambart, Earl of Cavan (1865–1946)

The Earl of Cavan was possibly one of the most successful British commanders of World War I, and certainly the best of the so-called 'dug-outs', retired officers recalled to the colours on the outbreak of war. A veteran of the Boer War, he retired in November 1913 as the acting Guards Brigade commander. When war broke out, he was sent out to France, and from this point his career developed rapidly. He was appointed as GOC 50th Division in June 1915, and then in August was transferred to command the newly created Guards Division. A successful period in command at divisional level led to his appointment as GOC of XIV Corps in January 1916, and he led this formation until March 1918, when he was made commander-in-chief of British forces in Italy. The Italian Tenth Army was part of his command, and played a vital role in the victory at Vittorio Veneto in the autumn of 1918. Cavan remained in the army after the war, until he retired once more in 1926.

balance in favour of the defenders. By 29 November, the Austrian Edelweiss Division was down to 2000 fit men, while the other troops in the area were beginning to suffer from a lack of food and winter clothing. This prompted Ludendorff to urge that

Although the situation in Italy was bad, the Italians were able to set up a new defensive line on the Piave River. The troops opposing them, such as these Germans in Belluno, were also exhausted and distracted by a need to forage for food.

the offensive be called off to allow the Austrian and German forces to regroup, and on 2 December Emperor Karl agreed that the time had come to halt what had been one of the most successful attacks of the entire war. Ironically, it was not perceived as such by a number of the senior commanders involved. Recriminations broke out between the Austrians and Germans, since many on the Habsburg side felt that the chance of decisive victory had been lost as the

result of German vacillation, a charge which ignored the fact that Ludendorff had only agreed to join the attack for political reasons and not because he thought it capable of shattering the Italian will to resist. As far as the French and British – and the Americans, for that matter – were concerned, the events in Italy were an irritating diversion from the main effort on the Western Front, and Ludendorff realized that it was here that any decisive victory would be achieved.

Sir Herbert Plumer (1857–1932)

Having attended Staff College, Plumer served in the Matabele and Mashona uprising of 1893, and the two Boer wars. At the outbreak of war, he was in charge of Northern Command. On 1 January 1915, he was sent to France to command V Corps, but in April the resignation of Sir Horace Smith-Dorrien, the commander of the British Second Army, led to Plumer being appointed Army commander. He held this position for the remainder of the war. Despite bearing a startling resemblance to the cartoonist David Low's portrayal of 'Colonel Blimp', a character who became the symbol of arch reactionary attitudes within the inter-war British Army, Plumer was anything but hidebound, being one of the most effective commanders of World War I, as his long tenure in charge of Second Army demonstrated. He took a brief period away from the Western Front to take charge of British forces in Italy, but returned to Second Army in time to meet the German Spring Offensives of 1918.

AUSTRO-HUNGARIAN TROUBLES

As the offensive at Caporetto drew to a close, the Austro-Hungarians suffered a notable upheaval: the new Hungarian Prime Minister, Alexander Wekerle, informed Emperor Karl that his aspiration for the survival of the Dual Monarchy after the war, based upon a renewal of the Compromise of 1867 that had rescued the empire from the verge of a previous possible implosion, would require concessions on his part. Chief among these was the creation of a separate Hungarian army. Karl's war minister, General Rudolf Stöger-Steiner, skilfully persuaded Karl that he should accede to the request, since this could be presented as a further illustration of the Habsburgs' commitment to dualism, while neatly delaying discussion of a potentially divisive issue that might risk tearing the army apart. Stöger-Steiner had few illusions about the state of the Austro-Hungarian forces, and long before the Caporetto offensive had decided that outright military victory was not possible, a view that he had put to Karl in a detailed memorandum. Almost all the troops were poorly fed and equipped, while the sheer scale of losses was almost unimaginable. Troops based in the rear were suffering increasing numbers of cases of malnutrition, and it was estimated that even basic staples such as potatoes would be unavailable by the middle of 1918. Training had fallen well below

The Czechs were not keen on fighting for Germany and Austria-Hungary. Many deserted and others who had been captured preferred to fight against their former masters than to be prisoners of war. Italy used Czech troops in support units at first, but formed a combat formation in April 1918.

the standard that had been possible in peacetime, not least because the number of officers and non-commissioned ranks had declined dramatically; the War School had been closed because of a lack of staff.

The transport situation was similarly dire. Thousands of horses had died in the last few months of 1917 as a result of a lack of feed and many others had been butchered for their meat. Coal production was teetering on the brink of complete collapse, and despite the needs of the army for manpower, the need for coal was such that all soldiers who had been miners in civilian life had been removed from their units and sent back to work in the pits. They at least had the consolation of being given increased rations. Even with the effort to increase output, the situation by the turn of the year had reached the point where the distribution of coal to civilians was a cause of major concern, since it seemed that civil insurrection

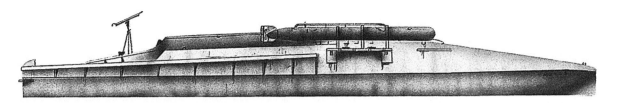

might be sparked by a lack of heating fuel. Food supplies were only just being maintained, and this was only thanks to increased supply of foodstuffs from occupied territories such as Poland. Requisitioning the food was one thing, but conveying it to Austria-Hungary was a challenge, since the railway network was in a parlous state and had suffered a sharp decline in efficiency. Train speeds had been reduced and were to be reduced even further so as to ensure that the tracks did not wear out as quickly; once rails had become unfit for use, it was not clear when replacement track would be available.

Although the Austro-Hungarian fleet spent most of the war in port, it still tied down many Allied warships that could have been useful elsewhere. Italian torpedo boats were used to attack Austrian ships in harbour. This boat, *MAS 9*, sank the Austrian battleship *Wien* in December 1917.

Transporting food to the civilian population was also a major and increasing concern, and the risk of strike action had increased. Stöger-Steiner was concerned that a wave of industrial unrest might be fatal to the hope that the empire could survive through 1918. To complicate matters further, the already uneasy relationship between Austria and Hungary was being challenged by rumours in Austria that the Hungarians had plentiful supplies of food but were unwilling to transfer stocks over to the hungry Austrians.

Stöger-Steiner's report was not regarded as being overstated, and concern over the position of Austria-Hungary only grew. By November, the army was warning again of the serious problems it faced in terms of attempting to train new soldiers, and that the lack of reserves had forced the size of infantry companies to be reduced by approximately a platoon's worth of men each. The number of doctors had fallen dramatically, a serious matter given the increased reliance upon returning wounded men to the front as quickly as possible, and the medical services as a whole were suffering. To compound the manpower problems, the army was suffering from greatly increased desertion rates, which required an increase in the numbers of military policemen to attempt to find the deserters and to force them back into the line. Hans von Seeckt, reporting to the German high command shortly before the Caporetto offensive, confirmed that the Austrians were in a desperate state, with no obvious means of overcoming their difficulties. Even the return of former prisoners of war after the Russian capitulation in early 1918

Food was in short supply in Austria-Hungary in 1918. Combat units and civilians alike were forced to forage for whatever they could obtain. Civilians such as these were forced to compete with roving bands of brigands and deserters from the army.

did not help matters: many of them simply formed into gangs of brigands roaming the countryside and living off the land, and by the middle of 1918 it was estimated that they numbered as many as a quarter of a million strong.

Those returned prisoners who did not succumb to the temptation to desert were far from happy at being put into the front line once more, and complained that while former German prisoners were welcomed back as heroes, they were given second- or third-hand uniforms, returned to the front and then fed less well than they had been while captive in Russia. Unsurprisingly, such levels

of discontent led to incidents of indiscipline and even the occasional mutiny. The high command recognized that the only way to end such outbreaks was to address the source of their concerns – namely lack of food and poor leadership. However, how this was to be achieved was unclear.

Finally, in January 1918, the discontent amongst the civilian population could no longer be contained. When the government announced a reduction in the flour ration, a wave of strikes broke out across the empire. Protestors demanded an increase in food production and an end to the war, and by 18 January it was estimated that half a million people were refusing to work. The situation was saved by the Bavarian state government sending food supplies, which it could ill afford. This helped to bring many strikes to an end; however, industrial unrest now became a major feature of domestic life throughout the Austro-

Hungarian Empire, while the Austrian Government in particular became increasingly concerned at censors' reports suggesting that rural areas were showing signs of sympathies towards Bolshevism. To make matters worse, the Adriatic fleet mutinied on 1 February. The uprising had to be put down by force, aided by the arrival of German U-boats, which made it clear to the mutineers that if they attempted to set sail their ships would be torpedoed.

THE DRIVE FOR A NEW OFFENSIVE

By spring 1918, while the Italians were growing in confidence as they recovered from the shock of the events on the Isonzo front, the Austro-Hungarian Army had reached a point where deputations of troops approached senior commanders pleading for them to launch another offensive, since this would give them the opportunity to loot Italian food dumps. As if this were not enough, the Austrian high command began to be bombarded by plans for a new offensive from Conrad, who despite his removal from supreme command, still wished to influence

the conduct of the war. His view was simple: Austria-Hungary could wait for its collapse, or it could make one final effort to defeat the Italians, and bring about an end to its problems with the conclusion of the war. It seems that Conrad himself was not convinced that this was possible, but he thought it the least worst option facing the Dual Monarchy. Arz von Straussenburg did his best to ensure that Conrad's appeal for forces to carry out a new offensive went unheeded, but there were increasing signs that some sort of attack would have to be carried out, both because of the need to do something to try to rescue the situation, and because a successful attack might help suppress the growing wave of mutinies breaking out amongst reserve units. Conrad's constant suggestions for a new offensive were joined by similar demands from Boroevich, although both

As the Austrian manpower and supply shortage became ever more critical, the Italians firmed up their new defensive line on the Piave. A renewed effort to break through and take the Italians out of the war required more German troops, such as these moving towards the Piave Valley.

commanders produced plans that were unrealistic. Boroevich proposed a frontal assault across the Piave, ignoring his better judgement that such an attack would be suicidal, while Conrad's proposals demanded manpower, ammunition and food stocks that were impossible to obtain.

While Arz von Straussenburg did his best to restrain Conrad and Boroevich, he could do nothing in the face of an intervention by Emperor Karl. As Holger Herwig has observed, Karl appears to have laboured under the misapprehension that he had an understanding of military strategy, and this convinced him that he should authorize an offensive. On 11 April 1918, he summoned Conrad for an audience and revealed that he was going to allow this. Conrad and Boroevich would attack the Italians out of the Tyrol and across the Piave respectively, using a combined force of 23 divisions. Karl overlooked the fact that launching a two-pronged assault almost guaranteed failure, since neither arm of the attack would have the manpower to be decisive. Although there was considerable concern amongst other senior Austro-Hungarian commanders, the need for an offensive became paramount after a disastrous diplomatic faux pas with the Germans.

For reasons best known to himself, the imperial foreign minister, Count Czernin, told a meeting of the Vienna Municipal Council that the French had been prepared to negotiate a peace settlement in 1917, but that this had failed to materialize because French Prime Minister Clemenceau had insisted upon the return of Alsace-Lorraine to France. Czernin, presumably in a bid to show loyalty to the Germans, claimed that he had rejected the demands. He had failed to take account of the possibility that Clemenceau might respond to accusations that he had blocked a peace settlement, and was horrified – as was the entire government of the Dual Monarchy – when Clemenceau released the letter written to him

After the shock of the collapse at Caporetto, Italian morale began to recover, especially once British and French help were forthcoming. The Piave line was reinforced with additional troops, and the prospects for a new offensive to remove the Central Powers from Italy improved.

by Prince Sixte in which Karl had attempted to open peace negotiations. The letter clearly stated that Karl recognized that France's claim on Alsace-Lorraine was legitimate. This would have been enough to infuriate Berlin even without the fact that it came as part of a secret attempt to conclude a separate peace. Karl had one chance to save the situation – namely to blame his hapless foreign minister and disclaim all knowledge of the letter. Out of pity towards his understandably distraught foreign minister, Karl made the matter worse by claiming that the letter was a forgery, part of a propaganda effort by the French to spoil relations between the Dual Monarchy and Germany. His protests, however, were unconvincing, and the Germans refused to believe him. To make matters worse, the Allies concluded that Karl was capable of great duplicity, and the chances of them reaching a favourable settlement with the Habsburgs were greatly reduced.

As a result of this farce, Karl travelled to the German headquarters at Spa and met Kaiser Wilhelm to offer his apologies the day after he had informed Conrad of his plans for an offensive. It now seemed imperative that the offensive be launched without any further debate, since this might do something to restore Austria-Hungary's reputation in the eyes of the Germans. Despite the serious misgivings held by many of his military commanders, Karl ordered Conrad and Boroevich to launch their attack on 28 May 1918.

THE 'HUNGER OFFENSIVE'
A sign of the difficulties facing the planned operation came with the decision that the 28 May start date was impractical because of major supply problems. The front-line troops, aware of the fact that an attack was in the offing because of the preparations being carried out, began to refer to it as the 'hunger offensive', a grim jibe based partly on the belief that an attack was the only way to obtain food, and partly because the troops carrying out the attack would undoubtedly cross the start line hungry. By 27 May, the Austrian Eleventh Army was down to its last three days' flour stocks, meaning that the

army would run out of bread. Food was not the only problem facing the unfortunate Austro-Hungarian soldiers. There was a serious shortage of artillery, and the batteries that were available had few gas shells. Furthermore, the type of gas available was not the highly efficacious 'yellow cross' variety that rendered the filters on Italian respirators almost useless, but a much weaker and therefore less effective formula. The shortage of horses prevented the prompt arrival of the bridging equipment for crossing the Piave. The fact that the operational plan underpinning the attack was fundamentally flawed only compounded this parlous situation. Further postponements delayed the start of the assault until it was finally decided that the attack would begin on 15 June. It was to be preceded by a

With the Piave bridges destroyed, the Austro-Hungarians needed bridging equipment to make an effective crossing. However, supply shortages meant that there were not enough horses to bring this into position – a critical problem that made success very unlikely.

diversionary attack two days beforehand against the Tonnale Pass, which was at the western end of the Austrian positions. It was hoped that the Italians, French and British would move forces over to meet this attack, weakening the positions directly in front of the real venue for the offensive.

Unfortunately for the Austro-Hungarians, the 13 June attack was a failure. The Italians had been active in the area for some weeks beforehand, and had conducted a minor attack around the Tonnale Pass on 25 May, during the course of which they had moved 200 artillery pieces forward. The Austrian commander in the area, Lieutenant-General Metzeger, had approved a counterattack on 12 June, but this had failed as a result of appalling weather conditions. Metzeger then switched his forces to the diversionary attack the following day, but this created the impression that the attack planned for the 13th was nothing more than a continuation of the limited action of 12 June; also, this attack quickly

bogged down in the face of heavy defensive fire. Attempts to recover the situation failed.

After a week of heavy rain had made the conditions for an attack even more challenging, Conrad launched his assault early in the morning of 15 June, attacking along a wide front between Astico and the Piave River. After making some early progress, the Austrians ran into the French and British, and were thrown back with heavy losses. Conrad lost control of elements of the battle as the British and French artillery caused havoc with the Austrians' communications, breaking landlines and destroying telegraph wires. The Austrian artillery was helpless in the face of the Allied guns, and it became impossible for their forces to advance. They were compelled to fall back to their start line, having sustained some 46,000 casualties. Unable to break into the Allied lines, the troops had failed to seize enemy food rations, so within 48 hours of the offensive starting, Eleventh Army was back where it had begun, cold, starving and demoralized.

This left the field to Boroevich, who began his attack in the direction of Oderzo and Treviso. His troops crossed the Piave at 5.30am, and managed to establish a solid bridgehead some 8km (five miles) deep into Allied lines. Fate then turned against Boroevich, as the river rose to three times its normal level. This made the Austrians reliant upon their pontoon bridges, which were immediately subjected to fierce strafing and bombing attacks by Allied aircraft. A combination of the raging torrents of the Piave and air attack accounted for the destruction of all the pontoon bridges by the end of 18 June.

Boroevich was left facing the prospect of a vigorous Allied counterattack with troops whose morale was declining, and without the necessary supplies of food

The defences of the Piave line, which the Austro-Hungarians would have to breach, were well constructed and strongly manned. This section of trench is held by British troops. They, and their French counterparts, beat off the attacks that reached them without undue difficulty.

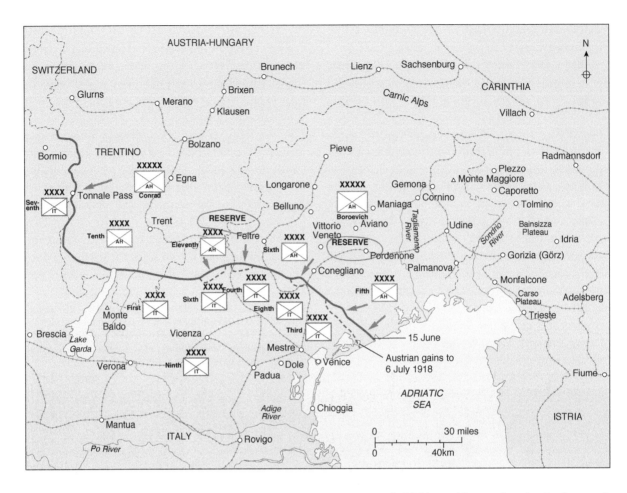

The Battle of the Piave came about in part due to the desire of the Central Powers to finish off Italy before American manpower and industrial strength made itself felt. The offensive was undertaken with inadequate supplies and resulted in a disastrous defeat for the Central Powers.

and ammunition to sustain his men. As if his situation was not bad enough, he was informed by his chief logistician that the very last supply trains had been sent to the front line, and there would be no more: the Austro-Hungarian logistic system had finally toppled over the edge of the precipice upon which it had been teetering for several months.

The imminent disaster facing his troops on the Piave prompted Emperor Karl to rush to the front to consult his commanders. He was horrified to discover the extent of the failure, particularly that which had befallen Boroevich; Karl's pleas to the general to

attempt to hold his position and maintain the attack fell on unsympathetic ears. Boroevich politely yet pointedly reminded the emperor that he had argued against splitting the weight of the attack between his and Conrad's forces, and that events had demonstrated the reason he had been so forceful in his contention that a two-pronged assault could not work. On 20 June, the chastened Karl called off the offensive, leaving Boroevich with the thankless prospect of attempting to extricate his troops from the wrong side of the Piave. Boroevich held out little hope of carrying out the withdrawal successfully, but thought that he might stand a chance if security was maintained and the withdrawal carried out in an orderly fashion. Unbeknown to Boroevich, General Diaz had decided that his troops were in need of a rest, and that an immediate, vigorous pursuit of the Austrian forces would be unwise, preferring to wait for a short period before shifting over to the counterattack. This was to prove a considerable aid to the successful retirement of the Austrians. Over the course of the night of 21/22 June 1918, all those units not essential to maintaining a foothold over what was left of the bridgehead were evacuated, along with the wounded. During the course of the next day, following Boroevich's strict orders that no movement was to be carried out in daylight, the Italians and Austrians faced one another without the potentially decisive thrust from the Allied lines materializing. Boroevich then withdrew the remainder of his force over the Piave. The Italians eventually realized that a major retirement was under way in the early morning of 23 June, too late to stop it. However, they were able to inflict a large number of casualties upon the retreating enemy.

The extent of the failure of the Austro-Hungarian offensive became apparent over the next few weeks.

This bolstered Italian confidence, while morale amongst Austro-Hungarian units rapidly declined. Desertion became a major problem for the Austrians as hungry soldiers abandoned their positions and began scouring the countryside for food. Many of the deserters banded together and raided Austrian storage dumps, depriving those troops in the front line of desperately needed rations. Although the defeat of the offensive on the Piave did not bring about an end to the war, it had profound effects, both on the Austro-Hungarians and the Germans. The Austrians became increasingly gloomy about the prospects of success, and Karl's view that a peace settlement was required with some urgency was only reinforced. The Germans,

The Piave offensive was launched partly for political reasons and largely because success would give access to Italian food stocks. These Austrian troops have captured a wine cellar. It was not uncommon for soldiers in such circumstances to drink themselves insensible.

The offensive did manage to throw a bridgehead across the Piave before it bogged down and ground to a halt. Pontoon bridges such as this one allowed the forward elements to be reinforced and resupplied as best could be. Pack animals and horse-drawn wagons carried the bulk of the army's supplies.

meanwhile, were alarmed at the realization that the Austro-Hungarians could no longer be regarded as a source of potential manpower in the battles they expected in the west; rather, they were a liability.

Tasked with providing an assessment of the reasons for failure, General Arz von Straussenburg made a rather optimistic claim to have tied down Allied troops and thus aided the German war effort before making some more reasoned judgements as to the causes of failure. He pointed to the fact that the gas attacks against Italian positions had failed, partly because many of the Italian units had been equipped with far superior British gas masks. The Italians had thus been able to put up much stiffer resistance in those areas where it had been assumed that gas attacks would give the attacking troops the edge. He also made the frank admission that it was now obvious that Austro-Hungarian soldiers were not as good as their German counterparts. Events since as early as the fight against Serbia had demonstrated the truth of this statement, but it had been impossible for the

Habsburg forces to make the fundamental alterations to training required at all levels. Furthermore, Arz noted sadly, the very nature of the imperial forces, drawn from a variety of nationalities, not all of which were committed to the continuance of the Habsburg Empire, meant that they could never hope to achieve the level of cohesion enjoyed by German formations.

The failed battle represented the final denouement for the broken Conrad, who was elevated to the rank of count and removed from command of what remained of the Eleventh Army on 15 July. Arz submitted his resignation, but the ever-loyal Karl refused to accept it. Boroevich , being a Croat, suffered the brunt of the blame handed out by the Austrian general staff, with some going so far as to accuse him of treason, putting his nationality ahead of loyalty to the emperor – a quite ludicrous suggestion. While the battle on the Piave was not a decisive blow in terms of bringing the war to an end, it marked the point at which the Habsburg Army ceased to be a viable fighting force and began to disintegrate.

THE END OF BULGARIA

After the removal of General Sarrail as commander in Salonika, relationships between the Allies improved considerably thanks to the diplomatic skills of General

Marie Louis Adolphe Guillaumat (1863–1940)

A brilliant student of the Saint Cyr Military Academy, Guillaumat was given command of the 33rd Division in September 1914, a position he held during the German attack on Verdun and the Allied offensive on the Somme in 1916. He was given command of the French Second Army in December 1916, and led it through the difficult period when the French armies were beset by mutinies in the aftermath of the ill judged Nivelle offensives of spring 1917. He was then posted to succeed Sarrail as commander-in-chief Salonika. Guillaumat's formidable diplomatic skills repaired much of the damage done to the coalition effort in Salonika, and he was responsible for planning the 1918 offensive there. His reputation, however, meant that he was recalled to France during the crisis caused by the German Spring Offensives of early 1918 to become military governor of Paris. Appointed to command the French Fifth Army in October 1918, he led this formation in the last days of the war.

Guillaumat (right) in discussion with Joseph Joffre (left) and Fernand de Langle de Cary (centre).

Guillaumat. The latter arrived on 22 December 1917, with instructions to prepare for an offensive in the summer of 1918. As he did so, he used the opportunity to liaise closely with alienated Allied commanders to rebuild the understanding that the high-handed Sarrail had undermined. While the planning process was being completed, the Allies launched a number of minor assaults, with the intention of keeping the Bulgarians off balance. The French and Italians gained some ground in Albania, while a combined Franco-Greek attack seized high ground at the Skra di Legen. The Earl of Cavan's XVI Corps defeated the Bulgarians in an attack on the Sturma, but all of these actions were merely a prelude to the effort that would be made with the intention of smashing through the enemy lines. However, Guillaumat was under few illusions that this offensive would not be a decisive battle, since his orders were explicit in outlining that the offensive was to be limited in scope and ambition.

Nonetheless, Guillaumat oversaw the construction of a series of railway lines and roads to improve the flow of supplies to the front line, which would be essential when the offensive came. However, as Guillaumat entered the final stage of planning, the Germans launched their Spring Offensives on the Western Front. Guillaumat was well regarded by the French Premier, Clemenceau, and he was recalled to become the military governor of Paris. This necessitated the dispatch of a new commander for the Salonika front: General Franchet d'Espérey.

Franchet d'Espérey had built a considerable reputation during the course of the war, and was in many ways an even better choice to lead the forces in the Balkans than the emollient Guillaumat. Franchet d'Espérey had taken the minority view that the war could be won in the east, rather than espousing the 'western' perspective that dominated the strategic planning of the war in Paris and – despite the efforts of Lloyd George – London. He had held the view that

the Balkans would be a vital theatre in any future war for some time, and he had spent a great deal of his leave prior to the war travelling through the Balkans, providing him with a considerable amount of local knowledge. Franchet d'Espérey also held views that were not well suited to the war in the west: he believed that an attritional approach to war was inferior to campaigns conducted around fast manoeuvre over a wide front, making use of cavalry wherever possible. His vision of warfare could not be realized on the Western Front, but Franchet d'Espérey was of a sufficiently flexible mindset to adapt to the static warfare that had ensued in France since the end of 1914, and his skills as a general were widely recognized. While he had a fiery temper, which he sometimes displayed to his disadvantage, he had considerable personal presence and had an innate ability to inspire the men under his command. He also enjoyed support from Guillaumat, who was

Louis Félix Marie François Franchet d'Espérey (1856–1942)

Born in Mostaganem, Algeria, Franchet d'Espérey graduated from the Saint Cyr Military Academy in 1876. He saw action in Tunisia in 1881, Indochina, and in the Boxer Rebellion in China in 1900. In 1913, he was given command of the French 1st Corps at Lille. When war broke out, Franchet d'Espérey took his corps into battle at Charleroi, where he performed well. This established his reputation and he took command of the French Fifth Army at the Battle of the Marne. He was then appointed as commander of Eastern Army Group in 1916, before moving to take over Northern Army Group in January 1917. During the crisis caused by the German offensives of early 1918, the recall of General Guillaumat from Salonika to take over as military governor of Paris led to a reshuffling of commanders, and Franchet d'Espérey was sent to Salonika in Guillaumat's place. Following the successful campaign in Salonika in autumn 1918, Franchet d'Espérey's forces had reached Hungary by the end of the war.

Emperor Karl of Austria-Hungary visiting the front in 1918. By this time his army had ceased to be an effective fighting force, with desertions common and many troops wandering the countryside in search of food. Peace with the Allies was, by now, the only real hope for the Dual Monarchy.

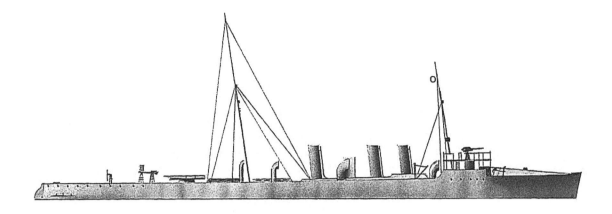

convinced of the importance of an attack in the Balkans and expressed his view at meetings of the French War Council in Paris.

Franchet d'Espérey arrived in theatre and almost immediately set about attempting to inculcate an aggressive spirit amongst his subordinate commanders. His dynamic approach earned him the nickname of 'Desperate Frankie' from the British, reflecting a wry (but respectful) view of his bustling, eager attitude.

As part of this dynamic approach to his new command, Franchet d'Espérey set about reviewing

Operations at sea were always hazardous, even without the threat of enemy action. The Italian *Soldati*-class destroyer *Garibaldino* was sunk off Villefranche on 16 July 1918 after a collision with the Royal Navy ship HMS *Cygnet; Cygnet* survived the impact.

all the plans for offensives that his predecessors had drawn up, but felt that amendments were required. All the previous plans had been based upon the premise that an attack on the Bulgarians would require a frontal assault on the Vardar River valley. Franchet d'Espérey felt that the Bulgarian defensive

plan would be based upon exactly the same premise, and that it would be difficult to gain any element of surprise there. He also felt that the orders for a limited offensive were unnecessarily cautious, and was delighted to discover that the Earl of Cavan, Prince Alexander and General Mishich all held the view that the Bulgarian forces against them would succumb in the face of a full offensive. This confirmed Franchet d'Espérey's perspective that there was little point in carrying out the proposed limited offensive if something of a larger scale stood a good chance of breaking Bulgarian cohesion and possibly driving them out of the war. Franchet d'Espérey therefore set out to reconnoitre his front line, attempting to work out the sector from which he might conduct a surprise attack that would unhinge the Bulgarian defences.

It took Franchet d'Espérey just three weeks to oversee the development of an initial plan that aimed not only to break through the Bulgarian lines, but to drive them 480km (300 miles) back to the Danube. Franchet d'Espérey realized that he faced a considerable obstacle to success even before any of his troops crossed the start line: the Supreme War Council. He put his proposals before the council on 3 July 1918, and met with opposition. Those senior leaders committed to winning the war on the Western Front were convinced that the offensive planned for the Balkans was an unnecessary and potentially dangerous diversion. Although the German offensives had finally been halted and a counterattack was underway in the west, there was concern that committing resources to a relatively minor theatre of war might militate against success in the west. Furthermore, even a dedicated 'Easterner' such as Lloyd George was not convinced, since he hoped to send troops from Salonika to Palestine. As a result of this opposition, it was decided that the matter should be put before a subcommittee, which would make the final recommendation as to whether the attack would take place. The subcommittee took a month to examine Franchet d'Espérey's plan, and reported that they felt it should be carried out, although they added the proviso that the offensive should not divert any shipping from the Mediterranean, nor should it impinge upon operations on the Western Front. Even this recommendation was not the end of the matter, since the British Chief of the Imperial General Staff, Sir Henry Wilson, was opposed to the idea. It was at this point that Guillaumat's diplomatic skills were employed: he was sent to London with the aim of winning Prime Minister Lloyd George's support for the offensive. On 4 September 1918 he succeeded, despite objections from Wilson. Guillaumat was then sent to Rome, where the Italian Government had expressed reservations about the plan, and once again managed to win support. At last, on 10 September, Franchet d'Espérey received permission to carry out the offensive as he had intended. The day of the attack was set for 15 September.

THE PLAN
Franchet d'Espérey had continued planning even while awaiting approval from Allied leaders, and from the first week in August massive efforts to build even more roads for the movement of supplies had begun. This had been accompanied by a strenuous effort to maintain security, even though disguising construction on such a large scale was a difficult prospect. However, Franchet d'Espérey had one advantage, which was that the Bulgarians and their German advisers did not believe that it was possible for an offensive to be conducted in the region that had been chosen for the offensive. In this belief, they had interpreted the development of the transport infrastructure as being an upgrading of the communications links rather than as a sign that an offensive in the area was imminent.

In fact, Franchet d'Espérey had taken particular care to choose the area for the offensive, and was convinced that it was practical. At the suggestion of the Serbian leadership, he had chosen the Moglenitsa Mountains as its starting point, even though it appeared that the area was a most unfavourable location from which to mount an offensive. The difficult terrain meant that it would be hard to obtain the concentration of artillery that was thought necessary for an attack, while the Bulgarians had built strong fortifications to protect their line against an assault. However, they were not expecting an attack, and this meant that some of the potential disadvantages caused by the terrain might not be such an issue if the Allies were able to exploit the benefit of surprise and break into the enemy positions before they had an opportunity to react.

The Serbs had managed to capture one of the summits of the Moglenitsa in September 1916, but they had not managed to achieve any further successes as the Bulgarians had established firm positions along the mountains, with the key to

their defences being the mountain peaks rejoicing in the descriptive names of Sokol (The Falcon) and Ventrenik (The Windswept One), linked by the Dobropolje Ridge. While the Bulgarians assumed that the difficulties inherent in assaulting these positions would prevent the Allies from mounting an attack,

Leading his aggressively counterattacking corps from horseback, General Franchet d'Espérey won the admiration of British troops, and his nickname of 'Desperate Frankie', during the chaotic early months of the war. He went on to gain a reputation as an energetic and capable commander.

Franchet d'Espérey saw the potential rewards as being well worth the risk. If the Bulgarian positions along the Dobropolje could be taken, this could provide a springboard to the second enemy defensive line on the Kozyak Mountain. If these positions were taken, then it would be possible to drive up the Vardar, turning all of the Bulgarian defensive line.

This encouraged Franchet d'Espérey to do everything possible to mitigate the difficulties of operating in such difficult terrain. His artillery commanders and logisticians managed to bring heavy artillery up the mountain. A dozen guns were moved into place by a combination of tractors and muscle-power, with block and tackle being used to get the guns into their final locations. The effort placed the guns at over 2200m (7,500ft) above sea level, giving them a commanding field of fire over the Bulgarian

In the late stages of the war, British and French troops on the Salonika front were able to advance into Serbia and help in the driving out Bulgarian forces. Transportation was primitive in this part of the world, as these British troops and their oxcart show.

defences on the Dobropolje. Once these guns were in place, more artillery batteries were moved into similar positions on other peaks on the Allied side of the mountain, using similar methods. These guns were in a position to bring down fire upon the Bulgarian lines on Kozyak Mountain.

The Serbs were tasked with making the breakthrough on the Dobropolje, while a combined force of French, Serbian and Italian troops was to push forward from Monastir to the Vardar. Meanwhile, the two corps of British troops – XII and XVI – along with two Greek divisions would engage the Bulgarian First Army on the banks of Lake Doiran, with the aim of preventing them from moving to the right bank of the Vardar.

On 1 September 1918 elements of the British 27th Division attacked the Bulgarian positions on the right bank of the Vardar, a move designed to deceive the Bulgarians into believing that the Allied offensive would take two lines of attack into Serbia, namely along the Vardar Valley and through the Monastir gap. The deception appeared to have worked well,

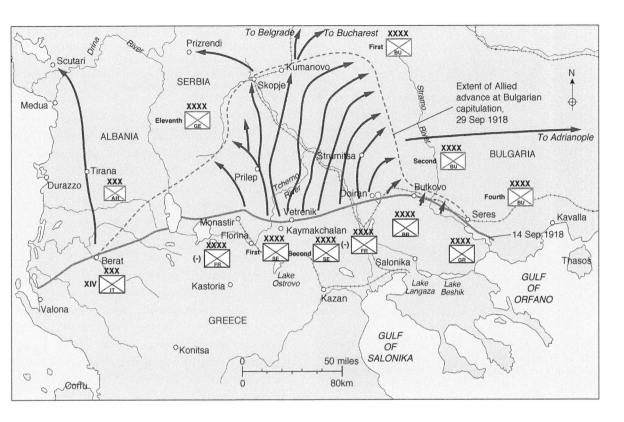

The following labels appear on the map:

To Belgrade • To Bucharest • XXXX First BU

Prizrendi

Scutari • Drina River • SERBIA • Kumanovo • Skopje

Medua • XXXX Eleventh GE

ALBANIA • Stramo River • Extent of Allied advance at Bulgarian capitulation, 29 Sep 1918 • N

Tirana • XXX AH • Prilep • Strumitsa • XXXX Second BU • BULGARIA • To Adrianople

Durazzo • Tcherno River • Doiran • Butkovo • XXXX Fourth BU • Seres • Kavalla

Berat • XXX IT • Monastir • Vetrenik • 14 Sep 1918

XIV • Florina • Kaymakchalan • XXXX BR • Thasos

Valona • XXXX (-) FR • First SE • XXXX Second SE • XXXX (-) FR • XXXX GR • Salonika • GULF OF ORFANO

Kastoria • Lake Ostrovo • Kazan • Lake Langaza • Lake Beshik

GREECE • Konitsa • GULF OF SALONIKA

0 — 50 miles • 0 — 80km

Corfu

As the Central Powers began to collapse, the Allies launched an offensive that drove into Bulgaria. This involved Greek and Serbian troops, who finally had a chance to avenge defeats suffered at the beginning of the war. The Bulgarians put up a stiff fight, but defeat was inevitable for them.

since the preliminary artillery bombardment along the mountains between Monastir and the Vardar on 14 September took the Bulgarians and the German units supporting them by surprise. The German commander, General von Scholtz, was impressed by the weight of fire brought down, but made a careful assessment of the situation and gave orders to move troops up to Monastir, since it appeared that this was where an infantry attack would come. By the time it became clear that Monastir was not going to be the focal point of the Allied attack, it was too late. At 5.30am on 15 September, the Serbs advanced, supported by a number of French and French colonial troops on the Dobropolje. The Bulgarian defenders put up stiff resistance, and it took the Serbs eight hours to reach the summit of the Vetrenik. Forty-eight hours of hard fighting ensued, but by the early hours of 17 September Franchet d'Espérey was content with progress. His forces had driven 10km (six miles) into the Bulgarian lines along a front 30km (20 miles) wide, and this had compelled the

Germans to withdraw some of their units to ensure that they would not be cut off. As the Bulgarians were attempting to regain their balance, Milne launched the Anglo-Greek contribution to the offensive on 18 September. The 22nd Division, supported by a Greek division, opened the attack around Lake Doiran, attempting to take the high ground surrounding the lake. The day was frustrating for the British, since they were unable to gain a foothold on the hills.

However, although the Anglo-Greek attack had failed, General Scholtz was already deeply concerned by events. He sent an urgent signal to Hindenburg calling for the dispatch of reinforcements, since he feared that there was a serious danger that the Bulgarians would be routed. It was clear from reports that the Bulgarians were reluctant to fight: their 2nd

plan was rejected by Scholtz, not least since a quick review of the plan illustrated that it required the use of the Bulgarian 3rd Division, elements of which were barely in a state to be considered a viable military force, let alone launch a major counter-stroke against the British, no matter how weakened they were. The Bulgarians enthusiastically suggested an alternative, which involved cutting off the Allies from their supply lines – again, a plan that took little account of reality. On 20 September, the Germans and Bulgarians were ordered to pull back, which had a deleterious effect on the morale of the Bulgarian First Army. Its men could not understand why it was being forced to retreat from such strong defensive positions; the troops who had faced the British were particularly bemused, since it appeared that they were likely to defeat all efforts to overcome them.

Nevertheless, the Bulgarians began their withdrawal on schedule in the evening of the 20th. Soon afterwards, disaster struck. British aircraft discovered the retreating column of Bulgarian troops, and it became obvious to Milne that the enemy was withdrawing directly along the Sturmica Road and into Bulgaria. He immediately set his small air component to work attacking the Bulgarian columns. Trapped in the ravines, there was little that the Bulgarians could do to avoid the heavy air attacks that now fell upon them. The British airmen inflicted heavy casualties amongst both men and horses, and much of the Bulgarian First Army's equipment was destroyed and left littering the road. The Bulgarian force broke up, taking to the mountains, a broken fighting force.

By midday on 22 September, the Serbs had reached the Vardar, and the French were making steady progress in their sector. However, the main breakthrough was made by the main cavalry force, based around a French colonial cavalry force under General Jouinot-Gambetta. Franchet d'Espérey

Division had retreated twice without waiting for the enemy attack to fall on their positions, while the 3rd Division had two regiments that were refusing to obey orders. Scholtz attempted to shorten his line, but by the end of 18 September he was painfully aware that the Franco-Serbian attack could be aiming towards the Vardar and the logistics base at Gradsko. If Gradsko fell, it would split Scholtz's defensive position in half. As he reviewed a stream of reports from staff officers, Scholtz concluded that this disaster would materialize within 72 hours.

The British attacks were renewed, but to little avail: casualties were heavy, although the offensive achieved its primary objective of fixing the enemy in place so that units could not be sent to aid in the defence against the French and the Serbians. The losses on the British side were so notable in some units that the Bulgarian First Army's commander, General Nerezov, proposed a counterattack against Salonika itself, aiming to drive through the weakened Anglo-Greek positions while Franchet d'Espérey was unable to break contact to defend against the counter. The ordered Jouinot-Gambetta to take his force to Skopje, a daring move which was to pay off handsomely, even though the advance demanded that Jouinot-Gambetta take his troops away from the road network and thus out of contact with Franchet d'Espérey's headquarters.

The British were the next to advance, as XVI Corps crossed the Bulgarian frontier on 25 September. They had 210km (130 miles) to cover if they were to reach Sofia as Franchet d'Espérey hoped, but to their considerable surprise encountered little organized opposition. On 26 September, a patrol from the Derbyshire Yeomanry was startled to be approached by a truce party, which expressed a desire to open peace negotiations. These began on a formal basis on 28 September.

As dusk fell on 28 September, Jouinot-Gambetta's force reached the Skopje railway, which they found completely unguarded. When the leading elements of Jouinot-Gambetta's force were sighted by Bulgarian troops in Skopje, the occupants of the town were astonished, not least since they believed that the enemy was at least 30km (20 miles) away. By 9am, the town was in French hands, and this, combined with the heavy losses that had broken the Bulgarian First

Army, led to an unravelling of the whole Bulgarian position. Mutiny broke out, and there was a series of anti-war riots in a number of towns, at which point it became clear that the Bulgarian will to fight had been broken. Franchet d'Espérey, confident that there was little the Bulgarians could do to resist, made clear his demands; these included the right to exploit the Bulgarian railway system so as to permit him to move his forces through Bulgaria so that they could be deployed against the Germans, Austro-Hungarians and Turks if required. The Bulgarians capitulated at midday on 30 September. Despite the apparent odds against success in a mountainous area, Franchet d'Espérey had managed to bring the Bulgarians to defeat in less than a month.

VITTORIO VENETO

As the offensive in the Balkans began, the Allies continued their run of successes on the Western Front, but endured frustration in Italy. The victory gained in

By the end of four years of war, these Austro-Hungarian troops had become prisoners of war in Serbia, with their nation about to be dissolved into its constituent parts; the empire was no more.

the summer had not been followed up, thanks to a lack of available reserves and the caution of the Italian high command, particularly General Diaz. The latter shared the view of a number of senior Allied leaders that the war would not be won in 1918, rather in the following year. Diaz felt that Italy's war aims would be met more readily if Italian troops played a major role in the decisive battles of 1919, and had no intention of seeing his troop strength reduced in minor battles preceding a main effort. While this point of view made a certain degree of sense from an Italian perspective,

it was a source of considerable annoyance to the other Allies, who felt that the Italians were not pulling their weight. Despite their attempts to persuade Diaz to make plans for an offensive against the Austrians, he refused to countenance the idea. However, events were to force a reassessment of Diaz's position.

Franchet d'Espérey's success against the Bulgarians, coupled with the advance of Serbian troops deeper into their homeland, began to create concerns in Italy that they would be left behind in any peace settlement if they had not played any notable role (the presence of some Italian forces under Franchet d'Espérey's command notwithstanding) in bringing about the collapse of the enemy. To add to this concern, the Germans and Austrians announced their willingness to negotiate with the Allies, using President Woodrow Wilson's Fourteen Points as the basis for discussion.

The Battle of Vittorio Veneto resulted in the final demise of the Austro-Hungarian Army as a fighting force. Although the Italians held only a modest superiority in men and artillery, their opponents were hungry, weary and had poor morale. After initial determined resistance, the Austro-Hungarian Army collapsed and a ceasefire was soon agreed.

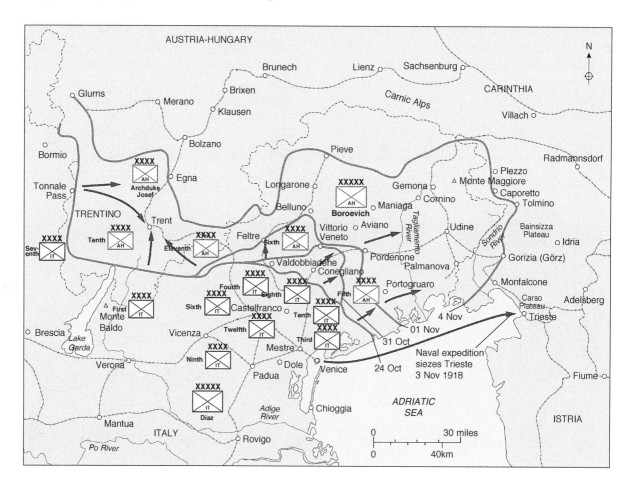

The Italian Government became alarmed at the thought that the war might end with enemy forces still within Italian territory and Italian influence at the peace conference miniscule, with the nation having done nothing to merit favourable consideration from its allies when the spoils of war were divided.

As a result of these political considerations, Prime Minister Orlando sent a dramatic signal to Diaz in which he declared that, faced with a choice between military inactivity or defeat, he would prefer defeat; he urged Diaz to act at once. Yet Diaz still dithered, sustained in his intent to conserve his forces by politicians less certain that the war was coming to an end. However, by the second week in October 1918, the Austro-Hungarian Empire had begun its terminal disintegration. On 6 October, the birth of what would become a united Yugoslavia was declared by Serbian and Slovene political leaders (aided by the gains being made by the Serbian Army, which was closing on Belgrade). A week later, the Czechs formed a temporary national government. In both cases,

there was nothing that Emperor Karl's government could do. Proposals for a federated empire with much greater autonomy for minorities had come to nothing, going too far for traditionalists in the Austro-Hungarian Government and not far enough for the various nationalities who would be affected by the proposals. The announcement of a federal constitution for the empire by Karl on 17 October failed to move the nationalists into staying their hand. Then, on 21 October, the Germans in Austria declared that they would form their own independent state, while the Hungarians were on the verge of declaring their intent to split from the control of the Dual Monarchy. Emperor Karl was on the verge of becoming an imperial ruler in name only, as his empire disappeared.

Losing artillery to the enemy has always been a military embarrassment. The fact that these guns were not directly captured by the Allies but were simply abandoned as the Austro-Hungarian Army disintegrated shows just how overwhelming the defeat of the Austrians had been.

President Wilson's Fourteen Points

Wilson delivered his vision of the terms upon which the United States wished to see the post-war peace settlements based. Although there was some cynical reaction – the French Premier Clemenceau observed that God had been happy with only 10 points – the Fourteen Points became the generally accepted terms of reference by which the Allies implemented the peace treaties after 1919.

I.   Open covenants of peace, openly arrived at, after which there shall be no private international understandings of any kind but diplomacy shall proceed always frankly and in the public view.

II. Absolute freedom of navigation upon the seas, outside territorial waters, alike in peace and in war, except as the seas may be closed in whole or in part by international action for the enforcement of international covenants.

III. The removal, so far as possible, of all economic barriers and the establishment of an equality of trade conditions among all the nations consenting to the peace and associating themselves for its maintenance.

IV. Adequate guarantees given and taken that national armaments will be reduced to the lowest point consistent with domestic safety.

V.   A free, open-minded, and absolutely impartial adjustment of all colonial claims, based upon a strict observance of the principle that in determining all such questions of sovereignty the interests of the populations concerned must have equal weight with the equitable claims of the government whose title is to be determined.

VI. The evacuation of all Russian territory and such a settlement of all questions affecting Russia as will secure the best and freest cooperation of the other nations of the world in obtaining for her an unhampered and unembarrassed opportunity for the independent determination of her own political development and national policy and assure her of a sincere welcome into the society of free nations under institutions of her own choosing; and, more than a welcome, assistance also of every kind that she may need and may herself desire. The treatment accorded Russia by her sister nations in the months to come will be the acid test of their good will, of their comprehension of her needs as distinguished from their own interests, and of their intelligent and unselfish sympathy.

VII. Belgium, the whole world will agree, must be evacuated and restored, without any attempt to limit the sovereignty which she enjoys in common with all other free nations. No other single act will serve as this will serve to restore confidence among the nations in the laws which they have themselves set and determined for the government of their relations with one another. Without this healing act the whole structure and validity of international law is forever impaired.

VIII. All French territory should be freed and the invaded portions restored, and the wrong done to France by Prussia in 1871 in the matter of Alsace-Lorraine, which has unsettled the peace of the world for nearly

50 years, should be righted, in order that peace may once more be made secure in the interest of all.

IX. A readjustment of the frontiers of Italy should be effected along clearly recognizable lines of nationality.

X. The peoples of Austria-Hungary, whose place among the nations we wish to see safeguarded and assured, should be accorded the freest opportunity to autonomous development.

XI. Romania, Serbia and Montenegro should be evacuated; occupied territories restored; Serbia accorded free and secure access to the sea; and the relations of the several Balkan states to one another determined by friendly counsel along historically established lines of allegiance and nationality; and international guarantees of the political and economic independence and territorial integrity of the several Balkan states should be entered into.

XII. The Turkish portion of the present Ottoman Empire should be assured a secure sovereignty, but the other nationalities which are now under Turkish rule should be assured an undoubted security of life and an absolutely unmolested opportunity of autonomous development, and the Dardanelles should be permanently opened as a free passage to the ships and commerce of all nations under international guarantees.

XIII. An independent Polish state should be erected which should include the territories inhabited by indisputably Polish populations, which should be assured a free and secure access to the sea, and whose political and economic independence and territorial integrity should be guaranteed by international covenant.

XIV. A general association of nations must be formed under specific covenants for the purpose of affording mutual guarantees of political independence and territorial integrity to great and small states alike.

Diaz was now in a position where he had little option other than to move onto the offensive, even though his concerns about a lack of available reserves remained valid. Nevertheless, he had begun to make preliminary plans for an attack, as the possible repercussions of a lack of action from Italian forces became more of a concern. Therefore, on 21 October, plans for an offensive on the Piave and the Grappa were finalized, which aimed to destroy the enemy forces in Italy.

The plan for the attack demanded that operations begin on the Grappa with the Fourth Army, while the Eighth and Tenth armies would attack 12 hours later on the Piave. The attack opened with a bombardment at 5am on 24 October, followed by the first wave of infantry two hours later. However, the weather conditions had worsened and the Piave had flooded, making it impossible for the second phase of the operation to begin. This left the Italian Fourth Army bearing the brunt of the offensive for the next 48 hours, making desperate efforts to break through the Austrian lines, all of which were rebuffed with heavy casualties. The Austrians counterattacked on 27 October, an assault that was finally driven back with significant losses on both sides. By the 29th the weather had become so bad that Diaz suspended operations. This gave time for a reappraisal, and it was decided to shift the focus from the Grappa to the operation on the Piave, which had finally started on 26 October when the river had subsided sufficiently to allow the first bridges to be thrown across it by engineers. Eighth Army had been only partially successful in its attempts to cross the Piave, but the Tenth, under the command of the Earl of Cavan, was first to cross in strength, followed by the Twelfth Army. This enabled the Eighth Army to cross the river, and the combined weight of the Allied assault finally began to tell. Although imperceptible at first, the degree of resistance from the Austro-Hungarians began to decline, and by the morning of the 29th the first major cracks in the Austrian line began to materialize, prompting the Austrian Government to begin efforts to secure an armistice. At 9am on 29 October, a party of officers approached the Allied lines under a white flag. There was some initial confusion as the intent of

Once the surrender of Austria-Hungary was complete, prisoners such as these were sent home. The newly created nations they went to were unable to object to any loss of territory, and nor were these men in any position to take up arms against a treaty imposed by their former captors.

the negotiating party was not recognized, and it came under fire. Fortunately, an order to cease fire came quickly from the Allied lines and the party was allowed to open discussions.

After two days, the armistice terms between Austria-Hungary and Italy were worked out, and the Austrian representative, General Viktor Weber von Webenau, finally signed the necessary agreement at around 2am on 3 November 1918. The war in Italy and the Balkans was over, and with it ended the Habsburg Empire. The empire continued its collapse, as the remnants of the army not taken into captivity made their way back to their homelands, many of which lay in brand new nations that had not existed when the soldiers left for the front. On 11 November, Karl accepted the inevitable, and surrendered political

power. He pointedly refused to abdicate, hoping that circumstances would allow him to reassume the throne in one of the nations that had once been part of his empire – circumstances that never emerged.

The final act of the war in Italy and the Balkans came at the signature of the peace settlements. Indicative of the demise of the Habsburg Empire, it took two separate treaties to end Austria-Hungary's war. The Treaty of St Germain on 10 September 1919 formalized the creation of Poland, Czechoslovakia and Yugoslavia, and the splitting of the Dual Monarchy. The new Austrian Republic was forced to cede territory to the newly created nations, as well as to the Italians (who were infuriated to discover that their allies were not prepared to grant them the territory that they thought they deserved). It took until 1920 for the peace treaty with Hungary to be arranged, but it was signed at Trianon on 4 June that year. The newly independent state lost 75 per cent of its territory and two-thirds of its former population as a result, surrendering land to the newly formed

states and to the Romanians. Just under six years after Gavrilo Princip had fired the fatal shots at Sarajevo that killed Archduke Franz Ferdinand, the world was finally, formally, returned to peace.

The peace settlement at the end of World War I altered the map of Europe significantly. Several new nations had appeared and others had vanished. However, not everyone got what they wanted or what they felt they deserved, resulting in tensions that still remain to this day.

FURTHER READING

Anderson, R., *Forgotten Front 1914–18: the East African Campaign* (Stroud, Tempus, 2004)

Buchanan, A., *Three Years of War in East Africa* (Uckfield, Naval & Military Press, 2006)

Clark, A., *The Eastern Front 1914–1918: Suicide of the Empires* (Witney, Windrush Press, 1999)

Clark, L., *World War I: an Illustrated History* (Abingdon, Helicon, 2001)

Crowe, J.H.V., *General Smuts' Campaign in East Africa* (Uckfield, Naval & Military Press, 2006)

Fendall, C.P., *The East African Force 1915–1919* (Uckfield, Naval & Military Press, 2005)

Herwig, H.H., *The First World War: Germany and Austria-Hungary 1914–1918* (London, Hodder Arnold, 1998)

Howard, M., *The First World War* (Oxford, Oxford University Press, 2003)

Lettow-Vorbeck, P., *My Reminiscences of East Africa* (Nashville, The Battery Press, 1990)

Liddell Hart, B.H., *History of the First World War* (London, Papermac, 1992)

Morselli, M., *Caporetto 1917: Victory or Defeat?* (Abingdon, Routledge, 2007)

Nicolle, D., *The Italian Army of World War I* (Oxford, Osprey Publishing Ltd, 2003)

Pirocchi, A., *Italian Arditi: Elite Assault Troops 1917–20* (Oxford, Osprey Publishing Ltd, 2004)

Schindler, J.R, *Isonzo: the Forgotten Sacrifice of the Great War* (Westport, Praeger, 2001)

Stone, N., *The Eastern Front 1914–1917* (Harmondsworth, Penguin, 2004)
—— *WW1: a Short History* (Harmondsworth, Allen Lane, 2007)

Strachan, H., *The First World War in Africa* (Oxford, Oxford University Press, 2004)

Wilks, E. and J. Wilks, *Rommel and Caporetto* (Barnsley, Pen and Sword, 2001)

INDEX

PICTURE CREDITS

Art-Tech/Aerospace: 8, 16, 198

Art-Tech/MARS: 44, 47(bottom), 63, 94, 100, 124, 128, 129, 136, 168

Cody Images: 67, 77, 83(top), 89, 90, 91, 93, 95, 96, 113, 133, 134, 176

Corbis: 11, 112, 160, 196

Nik Cornish @ Stavka: 21, 24, 27(top), 28, 30, 34, 36, 37, 39, 41(bottom), 42, 43, 47(top), 48, 51, 56, 60(top), 65, 66, 68, 69, 71, 76, 83(bottom), 88, 92, 97, 99, 102, 104, 105, 107, 108, 110(bottom), 117, 120(top), 123, 125, 132, 145, 148, 152, 153, 157, 161, 173, 177, 183, 187, 194, 201, 203, 207(bottom), 210, 212, 213, 218

De Agostini: 156, 179, 184, 215

E. W. W. Fowler: 81, 84

Getty Images: 126, 140, 143(top), 147, 174 (De Agostini)

Library of Congress: 12, 25, 26, 27(bottom), 41(top), 46, 49, 50, 53, 60(bottom), 64, 82, 85, 98(bottom), 106, 120(bottom), 121, 141, 151, 185, 191, 193, 205, 216

Bertil Olofsson/Krigsarkivet: 15, 72, 80, 86, 158, 162, 164, 169, 172, 180, 181, 188, 190, 192, 197, 200, 204

Photos 12: 206, 209

Photos.com: 10, 55, 116

Public Domain: 119, 130, 137

SMB Bildarkiv: 139

Suddeutsche Zeitung: 1, 6, 18, 20, 23, 29, 32, 40, 52, 57, 61, 165

TopFoto: 174(top)

Artworks

Art-Tech/Aerospace: 31, 98(top), 146, 155, 163

Art-Tech/John Batchelor: 110(top), 115, 131, 150, 166, 167, 175

Art-Tech/De Agostini: 38, 79, 111, 114, 122, 142, 143(bottom), 178, 195, 207(top)